THE
GUERRILLA
READER

A HISTORICAL ANTHOLOGY

THE GUERRILLA READER

A
HISTORICAL
ANTHOLOGY

Walter Laqueur

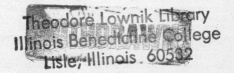
TEMPLE UNIVERSITY PRESS
PHILADELPHIA

TEMPLE UNIVERSITY PRESS, PHILADELPHIA 19122

Copyright © 1977 by Walter Laqueur

ACKNOWLEDGMENTS

Selections from PHILOSOPHY OF THE URBAN GUERRILLA: The
Revolutionary Writings of Abraham Guillen, translated by Donald C.
Hodges. Copyright © 1973 by Abraham Guillen and Donald C. Hodges.
Adapted by permission of William Morrow & Co., Inc.
Selected from REVOLUTION IN THE REVOLUTION by Régis Debray.
Copyright © 1967 by Monthly Review Press. Reprinted by permission
of Monthly Review Press.
"The Lessons of Arabia" by Thomas Edward Lawrence is reprinted from
the *Encyclopaedia Britannica*, 14th edition (1929).

Library of Congress Catalogue Card Number: 76-047279

International Standard Book Number: 0-87722-095-6

Published 1977

1 2 3 4 5 6 7 8 9

PRINTED IN THE UNITED STATES OF AMERICA

Contents

Part III: Partisan Warfare 1860-1938

Part IV: Socialism and the Armed Struggle

Part V: Guerrilla Doctrine Today

Preface

According to widespread belief guerrilla warfare is a new way of conducting unconventional war. Supposedly it was discovered in a stroke of genius by Mao Tse-tung and was later successfully applied in other parts of the world by left-wing revolutionary movements. Observers with a longer view point to Lawrence of Arabia as the great pioneer of modern guerrilla warfare, and some go back even further, pointing to the Spanish resistance against Napoleon which produced the term "guerrilla." In actual fact guerrilla warfare is as old as the hills and predates regular warfare. Throughout history guerrilla wars have been fought by weaker peoples against invading or occupying armies, by regular soldiers operating in the enemy's rear, by landless peasants rising against landowners, and by bandits, social and asocial.

The tactics of guerrilla warfare are neither complex nor shrouded in mystery; with slight variations they have been about the same since time immemorial. Typical guerrilla operations include harassment of the enemy, evasion of decisive battles, cutting lines of communications, and carrying out surprise attacks. Guerrilla tactics are based on common sense and imagination; they vary from country to country and are affected by geographical conditions, social and political processes, and changes due to technological innovations.

Guerrilla wars were rare in the eighteenth century when strict rules for the conduct of warfare were generally observed. Guerrilla methods were used in the Southern theater during the American War of Independence and during the Napoleonic Wars by partisans in occupied countries (Spain, southern Italy, the Tyrol, and Russia). Upon the emergence of mass armies in the nineteenth century, guerrilla warfare again declined. Nonetheless it still was practiced in major wars (the American Civil War, the Franco-Prussian War of 1870–1, and the Boer War) and in the campaigns of national liberation movements (in Poland, Ireland, and Macedonia). Furthermore, guerrilla tactics

1

played an important role in nineteenth-century colonial wars, of which the campaigns of the French against Abdel Kader and the Russians against Shamyl were the most noteworthy. In all these instances the guerrillas failed to achieve their aims except when they cooperated with regular armies. The imperial powers, as yet unfettered by moral scruples about imposing their rule on lesser peoples, were not deflected from their intentions by pinpricks: the Russians did not withdraw from Poland or the Caucasus of Central Asia; the French did not give up North Africa and the British did not surrender India. There was not one outright guerrilla victory in the nineteenth century. In some instances, however, guerrilla campaigns indirectly contributed to eventual political success. Thus the military outcome of the Cuban insurrection of the 1880s and 1890s, although inconclusive, helped to trigger America's intervention in 1898 which led to the expulsion of the Spanish. The dour struggle of the Boers after their regular armies had collapsed hastened the British decision to grant South Africa a large measure of independence. In Latin America guerrilla war continued to be the prevailing form of military conflict because of the absence of strong regular armies.

The First World War saw mass armies pitted against each other. The few instances of guerrilla combat (Arabia, East Africa) occurred in minor theaters of war and were not ideologically motivated. The Mexican, Russian, and Chinese civil wars of the twentieth century saw much partisan fighting, mainly because opposing sides were not strong enough to mobilize, train, and equip a large regular army. Guerrilla war in these circumstances was not so much a war of the weak against the strong as of the weak against the weak. Revolutionary movements had not yet opted for the guerrilla approach, the prospects for anticolonial struggle before the Second World War being unpromising. The Soviets established a large regular army as quickly as they could after the revolution. Twenty years later the Chinese communists tried to do the same, though, in their case, the guerrilla phase was to last much longer.

World War II brought a great upsurge in the fortune of guerrilla warfare. Hitler's predicament resembled Napoleon's insofar as his forces were dispersed over all Europe and his lines of communication and routes of supply were overextended and vulnerable. Also like Napoleon, the Germans lacked sufficient forces to impose full control on all the occupied territories or even to destroy partisan concentrations. Overall, the military importance of the partisan forces in the war was not very great and did not decisively influence its course. These forces' main impact was political, inasmuch as their presence resulted in the emergence of communist governments (i.e., in Yugoslavia, Albania—although both countries would have become part of the Soviet sphere of influence anyway) or caused protracted civil war (Greece, Malaya, the Philippines). The colonial powers, gravely weakened by the war, lacked the financial and military resources and political will to retain their overseas possessions against the rising tide of independence movements. Public opinion in the metropolitan countries, which had once regarded the possession of colonies as a source of pride, was no longer willing to shoulder the military and financial burden of empire; imperialism became morally reprehensible. This change of Western public opinion was decisive for the success of Asian and African national liberation movements. In the Far East and some African countries the leadership of the independence movements was taken over by communist or pro-communist forces. Their superior organization and their ideology, which corresponded with the cultural level and the emotional needs of the population, better equipped them to act as agents of modernization than their political rivals. Nevertheless, the wars of liberation in Asia and Africa were fought without exception under the nationalist rather than the communist banner. Even in the countries of Latin America which had been independent for almost one hundred and fifty years, the guerrilla campaigns had strong patriotic undertones.

The political context of guerrilla warfare has been and continues to be the subject of much confusion. Thus, it has been asserted that before the 1930s guerrilla movements were usually parochial and little more than of nuisance value and that they were ideologically conservative. Recent guerrilla movements, on the other hand, are said to be revolutionary. No longer spontaneous outbursts, they are considered part of a national (or international) political movement from which they derive greater cohesion than those movements of the past. There is some truth in these observations, but not all that much. It is certainly not correct that, until recently, guerrilla movements were all of local importance only. Nor are "wars of national liberation" a twentieth-century innovation. Guerrilla movements of the early nineteenth century were predominantly "right wing" in character, intensely patriotic, monarchist, and religious-fundamentalist, whereas modern guerrilla movements do appear more often than not to be left wing and revolutionary in inspiration. But on closer inspection the issues involved are not so clear. One detects strong populist, anti-aristocratic elements among the eighteenth-century guerrillas in Spain, Ireland, Italy, Latin America, and even in the Vendée in France. Also there were and are many movements which simply do not fit into ready categories of "right" and "left." Quite frequently their ideology has encompassed extreme left- *and* right-wing components (the Stern Gang, Dr. Habash's PFLP). The IRA and the Macedonian IMRO at various times in their checkered history had connections with fascism and communism (or Trotskyism). Latin American guerrilla movements quite frequently manage to combine a bewildering multitude of conflicting ideological attitudes. Even in communist-inspired guerrilla groups, nationalism almost always has been the most important factor. How much importance should be attributed to the political orientation of guerrilla movements? Or, to put it differently: are there perhaps certain basic nationalist-populist-revolutionary impulses underlying their political programs and slogans as well as a free-floating activism which may turn "right" and "left" according to political conditions and the changing fashions of the Zeitgeist?

Guerrilla warfare has been practiced throughout history, and its doctrine too is by no means of recent date. Guerrilla techniques were exhaustively described by eighteenth-century military writers and even more systematically by Lemière de Corvey, Decker, and others in the early nineteenth century. The experiences of the Napoleonic Wars provided much material for systematic analyses and descriptions. The Italian and Polish writers of the 1830s and 1840s were fully aware of the political aspects of guerrilla war. Their writings cover almost all the problems that were to preoccupy twentieth-century guerrilla theorists: the importance of bases and sanctuaries, whether a war should be short or protracted, whether it should be "pure" guerrilla war or conducted in coordination with regular forces, and whether guerrilla units should be gradually transformed into a regular army. Even the relationship between the guerrilla force and the political movement supporting it was discussed in the writings of Carlo Bianco and Mazzini. These precursors fell into oblivion. Mao and Ho Chi Minh, Castro, Guevara, and Debray were not in the least aware that their "own" ideas had been expounded before, and even tried, albeit not very successfully. The twentieth-century guerrilla theorists discovered their strategies through their own experience, instinct, and native traditions of guerrilla war, of which there were plenty in both Asia and Latin America.

The novelty of twentieth-century guerrilla warfare is not so much military as political in nature. The author of a recent study maintains that, on the one hand, revolutionary guerrilla war evolved out of Marxist-Leninist modes of political behavior and organizational principles, and out of the exigencies of anti-Western revolt in predominantly agrarian societies, on the other. In the light of historical evidence this thesis is tenable only if it is subjected to far-reaching reservations. The character of guerrilla war has of course changed greatly over the ages, partly due to technological developments and to changing social and political conditions. But on the whole, too much importance is attributed to the impact of Leninist doctrine upon the changing guerrilla context and too little to that of the nationalist-populist component upon the motivation and ideology of these movements. It is not just that the interest in the subject of guerrilla war of Marx, Engels, and Lenin was very limited; many twentieth-century guerrilla movements, from that of Pancho Villa in Mexico to that of the Mau Mau in Kenya, from the IRA to the Irgun and from Fatah to the Cypriot EOKA, owe nothing to Leninism. Neither the Algerians in 1954 nor the Cubans in 1958 were influenced by this doctrine. Even Chinese and Indochinese guerrilla wars evolved more in opposition to classical Marxism than in accordance with its basic tenets. The impact of Marxism-Leninism among contemporary guerrilla movements has been strongest with regard to the role of the political party in mobilizing the masses, the function of propaganda in the struggle, and the emphasis placed on organization. But political propaganda and organization were not unknown in nineteenth-century guerrilla movements, and women too participated in struggles well before those led by Mao and Fidel.

These new developments in the character of guerrilla movements should not be belittled, but neither should Marxist-Leninist ideology be regarded as the master key to understanding them. Communist guerrilla movements have failed, and non-communist groups have succeeded.

The importance of guerrilla movements in general was underrated for a long time. More recently the pendulum has swung to the other extreme, and the general tendency has been to exaggerate their political importance and historical role. The historical record shows that guerrilla warfare, with one exception (Cuba), has succeeded only against colonial rule or during a general war. With the end of the colonial period and in the absence of a general war, the prospects for guerrilla warfare have diminished. It has been argued that, although the state is always immensely stronger than the insurgents, the government's ability to use its power is severely restricted by both world opinion and domestic constraints. This applies, however, only to liberal-democratic regimes, that is, to a relatively small (and shrinking) part of the world community. It is too often forgotten that guerrilla or terrorist movements have never had the slightest chance of success against a real tyranny; there was no organized armed resistance in Nazi Germany or Fascist Italy; there is none now in the Soviet Union or in communist China. The guerrilla needs the permissiveness of a democratic society—or the inefficiency of half-hearted autocracies—as the fish needs water, to rephrase Mao's famous dictum. The tendency to regard guerrilla warfare and terrorism as a worldwide problem should be resisted; for modern, reasonably effective dictatorships, regardless of their political persuasion, this problem simply does not exist. The record of guerrilla movements shows that it has been infinitely easier to succeed against foreigners, however strong, than against native incumbents, however ineffective. Furthermore, the record reveals that the success of guerrillas in relatively liberal societies has been their undoing. What Regis Debray said about the Tupamaros applies *mutatis mutandis* to most guerrillas and terrorists operating in democratic regimes: by digging the grave of the "system," they dig their own grave. As long as the guerrillas are no more than a nuisance, public opinion will strongly resist the use of efficient but illegal measures against them. But as insecurity spreads and as wide sections of the population are adversely affected, demand will grow for tougher action by the government, even if this should involve occasional (or systematic) infringement of human rights. Only ten or fifteen years ago it was widely believed that guerrilla warfare and terrorism were a revolutionary panacea for the Third World and industrial countries alike and that public opinion would prevent the application of any effective counter-guerrilla strategy. These expectations have proved false. Unless the moral fiber of a regime is in a state of advanced decay and its political will paralyzed, the guerrillas will fail to make headway beyond the stage of provocation in which, according to plan, public opinion should have been won over to their cause. But even if the authority of the state is fatally undermined, even if a power vacuum exists, there is usually a far stronger contender for power—the army. Military coups have become more frequent; in the future they may be the normal form of political change in many parts of the globe. These coups can with equal ease turn right or left, the difference frequently being only semantic in character. Those with a left-wing bias will steal much of the guerrillas' thunder because their inspiration is more or less the same—nationalist and populist. Those inclined more to the right will effectively suppress them. A guerrilla campaign is still possible if it has the support of a major outside power and if attacks can be launched from sanctuaries across state borders. But in this case traditional guerrilla operations turn into war by proxy, which belongs to another species of armed conflict.

The predicament facing the guerrillas has resulted in the transition from rural to urban guerrilla warfare. The phrase "urban guerrilla" is a misnomer whose general use should be regretted. Insurrections and revolutions have occurred in cities and so have acts of terror, but urban guerrilla warfare has happened only on the rarest of occasions—when armed bands freely roam cities following the breakdown of state power. Such a situation is usually not likely to last longer than a few days, after which time either one side or the other will have won a decisive victory. The essence of guerrilla warfare lies in the fact that the guerrilla can hide in the countryside, in nature, which he cannot do in the city. The distinction is of more than academic importance. There have been guerrilla units of ten thousand men and women, but urban terrorist units rarely comprise more than a few people and urban terrorist "movements" very seldom consist of more than a few hundred members. What is now commonly called "urban guerrilla warfare" is only terrorism in a new guise. (It is quite understandable that the terrorist should prefer the "urban guerrilla" label because the image of the guerrilla is so much more attractive than that of the terrorist.) The general tendency in recent years has been to overrate the importance of urban terror, perhaps due to its highly dramatic—or melodramatic—character and to the fact that, unlike guerrilla operations, urban terror usually has many spectators. The attitude of the media toward "urban guerrillas" reminds one of T. E. Lawrence's descriptions of his Arab levies: they thought that weapons were destructive in proportion to the amount of noise they made. Urban terror certainly creates much noise and causes some destruction and indiscriminate killing. Its political significance, however, is very much in doubt.

All this is not to say that the history of guerrilla warfare has come to an end. The conditions that cause insurgencies have certainly not disappeared; men and women are still exploited, oppressed, deprived of their rights, and alienated. There will always be people with grievances, some of them legitimate, others devoid of any foundation, and yet others somewhere in between. "Objective revolutionary situations" still abound and will continue to exist. But the prospects for conducting successful guerrilla war in the post-colonial period have certainly worsened, except perhaps in the secessionist-separatist context. Guerrilla war may not entirely disappear, yet, seen in historical perspective, it is on the decline following the eclipse of the colonial powers and the emergence of dictatorships of various kinds in many parts of the world. It is said that the importance of terrorism will grow enormously as the destructive power of weapons increases. This danger does indeed exist as missiles, nuclear material, and highly effective poisons become more available. But it is part of a much wider problem, that of individuals blackmailing society. To engage in nuclear ransom one does not need a terrorist "movement"; a small group of people or perhaps a single individual will be equally effective, perhaps even more so, because the smaller the group, the more difficult it is to be identified and combatted. To apply the term "guerrilla" to such an individual or small group of individuals is as senseless as the indiscriminate use of "guerrilla" with regard to all and every manifestation of revolutionary politics, civil war, peasant war, insurrection, hijacking, and kidnapping, not to mention happenings in the theater, the arts, and even the kindergarten.

The present collection of texts is the first of its kind. It contains material new even to the specialist. While working on a study of guerrilla theory and practice since the eighteenth century, I realized that the existing sociological and psychological studies of guerrilla motivation and behavior are not of great help in understanding the phenomenon and that there is no reason to assume that more refined techniques will result in superior insights. The multiple "objective" and "subjective" factors involved in guerrilla warfare and their complicated interaction rule out all-embracing formulas and explanations that are scientific in the sense that they have predictive value. In other words, to understand guerrilla warfare one has to study its history. But to say that the historical sources for a study are no longer readily available would be a gross understatement. Carlo Bianco's *Trattato,* Lemière de Corvey's *Des Partisans* . . . or Johann Most's *Revolutionäre Kriegswissenschaft* (to choose three examples at random) are among the most important works in the field, yet the reader would look for them in vain at the British Museum, the Library of Congress, and other leading libraries. The same refers to many other sources used in this anthology. In brief, much important material has become exceedingly rare; much has never before been published in English.

I would like to record my gratitude to the following for providing translations:

Anthony Wells (Clausewitz, Ewald, Emmerich, Valentini, Chrzanowski, Boguslawski, Rüstow, Hron, Ehrhardt, Most)

Janet Langmaid (De Grandmaison, De Jeney, Blanqui, Lemière de Corvey, Decker, Gingins, Cabral)

Zeev Ben Shlomo (Stolzman, Tukhachevski)

Hilary Sternberg (Davydov)

Marion Rawson (Carlo Bianco)

Above all, I would like to thank Kimbriel Mitchell for having provided research and editorial assistance throughout this project.

This anthology includes a short bibliography; the reader interested in the historical background of guerrilla theory and practice will find a more detailed account in my *Guerrilla* (London and New York, 1976) and *Terrorism*, to be published in 1977. In a sequel to the present anthology, *The Terrorist Reader*, the development of terrorist doctrine will be reviewed in historical perspective.

Washington, December, 1976

PART I

The Age
of Small War

Introductory Note

Guerrilla and partisan wars have been fought throughout history, but a systematic doctrine of the small war first appeared only in the eighteenth century. The Austrians freely used semi-regular Hungarian and Croatian units during and after the Spanish War of Succession. Under daring commanders such as Von der Trenck these highly mobile units effectively disrupted enemy lines of supply and communication. Their discipline was low, however; they robbed and burned without discrimination, and there were complaints that they did as much harm to their own side as to the enemy. The French had some free corps even before 1740, and more were established in subsequent years.

The leading military thinkers of the period differed sharply in their appraisal of the value of these units. Guibert claimed that they were useless; neither Gustavus Adolphus nor Turenne had believed in them. But with the (harmful) expansion of armies a function had to be found for the many new cavalry units. As a result, observers came to attribute to the small war a role out of all proportion to its real importance. Frederick II of Prussia thought that the small war would never be decisive and, though he had suffered some unpleasant setbacks as the result of surprise attacks by Austrian irregulars, he preferred to ignore them rather than to be deflected from his course of action. Napoleon also took a dim view of irregulars, whether they appeared as partisans (in Spain, Russia, or Tyrol) or militias; they would never decide the fate of a campaign, let alone a war. Other lesser writers of the period attributed more significance to the small war: because armies had grown so much, their losses had increased, and they had become more dependent on supplies. Was it not true that, as a result, the cost effectiveness (as one would now say) of small, semi-independent units had become much greater? They would not be able to force a decision, but, by gathering intelligence, cutting off the enemy's lines, and harassing and misleading him, they could

make a major contribution to victory. Only later on, in the Napoleonic Wars, did the idea of national resistance appear—or to be
precise, reappear. Even if the regular army was defeated and the
capital of the country occupied, the war against the invader could
and should be continued.

Maurice, Count de Saxe (1696–1750), Marshal of France, was
an early convert to the importance of the small war. The excerpt
reprinted within is part of a letter to Augustus II, King of Saxony,
dated 1732 and first published in his *Mes Rêveries (Reveries or
Memoirs Upon the Art of War* [London, 1757]). Little is known
about De Grandmaison and De Jeney. The former was a lieutenant-
colonel of cavalry in the "Corps des Volontaires de Flandre"; De
Jeney served with the French army of the Rhine.[1] De Jeney's work,
which was translated into German and English, was the first systematic treatise on partisan warfare; it included maps, sketches, and
even advice on first aid. Andreas Emmerich (1737–1809) and his
contemporary and compatriot, Johann von Ewald (1744–1813),
were the leading partisan theoreticians of the late eighteenth century;
both were Hessian officers who saw service in the British army during
the American War of Independence. Von Ewald became a lieutenant-
general in the Danish army; Emmerich, called by Von Ewald "the
first partisan of our age," was executed by the French following the
Marburg insurrection in 1809.[2] Georg Wilhelm Freiherr von Valentini
(1775–1834), subsequently a Prussian lieutenant-general, participated as a young officer in the war against the French Republic in
1792–94. On the basis of his experience, he wrote a treatise on the
small war which was at the time of its appearance the most compre-
hensive work on the subject.[3] The authors mentioned so far were
almost exclusively preoccupied with the technique of the small war
within the wider framework of a large war. Carl von Clausewitz's

---

[1] De Grandmaison, *De la petite guerre* . . . (Paris, 1756); De Jeney, *Le
partisan, ou l'art de faire la petite guerre avec succès, selon le génie de nos
jours* (La Haye, 1759).
[2] Von Ewald, *Abhandlung über den kleinen Krieg* (Kassel, 1790); A. Emmerich,
The Partisan in War or the Use of a Corps of Light Troops to an Army
(London, 1789); the English original could not be located and it has been
translated here from the German translation of *Der Parteigänger im Krieg*
(Dresden, 1791).
[3] Von Valentini, *Abhandlung über den kleinen Krieg und über den Gebrauch
der leichten Truppen* (Berlin, 1799).

(1780–1831) writings after the Napoleonic Wars shift the discussion to the strategic, and political, function of the people's war. The excerpts published below are from Chapter 26 of *On War* and from a lecture course in 1810–11 on small wars. Major von Clausewitz was addressing the Prussian War Academy. His copious notes, covering almost four hundred printed pages, were first published in 1966.[4]

[4] Von Clausewitz, *Schriften-Aufsätze-Studien-Briefe*, ed. W. Hahlweg, Vol. I (Göttingen, 1966).

Maurice, Count de Saxe

Hercules Against Schoolboys

Sir,

I was honored with your Majesty's letter bearing date the 20th of last month. My silence in the conversation which passed upon the subject of light horse proceeded from my ideas concerning the importance of the object: but, in compliance with your Majesty's commands, I shall now speak my sentiments with that martial freedom which you are so good as to require of those whom you condescend to admit to your friendship.

An army unprovided with light horse, or not having a sufficient number to oppose against those of the enemy, may be compared to a man armed *cap à pié*, who is to encounter a troop of schoolboys without any other offensive weapons than clods of earth: this Hercules will presently be obliged to retire, struggling for want of breath and confounded with shame.

In 1713, your Majesty had twelve troops of Walachians, which performed great things because the Swedes had no light horse, which was what gave us the superiority over them in the field; for the Walachians were perpetually insulting, even their grand guards: our

Maurice, Count de Saxe, *Reveries or Memoirs upon the Art of War* (London, 1757).

forages, and pastures were never exposed to the least interruption or danger, whilst theirs were frequently attacked; neither could they make any detachments of which we had not immediate intelligence, and were in a capacity to defeat . . .

But a superior number of light horse is, notwithstanding, far from being the most eligible remedy to obviate all these inconveniences, because they are attended with a great expense, and, as you are not to lay any stress or dependance upon them for solidity, do not add to your strength in cavalry on the day of action: large bodies of them upon the flanks of your army are even dangerous, which we have but too often experienced in the war with the Swedes in Poland, and that even at the battle of Kalish,* which your Majesty is very sensible of; it is necessary therefore to have recourse to other measures: the French have established certain bodies of light horse, under the name of free companies, to remedy these evils, which are posted in houses in the environs of their camps from whence they make some excursions; but, being no better mounted than dragoons, they are incapable of moving much from their quarters; and although they may contribute a little toward the ease and relief of the army, yet they are far from answering the purpose effectually.

There is not a sovereign in Europe who has it so much in his power to establish an excellent body of light horse, as your Majesty: your troops have been accustomed for these twenty-six years past, in different wars, to fight against light horse and to contend with superior numbers; the grand point is to keep steady and maintain their ground, which method of behavior they have naturally learnt from a consciousness of the impossibility of flying upon horses so large and heavy as theirs: if they were mounted upon light horses and lightly accoutred, I am persuaded they would presently put a stop to the insults of the enemy's irregulars, which proceed from nothing but the impunity that attends them, and the facility of their flight . . .

If then your Majesty approves of my reflections upon this subject, a thousand of the shortest-sized men must be chosen out of all your army, and such officers appointed to command them as are noted for courage, skill, and understanding: they must be formed into twelve troops, according to which division a troop will consist of

* The King of Poland was present at this battle.

about eighty; so that if, by any means, there should happen to be a future deficiency of even thirty, there will still remain fifty, which is the usual number of a troop of cavalry in time of war in all regular services.

I have already observed that the smallest-sized men are the best, because it has frequently been proved that a horse which will carry a man thirty leagues in a day whose weight does not exceed eight or nine stones, which is usually about that of a man of five feet two inches high, will hardly be able to carry one of from ten to twelve stone half that same distance; and, in swiftness, will lose from a hundred to a hundred and fifty paces in a thousand.

All their arms, as well as accoutrements, are to be extremely light. With regard to horses, your Majesty may furnish yourself with very good ones out of the strings brought by the Walachian dealers to Otakir, from Rougiac, from lower Arabia, and from Romelic, which are infinitely better, swifter, larger, and higher mettled than the Hungarian ones; neither will they cost more than those from Holstein, which are made use of in the Saxon cavalry . . .

De Grandmaison

The Uses of Small War

While the usefulness of troops engaged in small war and that of partisan leaders has been generally recognized throughout all ages and all nations, the necessity for them is even more strongly proved in our present century by the torrent of the Queen of Hungary's light irregular troops which has overwhelmed Bohemia, Bavaria, and Alsace in a situation where France finds herself entirely lacking in such troops.

Without harking back to when the Numidian cavalry rendered immense service to Hannibal, above all in the famous Battle of

De Grandmaison, *La petite guerre ou traité du service des troupes légères en campagne* (Paris, 1756).

Cannae, and when the Parthians preserved their liberty against the whole might of Rome by their swiftness and agility in combat, we may note that the French at various times and under different names have formed advance troops to fight in campaigns, obtain intelligence about the enemy, intercept his convoys, storm his outposts, and fall upon his equipment during an action. The Stradiots [light Albanian cavalry: scout (*estrader*)] did so at the Battle of Fornouë: by means of an unexpected charge upon the supply convoy of the army of King Charles VIII of France, they swung the balance of victory between him and the federated Princes of Italy, to whom the raid proved disastrous rather than advantageous because of this light cavalry's obstinate seizure of booty throughout the action.

In the following century, Captains Montluc and Bayard and their adventurers carried out some remarkable feats. Henri IV himself found it necessary to engage in partisan exploits on many occasions.

Under Louis the Great, the famous leaders Jacob-Pasteur, Lacroix, Dumoulin, Kleinholds, and others gave signal service to the state by their bold enterprises and lucky achievements. Lastly, France is not unaware of the harm which it suffered in the last war because of the abundance of nations subject to the Queen of Hungary whose troops were lightly equipped and nimbly mounted. They harried us incessantly, stormed our convoys, our sick quarters, our baggage, our foragers, our detachments, and great numbers of our raiders; and this destroyed the finest armies ever to cross the Rhine, who neither saw nor fought any troops other than Hungarians, Slavonians, Waradins, Lincanians, Croats, Rascians, Banalists, and Pandours, against whom we could oppose only a few French companies and two regiments of Hussars devastated by desertion and by the great superiority of their adversaries.

De Jeney

Some Qualities Required of a Partisan

Among all the branches of military service, there is none which in essence demands so many uncommon qualities as those of a partisan. Without entering into too great detail, I shall cite only the most indispensable: on the one hand the natural advantages, on the other the habits acquired by his own efforts, all of which he should have.

A good partisan should possess:

1. An imagination fertile in schemes, ruses, and resource.
2. A shrewd intelligence, to orchestrate every incident in an action.
3. A fearless heart in the face of all apparent danger.
4. A steady countenance, always confident and unmoved by any token of anxiety.
5. An apt memory, to speak to all by name.
6. An alert, sturdy, and tireless constitution, to endure all and inspire all.
7. A rapid and accurate glance, to grasp immediately the defects and advantages, obstacles and risks presented by a terrain, or by anything it scans.
8. Sentiments that will engage the respect, confidence, and affection of the whole corps.

Lacking such aptitudes, success in this art is impossible: it is useless for anyone to presume on some other talent or to flatter himself that, by taking pains or by good fortune, he may expect to win renown; experience, reason, and duty deny such a presumption: notwithstanding the value and excellence of his other virtues, his honor fails of its object.

Besides this, the partisan must know Latin, German, and French so as to make his meaning clear when he may meet men of all nations. He should also have a perfect knowledge of military prac-

De Jeney, *Le partisan ou l'art de faire la petite guerre* (La Haye, 1759).

tice, chiefly that of light troops, and not forget that of the enemy. He should possess the most exact map of the theater of war, examine it well, and master it thoroughly. It will be highly advantageous to him to keep some able geographers under his orders who can draw up correct plans of the armies' routes, their camps, and all places to be reconnoitered.

Nor should he be at all parsimonious, if he can thereby obtain from able spies sure information of the enemy's line of march, his forces, his intentions, and his position. All such disclosures will enable him to serve his general to great advantage; they will be of incalculable benefit to the army's security and to his own corps' standing, good fortune, and glory.

His own interest and his honor also require that he should retain a secretary to draw up the diary of his campaign. In it, he will cause to be set down all orders received and given, as in general all his troop's actions and marches; so that he may always be in a position to account for his conduct and justify himself when attacked by criticism, which never spares partisans.

As a leader, he owes to his troop the example of blameless conduct, entirely commensurate with the care and affection of a father for his children. He will thereby inspire them all with respect, love, zeal, and vigilance, and will win all hearts to his service.

Such an officer would run great risk should he entertain the least attachment to women, wine, or wealth. The first is conducive to neglect of duty and is often the cause of ruinous treachery. The second prompts dangerous indiscretions and always attracts contempt. The third leads to crime and extinguishes honor.

Johann von Ewald

Cunning, Skill, Speed, Secrecy

. . . By rights, the phrase "surprise attacks" should be unknown in wartime, and if all officers were to reflect upon the insulting implications of this term, there would be few, if any, cases of this kind. For to be attacked means in reality to have forfeited through one's own negligence, ignorance, or willfulness one's honor, freedom, and possibly life, as well as that of large numbers of others entrusted into one's care. Can, then, an officer who has brought such a calamity upon himself through his own fault suffer a worse insult than the comment: He was taken by surprise! Nevertheless, however much an officer who has been entrusted with a post in the field may be on his guard, cases of this kind will always occur in wars; for he who chances an attack will seldom fail, and it is those very attacks that the common run of men considers impossible that customarily meet with the greatest success.

The large measure of cunning, skill, speed, and secrecy that the launching of such "surprise attacks" requires is well rewarded when they are successful, for these attacks are of great use in wartime, dealing a harsh blow to the morale of those exposed to them. To be in a position to deal the enemy such a blow, one must first make a particular effort to get to know the terrain and region where the attack is to be staged. One must have both good scouts and good guides. The former are needed to inform us of the enemy's strength, how his outposts are manned and of what kind they are; to tell us whether he is neglectful of his duties, where and how far his patrols go, how strong they are, how often they are sent out, and how far the nearest outpost is to the one we intend to attack; and further, to discover what sort of man the commanding officer is, whether he is perhaps easygoing or given to extravagant behavior. The latter,

Johann von Ewald, *Abhandlung über den kleinen Krieg* (Kassel, 1790).

the guides, are necessary to lead us to the enemy by a roundabout route and to show us exactly where all the points of access are so that one can cut off the enemy completely. For if these lightning attacks are only half-successful, or fail, then one makes oneself look ridiculous in the eyes of the enemy and loses the respect of one's men. To take an example, on the occasion of the attack on Baumbruck in the spring of 1777, the English cavalry should have advanced a quarter of an hour earlier from the point where they crossed the Raritan River if they were to succeed in cutting the Americans off from the pass leading to Morristown. It was because they failed to do so that General Lincoln and all but two hundred of eight hundred men escaped. The same mistake was made on the occasion of the attack on the Marquis de Lafayette's corps near Germantown in the spring of 1778.

One must also know of more than one way back so that after a successful, or unsuccessful, raid one can find the shortest route home. The night is the most favorable time for such attacks, since at night panic rapidly spreads among the enemy. When he sees he is being attacked from all sides, he cannot make out our movements; he cannot distinguish between a real attack and false one; in his fright he sees two of everything and even mistakes trees and bushes for human beings. I myself have experienced a false alarm at first hand only once. It is difficult to imagine just how great an effect fear has on men who are groggy with sleep. The incident I refer to happened during the Pennsylvanian campaign, when General Howe was making to cross the Chalkill after the Battle of Brandywine River. The Hesse and Anspach rifle corps were encamped in a wood not far from French Creek. They had been told to act as rear guard and were resting, weapons in hand, ready to move at a moment's notice. A few shots were heard from the direction of one of the pickets. These sparked off shouting and screaming among the inhabitants of nearby plantations. All at once someone yelled: "Run for your lives; we're being attacked!" At this, the whole corps started to run amok. It took about an hour to calm down the men, and it was well nigh impossible to convince them that the "attack" was only a false alarm.

Fog, mist, strong winds with driving snow or rain contribute to the success of an attack, for in bad weather there are seldom any patrols on the roads because the enemy thinks the weather will prevent an attack. Fog enables one to creep up on the enemy unnoticed.

When strong wind and driving rain are blowing into the faces of the
sentries, they often drop their heads and forget themselves, turning
their backs to the wind and rain and making it easy to creep up and
kill them. I myself have succeeded in approaching very close to
sentries who, because they were guarding the most dangerous outposts, were constantly aware that the slightest negligence on their
part could bring death or disaster and have remained for some time
standing right in front of them without being discovered. At such
times, therefore, one cannot be too assiduous about visiting outposts.

Andreas Emmerich

The Partisan in War

No army can do without light troops in time of war because it depends upon them not only for what it can or cannot undertake but
also for its sustenance.

The detachments of light troops should be made up of fusiliers
with drawn muskets, light infantry with bayonets, and light dragoons
or hussars, though occasionally, as the English have done, they may
consist of battalions drawn from the light infantry of various regiments supported by grenadiers.

A corps made up of these three kinds of light troops should never
number below a thousand men or above seventeen hundred. Moreover, the troops recruited should be volunteers, as it would be dangerous to force people into this kind of service. . . .

It is important that the person commanding a corps of light troops
be an officer of proven good conduct and great experience and a
man in whom one can place great trust without risk. This is vital
because from time to time the commanding general may need to
divulge to him—depending on the nature of the mission—both the

Andreas Emmerich, *Der Parteigänger im Krieg* (Dresden, 1791).

password and the warcry, the discovery of which by the enemy could be of dire consequence for the whole army. It is of no less importance that he should be strong of body, lively of mind, and capable of enduring great hardships.

The other officers of a large partisan corps must be chosen with similar care, for without exception they must be men of proven moderation, energy, loyalty, and physical resilience. Their duties are more unsettled and exacting than those of any other kind of troops, as they are never encumbered with tents and as the security of the army largely depends upon their vigilance.

Conversely, if the partisan ever allows himself to be taken by surprise, he has no excuse. He may of course be attacked, even cut to pieces, but he must never, either in the field or in his quarters, let himself be taken by surprise. . . .

Earlier, I mentioned the qualities required of a partisan. Here I feel I must add that the skill necessary for this extremely important branch of military science is rarely acquired in the course of normal service. . . .

If a partisan discovers an enemy spy in his own camp, by judicious treatment he will be able to use him for the furtherance of his own interests; it is only good sense to defer all punishment until one has tried every means of bringing him over to one's side. One must have the spy's every movement carefully watched in order to discover whether he has an associate in the corps itself or in the vicinity of the post. The partisan should look for a favorable moment to approach the spy because, with his knowledge of this type of person, he will probably be able to elicit some useful information, if not indeed to persuade the spy to act on his behalf. If the partisan is successful in this latter attempt, the spy will have an important part to play in the execution of the partisan's plans since he has free passage into the ranks of the opposing army. The information he provides should, however, never be believed entirely until other information has substantiated it and removed all grounds for doubting the spy's loyalty and reliability. . . .

Of the duties of an officer, none requires more wisdom or adroitness than the management of spies. These people are as a rule motivated solely by greed, yet no commanding general can afford to do without them, much less a partisan who is continually in an advanced position and from whom his general thus expects the most precise information. It would be quite superfluous for me to describe the great variety of ways in which spies can be used. I shall limit myself to a few words on the subject as a whole.

Spies are to be found among all classes of society and even among both sexes. Should circumstances require their services, they must be paid well and punctually and never be made to wait even a second for their remuneration so that their identity does not become known to anyone—be he officer or soldier—but the commander who gives him his instructions.

Georg Wilhelm Freiherr von Valentini

What Kind of Training?

What I understand by the phrase "small war" are all those actions undertaken in time of war which further an army's or corps' operations without themselves being directly connected with the conquest or retention of territory. In other words the "small war" entails the protection, even the concealment, of the main army besides those operations intended to inflict minor injury on the enemy.

Although at first it might appear that the results of the small war have no significant bearing on the outcome of the war as a whole, they are nevertheless of importance: they contain the means whereby that higher goal of warfare may be attained. Moreover, a successfully conducted small war weakens the enemy by reducing his capacity to hold out in the field. Such was the case in the French Revolutionary War [1791–2]. The French, being untrained civilian soldiers and in no position to engage their properly trained enemy in open combat, fell back on a more natural form of fighting—that of marksmen.

Georg Wilhelm Freiherr von Valentini, *Abhandlung über den kleinen Krieg und über den Gebrauch der leichten Truppen* (Berlin, 1799), and many later editions.

Their *tirailleurs,* harrying and tormenting the enemy from every side like a pack of dogs, gave the armies of the Allies, which were accustomed to fighting only in serried ranks, not a moment's peace. When numbers, the lie of the land, and the time of year favored them, they gained the upper hand. Thus in the winter campaign of 1793, the Austrian army in Alsace, unable to hold out any longer, was forced to retreat from the Hagenau and Weissenburg lines, this momentous withdrawal occurring without any decisive battle.

Later, in the Netherlands, the French emerged the victors from much larger encounters and battles. Nevertheless, it was the systematic harrying of the defeated armies and the practice of continuously pestering and plaguing them with sharpshooters that proved the overriding reason why periods of respite in traditional winter quarters vanished from war and why the allied armies found no rest until they were back on the other side of the Rhine. . . .

Napoleon's furious campaigns, however, all but put an end to small war as we have defined it. "In recent times," Bevenhorst wrote in 1809, "large-scale warfare has almost entirely swallowed up the small war, for in the campaigns of 1805, 1806, and 1809 no real small war was fought. Perhaps fighting on a small scale will return in the future. But for the present, when Napoleon, in glorious isolation, is riding the crest of war like Neptune on the waves of the ocean, coursing ahead of all the unleashed sons of Aeolus, for the present, when overthrow and enslavement are the order of the day for kings and peoples, there will be little thought of that other trifling pastime of the goddess of war so long as this hero lives, breathes, and wages war."

Clearly, what the witty commentator whose words I have so gladly reproduced here was referring to were those small-scale, separate actions against the enemy for which Napoleon left us no time. Yet this prophecy that "fighting on a small scale" would perhaps return in the future was very soon fulfilled in Spain, where it was crowned with success surpassing even the boldest expectations. That the enemy was driven from the peninsula, and even put under pressure in his own country, was of course primarily due to the victories of the Duke of Wellington. But anyone who has merely glanced at the history of this war knows how the peasants' war—as it is called—contributed to those victories and how it prevented the enemy from enjoying in tranquillity the fruits of its initial successes.

Any defensive war in which the people play a purposeful role through supporting the operations of the allied forces by waging a small war in the enemy's rear will meet with the same grand success. Even after he has won a battle, the enemy will never be able to gain a firm foothold in the country, except in fortified places he has either overpowered or laid out himself. Every detachment he sends out and every fresh supply of reinforcements, armaments, or food are exposed to attacks by waiting partisans. Fought in this manner on a large scale, small wars become wars of extermination for the enemy armies.

The war in the Vendée, however, cannot be described as a small war. The peasants who fought there so bravely for king and country were intent upon *completely* destroying the opposing forces. Versed in the skills of hunting, they exploited to the full the hedges, bushes, and concealed meandering paths that ran among them to creep up on the blue hordes, surround them on every side, and shoot them down with well-directed musket volleys. Then, when this musket-fire had caused the enemy to falter, they would charge upon him at exactly the right moment and finish him off in the shortest possible time in hand-to-hand fighting. Artillery fire, the efficacy of which was considerably impaired by the restricted range possible in that wooded country, was rendered harmless by the peasants' practice of hurling themselves to the ground when the cannons were fired. Then they would overpower the artillery in the final assault.

When the war began, no more than a minority of the peasants were armed with muskets, and even some of these were ordinary hunting guns. The remainder of the peasants were used for close-quarter combat. Until the moment for the charge had arrived, the few muskets available were given to the best marksmen, while others reloaded them. Whenever they seemed to be getting the worst of a skirmish, the nimble peasants would jump over the hedges and vanish down winding lanes. There appears to have been no more than a minimum of leadership and organization among them. The volunteers were informed only of the purpose of a raid and the place where it was to take place; as the men involved were completely at home in the terrain, this was sufficient.

The war in the Tyrol affords a similar picture. It is striking how in mountainous areas and generally in regions where men must wrestle with nature to survive and make a living, the inhabitants receive a training of mind and body that well fits them for war; this training

instills in them a natural tactical sense suited to the terrain which is
almost impossible to inculcate by artificial methods. Teaching those
who live on the plains and pursue their trades in cities or in leisurely
fashion plowing the open fields how to wage war after the manner
of those pugnacious highland people will be no easy matter. . . .

I now come to the question of what kind of training the commanding officer of light troops, or a commanding officer in wartime in
general, should receive. It has long been a matter of dispute whether
war is to be considered a mathematical science or a game of chance.
I do not wish to enter into the argument here, but in my opinion the
partisan is of all leaders in war the most justified in tempting fate
and, by trusting to his own eye and talent for making snap decisions,
in thumbing his nose at the sacred rules constructed on mathematical
principles. In order that he may not be lacking in these qualities, let
him develop his military gifts to the highest degree and, above all,
let him acquire that *attentiveness* which allows us to exploit the
present moment to the full and enables us to learn more from practical life than from books. Let him spend more time in the fields
and woods than in his study or in company indoors so that he may
know his way around in the terrain that is to be the setting for his
actions. A speculative disposition and pettymindedness are two dangerous liabilities for any commanding officer in time of war. The
first estranges him from nature and people, preventing him from being
able to coolly reflect upon what is in front of his eyes; the second
causes him to miss the essential for the inessential. Most necessary
of all, however, to the man who would be a leader is that moral
courage which lifts us above events and carries others along with us
at the crucial moment.

Here we find the explanation of the successes of men who have
had no great preparation or long practice in peacetime and of half-
trained men who, placed at the head of armies or regiments by virtue
of their blood or turbulent times, nonetheless have led their troops
to glory and triumph in the field. They possessed this practical gift of
which I have been speaking; they did not allow their minds to be
ruled by a fixed idea. Thanks to this openness of mind they rapidly
acquired from experience the knowledge they needed to become great
generals.

It is thus experience, our own and that gleaned from military
history, that should be our mentor. It is by gathering together the

practical rules we have derived from experience and then applying them to the matter at hand that we form our theory of the small war. Examples illustrated in the actual terrain in which they took place will provide valuable practice both for eye and judgment, thereby giving the reader wide scope for the development of his own ideas. . . .

Carl von Clausewitz

A Battalion in Battle

. . . It is a characteristic of troops fighting in small-scale wars that, side by side with great audacity and daring, they show a far greater aversion to actual danger than do those fighting in large-scale war. The enterprising spirit of the lone hussar or fusilier and his trust in himself and his luck can scarcely be imagined by a man who has never been outside the ranks. Accustomed by experience to undertaking a variety of difficult missions, the former remains calm and collected when the latter would be nervous and fearful. But, in contrast, the hussar and fusilier are much more mindful of danger in a normal battle than are troops of the line. Unless absolutely necessary, the former will never expose themselves to danger and will withdraw and seek cover whenever they can. . . .

This characteristic of the light troops is a necessary one. If they did not possess this aversion, how could they ceaselessly place themselves right under the enemy's nose, how could they go on giving battle almost daily without being completely destroyed in one campaign? Therefore, I am by no means reproaching the light troops for their circumspection; it is a quality they must have. They must alternate between great daring and prudent caution according to different circumstances, and each man must be capable of both in equal

Carl von Clausewitz, *Schriften-Aufsätze-Studien-Briefe*, ed. W. Hahlweg, Vol. I, (Göttingen, 1966).

measure. No man needs to be taught a fear of danger; nor do the light troops. Natural instinct teaches them to avoid it. The same would be true of the other troops if one did not do everything to suppress it. In large battles, one must brave danger, for here the individual's cleverness and cunning can achieve nothing. It is in the broad planning of the commands of the main parties that cleverness and coordination are needed; in a particular position, great energy and the most ferocious defiance of danger make the best sense.

A battalion in a battle or large engagement will rarely have an opportunity to distinguish itself by clever maneuvers; it distinguishes itself by its bravery, courageous charge, and steadfast, disciplined endurance of hours of bombardment. To say that a battalion has lost half or two thirds of its men in a battle is to need to say no more. This is not true in the case of light troops. In a fixed battle, the masses of men are pressed up close to each other and small units have less opportunity for combinations. Provided that it had already been exchanging fire with the enemy, a battalion that recklessly threw itself against it without paying any attention to the battalions next to it might bring about its own destruction. Yet this danger does not compare with the advantage such an action might bring, for a charge at this spot might alter the course of the whole battle and perhaps lead to final victory. There is no telling how many victories such an action could lead to, and one wishes that many battalions would indulge in this kind of recklessness. In small-scale wars, a similar advance by an isolated troop may bring advantages, but they will rarely be large or decisive. Moreover, that the forces in small-scale wars are spread over large areas means there is much opportunity for combinations and that the advancing troop could easily be destroyed without creating any prospect of a great victory. It is the inventiveness and improvisation that small-scale wars permit and the skillful combination of boldness and caution (in other words, the happy composition of daring and fear) which make them so superlatively interesting.

Carl von Clausewitz

People's War

A people's war in civilized Europe is a phenomenon of the nineteenth century. It has its advocates and its opponents: the latter either considering it in a political sense as a revolutionary means, a state of anarchy declared lawful, which is as dangerous as a foreign enemy to social order at home; or on military grounds, conceiving that the result is not commensurate with the expenditure of the nation's strength. The first point does not concern us here, for we look upon a people's war merely as a means of fighting, therefore, in its connection with the enemy; but with regard to the latter point, we must observe that a people's war in general is to be regarded as a consequence of the outburst which the military element in our day has made through its old formal limits; as an expansion and strengthening of the whole fermentation process which we call war. The requisition system, the immense increase in the size of armies by means of that system, and the general liability to military service, the utilizing militia, are all things which lie in the same direction, if we make the limited military system of former days our starting point; and the *levée en masse*, or arming of the people, now lies also in the same direction. If the first-named of these new aids to war are the natural and necessary consequences of barriers thrown down, and if they have so enormously increased the power of those who first used them that the enemy has been carried along in the current and obliged to adopt them likewise, this will be the case also with people's wars. In the generality of cases, the people who make judicious use of this means will gain a proportionate superiority over those who despise its use. If this be so, then the only question is whether this modern intensification of the military element is, upon the whole, salutary for

Carl von Clausewitz, *On War* (J. J. Graham, trans.) (London, 1873).

the interests of humanity or otherwise—a question which it would be about as easy to answer as the question of war itself—we leave both to philosophers. But the opinion may be advanced that the resources swallowed up in people's wars might be more profitably employed if used in providing other military means; no very deep investigation, however, is necessary to be convinced that these resources are for the most part not disposable and cannot be utilized in an arbitrary manner at pleasure. One essential part that is the moral element is not called into existence until this kind of employment for it arises.

We therefore do not ask again: how much does the resistance which the whole nation in arms is capable of making, cost that nation? but we ask: what is the effect which such a resistance can produce? What are its conditions, and how is it to be used?

It follows from the very nature of the thing that defensive means thus widely dispersed are not suited to great blows requiring concentrated action in time and space. Its operation, like the process of evaporation in physical nature, is according to the surface. The greater that surface and the greater the contact with the enemy's army, consequently the more that army spreads itself out, so much the greater will be the effects of arming the nation. Like a slow, gradual heat, it destroys the foundations of the enemy's army. As it requires time to produce its effects, therefore whilst the hostile elements are working on each other, there is a state of tension which either gradually wears out if the people's war is extinguished at some points and burns slowly away at others, or leads to a crisis if the flames of this general conflagration envelop the enemy's army and compel it to evacuate the country to save itself from utter destruction. In order that this result should be produced by a national war alone, we must suppose either a surface extent of the dominions invaded, exceeding that of any country in Europe, except Russia, or suppose a disproportion between the strength of the invading army and the extent of the country, such as never occurs in reality. Therefore, to avoid following a phantom, we must imagine a people's war always in combination with a war carried on by a regular army, and both carried on according to a plan embracing the operations of the whole.

The conditions under which alone the people's war can become effective are the following—

1. That the war is carried on in the heart of the country.
2. That it cannot be decided by a single catastrophe.

3. That the theater of war embraces a considerable extent of country.

4. That the national character is favorable to the measure.

5. That the country is of a broken and difficult nature, either from being mountainous, or by reason of woods and marshes, or from the peculiar mode of cultivation in use.

Whether the population is dense or otherwise is of little consequence, as there is less likelihood of a want of men than of anything else. Whether the inhabitants are rich or poor is also a point by no means decisive, at least it should not be; but it must be admitted that a poor population accustomed to hard work and privations usually shows itself more vigorous and better suited for war.

One peculiarity of country which greatly favors the action of war carried on by the people is the scattered sites of the dwellings of the country people, such as is to be found in many parts of Germany. The country is thus more intersected and covered; the roads are worse, although more numerous; the lodgement of troops is attended with endless difficulties, but especially that peculiarity repeats itself on a small scale which a people's war possesses on a great scale, namely that the principle of resistance exists everywhere but is nowhere tangible. If the inhabitants are collected in villages, the most troublesome have troops quartered on them, or they are plundered as a punishment, and their houses burnt, etc., a system which could not be very easily carried out with a peasant community of Westphalia.

National levies and armed peasantry cannot and should not be employed against the main body of the enemy's army, or even against any considerable corps of the same; they must not attempt to crack the nut, they must only gnaw on the surface and the borders. They should rise in the provinces situated at one of the sides of the theater of war, and in which the assailant does not appear in force, in order to withdraw these provinces entirely from his influence. Where no enemy is to be found, there is no want of courage to oppose him, and at the example thus given, the mass of the neighboring population gradually takes fire. Thus the fire spreads as it does in heather, and reaching at last that part of the surface of the soil on which the aggressor is based, it seizes his lines of communication and preys upon the vital thread by which his existence is supported. For although we entertain no exaggerated ideas of the omnipotence of a people's war, such as that it is an inexhaustible, unconquerable element over which the mere force of an army has as little control as the human will has over the wind or the rain—in short, although our opinion is not founded on flowery ephemeral literature, still we must admit that armed peasants are not to be driven before us in the same way as a body of soldiers who keep together like a herd of cattle and usually follow their noses. Armed peasants, on the contrary, when broken, disperse in all directions, for which no formal plan is required; through this circumstance, the march of every small body of troops in a mountainous, thickly wooded, or even broken country becomes a service of a very dangerous character, for at any moment a combat may arise on the march; if in point of fact no armed bodies have even been seen for some time, yet the same peasants already driven off by the head of a column may at any hour make their appearance in its rear. If it is an object to destroy roads or to block up a defile, the means which outposts or detachments from an army can apply to that purpose bear about the same relation to those furnished by a body of insurgent peasants as the action of an automaton does to that of a human being. The enemy has no other means to oppose to the action of national levies except that of detaching numerous parties to furnish escorts for convoys to occupy military stations, defiles, bridges, etc. In proportion as the first efforts of the national levies are small, so the detachments sent out will be weak in numbers, from the repugnance to a great dispersion of forces; it is on these weak bodies that the fire of the national war usually first properly kindles itself; they are overpowered by numbers at some points, courage rises, the love of fighting gains strength, and the intensity of this struggle increases until the crisis approaches which is to decide the issue.

According to our idea of a people's war, it should, like a kind of nebulous vapory essence, never condense into a solid body; otherwise the enemy sends an adequate force against this core, crushes it, and takes a great many prisoners; their courage sinks; everyone thinks the main question is decided, any further effort useless, and the arms fall from the hands of the people. Still, however, on the other hand, it is necessary that this mist should collect at some points into denser masses and form threatening clouds from which now and again a formidable flash of lightning may burst forth. These points are chiefly on the flanks of the enemy's theater of war, as already observed. There the armament of the people should be organized into greater and more systematic bodies, supported by a small force of regular troops, so as to give it the appearance of a regular force and fit it to venture upon enterprises on a larger scale. From these points, the irregular character in the organization of these bodies should diminish in proportion as they are to be employed more in the direction of the rear of the enemy, where he is exposed to their hardest blows. These better organized masses are for the purpose of falling upon the larger garrisons which the enemy leaves behind him. Besides, they serve to create a feeling of uneasiness and dread and increase the moral impression of the whole; without them the total action would be wanting in force, and the situation of the enemy upon the whole would not be made sufficiently uncomfortable. . . . After these reflections, which are more of the nature of subjective impressions than an objective analysis, because the subject is one as yet of rare occurrence generally, and has been but imperfectly treated of by those who have had actual experience for any length of time, we have only to add that the strategic plan of defense can include in itself the cooperation of a general arming of the people in two different ways, that is, either as a last resource after a lost battle or as a natural assistance before a decisive battle has been fought. . . .

No state should believe its fate, that is, its entire existence, to be dependent upon one battle, let it be even the most decisive. If it is beaten, the calling forth fresh power, and the natural weakening which every offensive undergoes with time, may bring about a turn of fortune, or assistance may come from abroad. No such urgent haste to die is needed yet; and as by instinct the drowning man catches at a straw, so in the natural course of the moral world a people should try the last means of deliverance when it sees itself hurried along to the brink of an abyss.

However small and weak a state may be in comparison to its enemy, if it foregoes a last supreme effort, we must say there is no longer any soul left in it. This does not exclude the possibility of saving itself from complete destruction by the purchase of peace at a sacrifice; but neither does such an aim on its part do away with the utility of fresh measures for defense; they will neither make peace more difficult nor more onerous, but easier and better. They are still more necessary if there is an expectation of assistance from those who are interested in maintaining our political existence. Any government, therefore, which, after the loss of a great battle, only thinks how it may speedily place the nation in the lap of peace and, un-manned by the feelings of great hopes disappointed, no longer feels in itself the courage or the desire to stimulate to the utmost every element of force, completely stultifies itself in such case through weakness, and shows itself unworthy of victory, and, perhaps, just on that account, was incapable of gaining one.

However decisive, therefore, the overthrow may be which is ex-perienced by a state, still by a retreat of the army into the interior, the efficacy of its fortresses and an arming of the people may be brought into use. In connection with this it is advantageous if the flank of the principal theater of war is fenced in by mountains, or otherwise very difficult tracts of country, which stand forth as bas-tions, the strategic enfilade of which is to check the enemy's progress.

PART II

Napoleon
and After

Introductory Note

Following the Napoleonic Wars, greater attention was paid to the political aspects of partisan warfare. This section opens with the chapter on national war from *Précis de l'art de guerre* published by Antoine Henri de Jomini in Paris in 1838. Swiss by origin, General de Jomini (1779–1869) had served in Napoleon's army.

Francisco Espoz y Mina (1781–1836) was the best-known Spanish guerrilla leader of his time; he fought with less success in the first Carlist War. His *Memorias* were published posthumously; the excerpt presented here is from *A Short Extract from the Life of General Mina Published by Himself* (London, 1825).

Denis Vasilevich Davydov (1784–1839), Russian poet and cavalry officer, was the outstanding partisan commander among those fighting the French army near Moscow in 1812. He is the author of a fascinating diary about partisan operations, from which the present excerpts are taken,[1] and of a theoretical essay on partisan warfare (1821).

Lemière de Corvey (1770–1832) and Carl von Decker (1784–1844) are the authors of the two classic nineteenth-century books on partisan warfare. For many decades these works provided inspiration to authors all over Europe.[2] Lemière, also known as a composer, had fought as an officer in the Napoleonic army in the Vendée and Spain. He emphasized that partisan war, far from being primitive, was essentially novel, that it was pointless to treat partisans as mere brigands, and that the application of traditional military doctrine was of little use in combatting them. Major (subsequently General) von Decker also stressed that partisan warfare was more difficult than conventional war; even a mediocre talent could make a useful

[1] *Voennie Zapiski* (Moscow, 1940).
[2] Lemière de Corvey, *Des partisans et des corps irréguliers* (Paris, 1823). Carl von Decker, *Der Kleine Krieg im Geiste der neueren Kriegsführung* (Berlin, 1822).

contribution in regular warfare; partisan warfare, however, called for very special qualities.

In the political context the Italian and Polish guerrilla literature of the nineteenth century is by far the most important, for it provides the link between radical politics and partisan warfare tactics. The ideas of "bases," political indoctrination, the use of terrorism, and the gradual transformation of guerrilla war into regular war is found in the writings of the contemporary authors. The Polish and Italian writers represented in this section knew each other and collaborated on various occasions. Stolzman and Carlo Bianco helped to prepare Mazzini's ill-fated invasion of Savoy; Chrzanowski was chief of staff of the Piedmontese army at one time. Giuseppe Mazzini (1805–1872), the hero of the Risorgimento, was not a military leader, but among his writings were *Istruzione per le bandi nazionali* (1853), from which the excerpts below have been taken. More important as a military theorist was Carlo Bianco, Conte di St. Jorioz (1795–1843). The son of an ennobled Turin lawyer, he served in the army in Spain and later became a member of the radical-democratic wing of the Italian nationalist underground. His two-volume magnum opus was written and published in Malta.[3] His last years were spent in impoverished exile in France, Switzerland, and Belgium. Wojciech Chrzanowski (1793–1861) participated in Napoleon's invasion of Russia as a young lieutenant and was subsequently an officer in the Russian army. He was chief of staff of the rebel Polish units in 1831. Later he became a military and political adviser to the British government and a general in the Italian army. Karol Bogumir Stolzman (1793–1854) also participated in the last phase of the Napoleonic Wars and later served in the Russian army. He took part in the Polish insurrection of 1830 and, as an emigré, represented his native country on Mazzini's Young Europe committee. After 1835, England became his permanent home.[4]

---

[3] *Della guerra nazionale d'insurrezione per bande applicata all'Italia. Trattato dedicato ai buoni Italiani da un amico del paese*, 2 vols. (Italia, 1830). Soon after, an abridged and slightly modified version appeared from which these excerpts were taken, *Manuale pratico del rivoluzionario italiano* . . . (Italy, 1833).

[4] Chrzanowski's *O wojnie partyzanckiej* (Paris, 1835) was not accessible and the present translation is from *Über den Parteigänger-Krieg* (Berlin, 1846). Stolzman's main work is *Partyzanka czyli wojna dla ludow powstajacych najwlasciwza* (Paris, 1844).

Gingins-La Sarraz (1790–1863), author of *Les partisans et la défense de la Suisse* (Lausanne, 1861), was an amateur botanist and historian of some standing with a particular interest in medieval and regional history.

Antoine-Fortuné de Brack (1789–1850) began his military career in the Napoleonic Wars and later became known as a successful regimental commander, *beau sabreur,* and important military writer. The excerpts on partisan units are taken from the English translation of *Avant-postes de cavalerie legère—Advanced Posts of Light Cavalry* (London, 1850).

Antoine Henri de Jomini

National Wars

National wars, to which we have referred in speaking of those of invasion, are the most formidable of all. This name can only be applied to such as are waged against a united people, or a great majority of them, filled with a noble ardor and determined to sustain their independence: then every step is disputed, the army holds only its camp ground, its supplies can only be obtained at the point of the sword, and its convoys are everywhere threatened or captured.

The spectacle of a spontaneous uprising of a nation is rarely seen; and, though there be in it something grand and noble which commands our admiration, the consequences are so terrible that, for the sake of humanity, we ought to hope never to see it. This uprising must not be confounded with a national defense in accordance with the institutions of the state and directed by the government.

This uprising may be produced by the most opposite causes. The serfs may rise in a body at the call of the government, and their masters, affected by a noble love of their sovereign and country, may

Antoine Henri de Jomini, *Précis de l'art de la guerre* (Paris, 1838) [in English: Philadelphia, 1862].

set them the example and take the command of them; and, similarly, a fanatical people may arm under the appeal of its priests; or a people enthusiastic in its political opinions, or animated by a sacred love of its institutions, may rush to meet the enemy in defense of all it holds most dear.

The control of the sea is of much importance in the results of a national invasion. If the people possess a long stretch of coast, and are masters of the sea or in alliance with a power which controls it, their power of resistance is quintupled, not only on account of the facility of feeding the insurrection and of alarming the enemy on all the points he may occupy, but still more by the difficulties which will be thrown in the way of his procuring supplies by the sea.

The nature of the country may be such as to contribute to the facility of a national defense. In mountainous countries the people are always most formidable; next to these are countries covered with extensive forests.

The resistance of the Swiss to Austria and to the Duke of Burgundy, that of the Catalans in 1712 and in 1809, the difficulties encountered by the Russians in the subjugation of the tribes of the Caucasus, and, finally, the reiterated efforts of the Tyrolese, clearly demonstrate that the inhabitants of mountainous regions have always resisted for a longer time than those of the plains—which is due as much to the difference in character and customs as to the difference in the natural features of the countries.

Defiles and large forests, as well as rocky regions, favor this kind of defense; and the Bocage of La Vendée, so justly celebrated, proves that any country, even if it be only traversed by large hedges and ditches or canals, admits of a formidable defense.

The difficulties in the path of an army in wars of opinions, as well as in national wars, are very great, and render the mission of the general conducting them very difficult. The events just mentioned, the contest of the Netherlands with Philip II, and that of the Americans with the English, furnish evident proofs of this; but the much more extraordinary struggle of La Vendée with the victorious Republic, those of Spain, Portugal, and the Tyrol against Napoleon, and, finally, those of the Morea against the Turks, and of Navarre against the armies of Queen Christina, are still more striking illustrations.

The difficulties are particularly great when the people are supported by a considerable nucleus of disciplined troops. The invader has only an army: his adversaries have an army, and a people wholly or almost wholly in arms, and making means of resistance out of everything, each individual of whom conspires against the common enemy; even the noncombatants have an interest in his ruin and accelerate it by every means in their power. He holds scarcely any ground but that upon which he encamps; outside the limits of his camp everything is hostile and multiplies a thousandfold the difficulties he meets at every step.

These obstacles become almost insurmountable when the country is difficult. Each armed inhabitant knows the smallest paths and their connections; he finds everywhere a relative or friend who aids him; the commanders also know the country, and, learning immediately the slightest movement on the part of the invader, can adopt the best measures to defeat his projects; while the latter, without information of their movements, and not in a condition to send out detachments to gain it, having no resource but in his bayonets, and certain safety only in the concentration of his columns, is like a blind man: his combinations are failures, and when, after the most carefully concerted movements and the most rapid and fatiguing marches, he thinks he is about to accomplish his aim and deal a terrible blow, he finds no signs of the enemy but his camp fires: so that while, like Don Quixote, he is attacking windmills, his adversary is on his line of communications, destroys the detachments left to guard it, surprises his convoys, his depots, and carries on a war so disastrous for the invader that he must inevitably yield after a time.

In Spain I was a witness of two terrible examples of this kind. When Ney's corps replaced Soult's at Corunna, I had camped the companies of the artillery train between Betanzos and Corunna, in the midst of four brigades distant from the camp from two to three leagues, and no Spanish forces had been seen within fifty miles; Soult still occupied Santiago de Compostela, the division Maurice-Mathieu was at Ferrol and Lugo, Marchand's at Corunna and Betanzos: nevertheless, one fine night the companies of the train—men and horses—disappeared, and we were never able to discover what became of them: a solitary wounded corporal escaped to report that the peasants, led by their monks and priests, had thus made away with them. Four months afterward, Ney with a single division marched to conquer the Asturias, descending the valley of the Navia, while Kellermann debouched from Leon by the Oviedo road. A part of the corps of

La Romana which was guarding the Asturias marched behind the very heights which enclose the valley of the Navia, at most but a league from our columns, without the marshal knowing a word of it: when he was entering Gijon, the army of La Romana attacked the center of the regiments of the division Marchand, which, being scattered to guard Galicia, barely escaped, and that only by the prompt return of the marshal to Lugo. This war presented a thousand incidents as striking as this. All the gold of Mexico could not have procured reliable information for the French; what was given was but a lure to make them fall more readily into snares.

No army, however disciplined, can contend successfully against such a system applied to a great nation, unless it be strong enough to hold all the essential points of the country, cover its communications, and at the same time furnish an active force sufficient to beat the enemy wherever he may present himself. If this enemy has a regular army of respectable size to be a nucleus around which to rally the people, what force will be sufficient to be superior everywhere, and to assure the safety of the long lines of communication against numerous bodies?

The Peninsular War should be carefully studied, to learn all the obstacles which a general and his brave troops may encounter in the occupation or conquest of a country whose people are all in arms. What efforts of patience, courage, and resignation did it not cost the troops of Napoleon, Massena, Soult, Ney, and Suchet to sustain themselves for six years against three or four hundred thousand armed Spaniards and Portuguese supported by the regular armies of Wellington, Beresford, Blake, La Romana, Cuesta, Castaños, Reding, and Ballasteros!

If success be possible in such a war, the following general course will be most likely to insure it—viz.: make a display of a mass of troops proportioned to the obstacles and resistance likely to be encountered, calm the popular passions in every possible way, exhaust them by time and patience, display courtesy, gentleness, and severity united, and, particularly, deal justly. The examples of Henry IV in the wars of the League, of Marshal Berwick in Catalonia, of Suchet in Aragon and Valencia, of Hoche in La Vendée are models of their kind, which may be employed according to circumstances with equal success. The admirable order and discipline of the armies of Diebitsch and Paskevitch in the late war were also models, and were not a little conducive to the success of their enterprises.

The immense obstacles encountered by an invading force in these wars have led some speculative persons to hope that there should never be any other kind, since then wars would become more rare, and conquest, being also more difficult, would be less a temptation to ambitious leaders. This reasoning is rather plausible than solid; for, to admit all its consequences, it would be necessary always to be able to induce the people to take up arms, and it would also be necessary for us to be convinced that there would be in the future no wars but those of conquest, and that all legitimate though secondary wars, which are only to maintain the political equilibrium or defend the public interests, should never occur again: otherwise, how could it be known when and how to excite the people to a national war? For example, if one hundred thousand Germans crossed the Rhine and entered France, originally with the intention of preventing the conquest of Belgium by France, and without any other ambitious project, would it be a case where the whole population—men, women, and children—of Alsace, Lorraine, Champagne, and Burgundy should rush to arms? to make a Saragossa of every walled town, to bring about, by way of reprisals, murder, pillage, and incendiarism throughout the country? If all this be not done, and the Germans, in consequence of some success, should occupy these provinces, who can say that they might not afterward seek to appropriate a part of them, even though at first they had never contemplated it? The difficulty of answering these two questions would seem to argue in favor of national wars. But is there no means of repelling such an invasion without bringing about an uprising of the whole population and a war of extermination? Is there no mean between these contests between the people and the old regular method of war between permanent armies? Will it not be sufficient, for the efficient defense of the country, to organize a militia, or landwehr, which, uniformed and called by their governments into service, would regulate the part the people should take in the war, and place just limits to its barbarities?

I answer in the affirmative; and, applying this mixed system to the cases stated above, I will guarantee that fifty thousand regular French troops, supported by the National Guards, of the East, would get the better of this German army which had crossed the Vosges; for, reduced to fifty thousand men by many detachments, upon nearing the

Meuse or arriving in Argonne it would have one hundred thousand men on its hands. To attain this mean, we have laid it down as a necessity that good national reserves be prepared for the army; which will be less expensive in peace and will insure the defense of the country in war. This system was used by France in 1792, imitated by Austria in 1809, and by the whole of Germany in 1813.

I sum up this discussion by asserting that, without being a utopian philanthropist, or a condottiere, a person may desire that wars of extermination may be banished from the code of nations, and that the defenses of nations by disciplined militia, with the aid of good political alliances, may be sufficient to insure their independence.

As a soldier, preferring loyal and chivalrous warfare to organized assassination, if it be necessary to make a choice, I acknowledge that my prejudices are in favor of the good old times when the French and English guards courteously invited each other to fire first—as at Fontenoy—preferring them to the frightful epoch when priests, women, and children throughout Spain plotted the murder of isolated soldiers.

Francisco Espoz y Mina

Fighting in Spain

I kept in check in Navarre 26,000 men for the space of 53 days, who otherwise would have assisted at the battle of Salamanca, as they were on their march to join Marmont's army; and by cutting down the bridges, and breaking up the roads, I prevented the advance of 80 pieces of artillery, which would otherwise have been employed in that battle.

I contributed to the happy result of the decisive battle of Vittoria; for if, by the maneuvers, I executed, I had not prevented the junction

Francisco Espoz y Mina, *A Short Extract from the Life of General Mina Published by Himself* (London, 1825).

of the French divisions Claussel and Foi, which consisted of from 27 to 28,000 men, and intercepted their correspondence, the issue would have been very doubtful . . .

The French, rendered furious by the disasters they experienced in Navarre, and by their fruitless attempts to exterminate my troops, having begun a horrible mode of warfare upon me in 1811, hanging and shooting every soldier and officer of mine who fell into their hands, as also the friends of the volunteers who served with me, and carrying off to France a great number of families, I published on the 14th of December the same year, a solemn Declaration, composed of 23 articles, the first of which ran thus: *In Navarre, a war of extermination, without quarter, is declared against the French army, without distinction of soldiers or chiefs, not excepting the Emperor of the French.* And this sort of warfare I carried on for some time, keeping always in the valley of Roncal a great depot of prisoners, so that if the enemy hung or shot one of my officers, I did the same with four of his; if one of my soldiers, I did the same with twenty of his. In this manner I succeeded in terrifying him. . . .

I never suffered a surprise. Once, on the 23d April, 1812, at break of day, having been sold by the Partisan Malcarado, who had previously made his arrangements with General Panetier, and had withdrawn the advanced guard from before Robres, I saw myself surrounded in the town by 1,000 infantry and 200 cavalry, and was attacked by five hussars at the very door of the house where I lodged: I defended myself from these latter with the bar of the door, the only weapon I had at hand, while my attendant, Louis Gaston, was saddling my horse; and mounting immediately, with his assistance, I sallied forth, charged them, followed them up the street, cut off an arm of one of them at one blow, immediately collected some of my men, charged the enemy several times, rescued many of my soldiers and officers who had been made prisoners, and continued the contest for more than three quarters of an hour, in order that the remainder might escape. This Louis Gaston I always retain about my person as a friend. The next day I caused Malcarado and his attendant to be shot; while three alcaldes and a parish priest, likewise concerned in the plot, were hanging.

Amidst the numberless toils and anxieties by which I was continually surrounded, and which scarcely allowed me a moment's repose, *never having counted upon any assistance from the govern-*

ment, either pecuniary or otherwise (these very words are in the government's statement of my services), I found means to raise, organize, discipline, and maintain a division of infantry and cavalry, composed of nine regiments of the first and two of the latter class, whose total amount at the end of the campaign was 13,500 men.

My division took from the enemy, at different periods, 13 strong places and fortresses, and more than 14,000 prisoners (not including those made during the time that no quarter was given), with an immense number of pieces of artillery, quantities of arms, clothing, stores, and provisions, etc. etc. etc. The delivery of this number of prisoners at Valencia, Alicante, Lerida, the Cantabrian coast, and at other points to which I ordered them to be taken, I have officially authenticated.

From an examination of the returns of killed, wounded, and prisoners, the result is a loss on my side of 5,000 men, while that of the enemy, including their prisoners, does not fall far short of 40,000.

The Spanish prisoners whom I rescued amount to above 4,000; among them were some generals, many chiefs and officers, and not a few partisan leaders.

I was several times wounded by musket balls, sabers, or lances. I have still a ball in my thigh, which the surgeons have never been able to extract.

I had four horses killed under me, and several wounded in action.

A price was set upon my head by the enemy from the end of 1811 till the conclusion of the war.

Denis Davydov

Partisans Against Napoleon

In the meantime the hostile army was pressing on toward the capital. For a distance of thirty or forty versts it was followed along both sides of the road by countless numbers of baggage wagons, transports, and bands of marauders. Taking advantage of the prevailing anarchy, this riffraff indulged in excesses of violence and savagery. Fire was spreading over this wide band of devastation, and the populations of whole *volosts*[1] were fleeing, whither they knew not, from this all-consuming lava, taking what remained of their possessions with them. However, in order to gain a clearer picture of the situation of my own detachment, I was obliged to take a higher route. Our way became more dangerous as the distance between ourselves and the army increased. Even the places the enemy had left untouched presented us with numerous obstacles. Soon we encountered a general force of volunteer irregulars consisting of local peasants that blocked our way. The gates to every settlement were barred, and behind them stood the inhabitants, every man, woman, and child brandishing pitchforks, picks, and axes; some of them had firearms. Every time we drew near a settlement, one of us was obliged to approach the inhabitants and tell them that we were Russians come to help them defend the Orthodox Church. Frequently they answered us by firing a shot or powerfully swinging an axe, from whose blows we were saved only by the mercy of fate. We could have avoided passing through the settlements, but I desired to spread the word that the army was returning and to confirm the peasants in their intention to defend themselves. I also wished to dispose them to immediately inform us of the enemy's approach, for which reason we continued to parley with each settlement before entering its streets. When this had been done,

Denis Davydov, *Voennie Zapiski* (Moscow, 1940). •
[1] Districts.

the scene was transformed: once the people's doubt had given way to the certainty that we were Russians, our soldiers were presented with bread, beer, and pies.

After we had made peace with a village, every time that I asked the inhabitants, "Why did you suppose us to be the French?" they pointed to my hussar's cloak and answered: "Why, see here, old man, this looks a bit like their clothes, indeed it does." "But am I not speaking the Russian tongue?" "Yes, but they have all sorts and manner of people with them." It was then that I learned by my own experience that in a popular war one must not only speak the language of the mob but also adapt one's habits and dress to its own. Accordingly, I donned a peasant caftan and started growing a beard. Instead of the Order of Saint Anne the icon of Saint Nikolai hung around my neck. I also taught myself to converse with the peasants in their own language.

How insignificant, though, were these dangers compared with those that awaited us on the ground occupied by enemy detachments and transports! Our party was very small in comparison with each transport cover, even in comparison with each band of marauders. At the first rumor of our arrival in the neighborhood of Vyazma, powerful detachments came looking for us. The inhabitants, disarmed and trembling in fear of the French, were consequently quite liable to indiscretion. All this put us in fear for our lives.

To escape death, therefore, we passed the day in furtive vigilance on the heights near Skugorevo. As dusk fell, we lit fires a short distance from the village. Then, moving much farther away from where we had made our camp for the night, we lit more fires, and finally, we entered the forest and spent the night there with no fires. If in this place we chanced upon a passerby, we took him prisoner and kept him under surveillance until we resumed our march. Then, when he had had time to disappear from sight, we changed our position again. According to our distance from the object of our attack, we rose one, two, or even three hours before dawn to carry out our raids. Smashing whatever we could in one of the enemy's transports, we turned to the next; then, having struck yet another blow, we would return by a circuitous route to the forest which was our salvation and little by little steal our way through it to Skugorevo.

In this way we roamed about and fought from the 29th of August to the 8th of September. It was in this manner, I suppose, that Yermak[2] also started out. With a far greater talent than mine, he fought, however, for a tyrant, not for his fatherland. Never will I forget you, hardest of times! I had before and have since been in savage battles and passed nights standing on my feet, leaning against my horse's saddle, my hands on the reins. But never have I done so for ten days and nights in succession, not as a matter of honor, but of life and death.

Having learned that a band of marauders had arrived at the village of Tokarevo, we fell upon them at dawn on the 2nd of September and took prisoner ninety men who had been loading a string of transport wagons with goods and chattels stolen from the inhabitants of the village. Scarcely had the cossacks and peasants begun dividing the spoils among themselves when our secret pickets posted beyond the settlement let us know that a second band of marauders was approaching Tokarevo. The settlement lies on the slope of a hill beside the bank of the river Vorya. Because of this we were completely out of the enemy's sight and they filed past without the least caution. We mounted our horses, hid behind the cottages, and when the enemy were a few *sazhens*[3] from the settlement, we attacked them on all sides, noisily shouting and firing. Bursting in among the baggage wagons, we captured another seventy men.

Then I summoned the village *mir*,[4] to whom I pretended that a large number of our troops had arrived to help the *uyezds*[5] of Yukhnov and Vyazma. Distributing among the peasants the rifles and cartridges we had seized from the enemy, I urged them to defend their property and told them how to deal with bands of marauders whose numbers exceeded theirs. "Receive them amicably," I said, "and bow before them, for since they do not know the Russian tongue, they will understand bows better than words. Offer them all you have to eat and especially to drink so that they will lie down to sleep like drunken men. When you see that they have fallen asleep, seize their arms, which they usually place in a pile in the corner of the hut or outside it, and do that which God has commanded should be done with the enemies of Christ's Church and your native land. When you have

[2] The pioneer who first traversed Siberia.
[3] 2.13 meters = 1 sazhen.
[4] Council.
[5] Districts.

destroyed them, bury their bodies in a cattle shed, the forest, or some other impenetrable place. Take care that fresh or newly dug earth does not make the burial place conspicuous. Conceal it by throwing on it heaps of stones, sticks, cinders, or anything else. Burn all the military spoils—uniforms, helmets, waist-belts, and suchlike—or bury them in places like those where you will bury the bodies of the French. This caution is necessary, for if another band of infidels sees the fresh soil, they will be sure to dig it up, thinking to find money or even your own possessions. But should they discover instead the bodies of their comrades and articles that belonged to them, they will kill you and burn down your village.

"As head man of the village, my brother, I charge you with the supervision of all I have ordered. Moreover, you should order three or four men to be always ready outside your house so that, when they catch sight of a very large company of French, they can mount their horses and gallop off in separate directions to find me. I shall come to your assistance. God commands Orthodox Christians to live in peace among themselves and not to betray one another to our enemies, especially to the children of the Antichrist who do not spare even our places of holy worship. All that I have told you, tell your neighbors."

I did not dare issue these instructions in writing, fearing lest they might fall into the hands of the enemy and so inform him of the ways and means of destroying the marauders I had suggested to the inhabitants . . .

I have observed that certain guerrillas leading a unit of troops think they command not a detachment but an army and regard themselves not as guerrillas but as military captains. For this reason they are obsessed with a single idea—to *cut the opposing party off* from the army to which it belongs and to take up positions according to the Austrian methods. They should know once and for all that the best position for a detachment is for it to be continually on the move, thus causing uncertainty about its proper location and requiring the sentries and mounted patrols guarding against it to be unceasingly vigilant. They should also know that there is no possibility of cutting off the [enemy] detachment and that they should stick to the Russian proverb: *kill and get away*. This, in essence, is the tactical duty of the guerrilla. My opponent did not know this; therefore it was easy for me to get the better of him.

After sending our booty to the town by the means I had used before, we continued toward the high road, passing close by it—with little gain—until the 29th.

Denis Davydov

On Guerrilla Warfare

The concept of guerrilla warfare which still predominates is the result of a one-sided attitude or an apparently cautious view of the subject. Seizing prisoners and making them talk, committing to flames one or two enemy storehouses located near the army, suddenly smashing the advance guard, or viewing the multiplication of small detachments as the systematic and pernicious fragmentation of the army's effectiveness—these are usually the essential definitions of this type of warfare. All are erroneous! Guerrilla warfare consists neither of quite minor enterprises nor of those of the first order of magnitude, for it is not concerned with the burning of one or two granaries, nor with smashing pickets, nor with striking direct blows at the main forces of the enemy. Rather, it embraces and traverses the whole length of the enemy lines, from the opposing army's rear to the area of territory assigned for the stationing of troops, provisions, and weapons. Thus, guerrilla warfare stops up the source of the army's strength and continuing existence and puts it at the mercy of the guerrillas' own army while the enemy army is weakened, hungry, disarmed, and deprived of the saving bonds of authority. This is guerrilla warfare in the fullest sense of the word!

There is no doubt that this kind of warfare would be less effective were it waged only between low-powered armies that did not require large quantities of food and supplies and that fought only with cold steel. However, the invention of gunpowder and firearms, the great increase in the size of military forces, and the preference for the concentration rather than fragmentation of forces posed impossible obstacles to the procurement of food supplies from the occupied territory. Also immense difficulties were encountered in the manufacture of charges in laboratories, the training of recruits, and the mustering of reserves amidst the alarms, engagements, and general accidents of war.

Under these circumstances, it became necessary to provide troops with all the necessities of war in a way that would not entail their procurement from the occupied area, something which would be impossible because of the disproportion between the number of consumers and the amount producible. The solution was to obtain the necessities from areas beyond the range of military operations. Hence there came about the division of the theater of war into two fields, the battlefield and the reserves field, the former being supplied by the produce of the latter. This produce would come not all at once or in bulk but as the army used up the provisions and military equipment it carried with it. Thus troops would not be burdened with excessive loads that would hamper their movement. Naturally, however, this invention led to a counter-invention with which the enemy could obstruct the delivery of supplies of the produce so vital to the efficiency of the opposing side. Two ways of achieving this aim were immediately obvious: action on the battlefield by detachments against the rear of the army where newly supplied ammunition and provisions are distributed and newly arrived reserve troops deployed, or action by these same detachments on the reserves field itself.

But then it was discovered that the first of these, the battlefield, was difficult of access owing to the close proximity of the enemy to the place appointed for the attack and that the second, the reserves field, was usually protected by fortifications enclosing the stores of provision, the ammunition factory, and the reserve formations. There remained the ground over which these three items were transported to the army. This is the field of guerrilla operations. It presents none of those obstacles that abound on both the battlefield and the reserves field because the enemy's main forces and fortifications, being located at its extremities, are in no position to defend it—the former because all their efforts are directed at fighting the main army of their adversary, the latter by reason of their natural immobility.

Hence it follows that guerrilla warfare cannot exist when the opposing army is situated on the reserves field itself. But the greater the distance separating the battlefield and the reserves field becomes, the more effective and decisive guerrilla warfare can be. Prudent commanders do not fail to provide the entire length of the main supply route across the aforesaid territory with fortified stages or shelters to protect transports during halts or night stops and to supply troop detachments to cover these transports while they are on the march between stages. These sensible measures are nonetheless vastly inadequate in the face of attacks by numerous active brigades, as indeed any defensive operation is inferior to an offensive one. Another consideration is that the fortified stages, however spacious they may be, cannot accommodate the number of carts that go to make up even the smallest transport required by the armies of our times. The cover, however numerous it may be, can never operate as a single body for the reason that, in order to protect the entire length of the transport, it is obliged to spread out along its whole length during marches and therefore must always be weaker at any pressure point than a detachment operating as a whole. In addition to these inconveniences, much military strength is required to provide the army with fortified halts, the number of which increases as the army advances, its successes luring it farther away from its reserves field.

As a definitive illustration of the great importance of guerrilla warfare in modern operations involving huge armies and concentrations of supplies, let us ask some questions and give the answers. First: by whom is war waged? By people, joined together in an army.

Second: can people do battle empty-handed? No. War is not like fist-fighting. These people need weapons. But now that gunpowder has been invented, even weapons alone are insufficient. Soldiers need cartridges and charges for their weapons. As these charges and cartridges are almost completely discharged during the course of each battle and since their manufacture is difficult during troop movements and operations, new supplies must be sent directly from the place where they are prepared. This is a clear demonstration that an army with weapons but without cartridges and charges is no better than an organized crowd of people with bear spears, a crowd which will scatter at the first shot from the enemy or, if it accepts battle, which will perish in so doing. In short, there is no strength in an army, for since the invention of gunpowder, an army without charges and cartridges is no army at all.

Third: does an army require reinforcement during the course of a war? Yes, it does. Men and horses are lost in battles, skirmishes, and exchange of fire; they become casualties to wounds received in battle or to diseases which run increasingly rampant because of the intense pressure of campaigns, inclement weather, and strains and shortages of all kinds. An army unable to refurbish itself will inevitably dwindle and disappear.

The fourth and final question seems superfluous: does the soldier need food? A man without food cannot exist, let alone fight. Because of its large size, the army of modern times cannot make do with the produce of the area it occupies. It therefore needs regular food supplies. Without these it will either die of hunger or scatter beyond the radius of military operations in search of sustenance, thereby degenerating into a corrupt horde of robbers and vagrants that will perish without protection or glory.

Thus, what method should be selected to deprive the enemy of these three fundamental elements of the vital strength and military might of his army? There is no other method than to destroy them by guerrilla warfare while they are being transported from the reserves field to the battlefield. What venture will an enemy embark upon without food, ammunition, or replacement troops? He will be compelled to cease his operations either by making peace, surrendering into captivity, or scattering with no hope of being reunited—three dismal consequences totally opposed to those an army seeks when it opens hostilities. Besides the mortal threat that guerrilla warfare represents to these three fundamental elements of the strength and existence of an army, it poses danger to the secondary needs of an army that are so closely bound up with its welfare and no less exposed to danger than food, or ammunition, or transports of reserves. These secondary elements are clothing, footwear, and arms to replace those worn by excessive use or mislaid in the chaos of battle; surgical and hospital equipment; and messengers and aides-de-camp sometimes carrying vitally important orders to and from enemy headquarters and remote areas in the rear, command posts, and particular corps and detachments. The combined action of these units is disrupted and destroyed by guerrilla operations. Other targets may be transports of sick and wounded men on their way from the army to hospitals, teams of invalids who have recovered and are returning from hospital to the army, high-ranking officials traveling from one place to another to inspect particular units or take up a particular command, and so forth.

But this is not all. Guerrilla warfare can also have an effect upon the main operations of the opposing army. The army's strategic movements during the course of a campaign must inevitably encounter enormous difficulties when they can immediately be reported to the commander on the opposite side by guerrilla units or when they can be delayed by these same units building abatis or destroying fording-places. Also an army can be attacked by all the opposing forces when it has left one strategic point but not reached the next—a situation reminiscent of Seslavin at Maloyaroslavets. Similar obstacles are also a threat to the enemy during his retreat. Erected and defended by guerrilla detachments, these barriers allow the pursuing army to constrict the retreating one and exploit the advantages of the locality to bring about its final destruction—a spectacle we witnessed in 1812 during the retreat of the Napoleonic hordes from Moscow to the Nieman.

Still this is not all. Scarcely less important than the material aspect of this kind of operation is the moral one. Raising the lowered spirits of the inhabitants of areas in the enemy rear; distracting mercenary-minded troublemakers from giving assistance to the enemy by seizing all kinds of spoils from the enemy army and dividing them among the inhabitants; boosting the morale of one's own army by frequent deliveries and parades of captured soldiers and officials, transports and provisions, stock, and even guns; and, besides all this, stunning and disheartening the men in the opposing armies—such are the fruits of skillfully directed guerrilla warfare. What consequences will we not see when the success of guerrilla detachments leads to their winning over the entire population of regions in the enemy rear and when news of the horror sown along the enemy's lines of communication is broadcast among the ranks of its army? When the realization that there is no escape from the guerrilla bands robs each soldier of his reliance on the reserves field, the effect will be to cause timidity and circumspection and then looting, which is one of the chief reasons for a fall in discipline, and with it, the total destruction of an army.

Carl von Decker

On Partisan War

Insufficient importance is attached to partisan warfare; it is thought easier than it really is. Hence so many men reckon themselves, far from truly, as good partisans.

Partisan war can be more difficult than large-scale war since the partisan rarely possesses adequate resources. Such warfare requires special talents in the commander and unusual qualities in the men. By contrast, large-scale war provides a suitable place even for the most ordinary talents, and all rankers, if only they are brave, find their proper function . . .

In all cases, the selection of new men should be guided by the utmost discretion. Even more is this so in creating a band of partisans; success depends upon making a good choice.

Partisan leaders should never forget that a handful of brave soldiers can do wonders, whereas with a host of cowards not even an expedition of the smallest value can be mounted against the enemy. Above all, they will beware of cashiered officers or those who have been obliged to leave their regiments under a cloud. They will not accept the view that in wartime a man's past is of no moment. True courage in an officer is founded on blameless morality; blind and unthinking boldness is no more than a fleeting access of intoxication. In general, partisan actions are carried out with small numbers; hence, an officer must choose his men well because their usefulness lies not in number but in intrinsic merit. If the ranks possess this value as individuals, some whims may be overlooked—for example, theatrical uniforms or some eccentricities in their dress. However, where there are no real and material qualities to excuse such childishness, the free corps will rather resemble the well-known "travestied Aeneas" (Énée Tombolino) and his operatic heroes.

Carl von Decker, *Der Kleine Krieg im Geiste der neueren Kriegsführung* (Berlin, 1822).

A partisan will endeavor in every possible way to win over the local inhabitants. If he does not succeed in this or if the nature of things is unfavorable, he will never be of great use: this was clearly proven by the best-known partisans of the allied armies during the French campaign of 1814.

However, even when a partisan has the people on his side, he ought never to stay long in one place but be nowhere and everywhere.

A partisan, furthermore, must be able at all costs to win over spies and secret agents of all classes. Therefore, he should possess a knowledge of the world, an elegant manner, and authoritative, persuasive, and ingratiating ways. If he can invest himself with a certain brilliance, so much the better. If he knows how to achieve influence over women, he will take care not to neglect this approach; he will owe his surest information to them. A secret which neither women nor clergy can divulge will probably never be revealed.

The partisan must be welcome everywhere; to this end, he will maintain strict discipline in his band and will know how to present himself in a disinterested guise. He should be able to have the elements to fulfill his needs brought to him without having to take them; but when he must requisition them, he will ensure that everything is paid for in ready money so that he is not classed with freebooters. The country should consider him its liberator, shielding it from enemy vexation, and gratefully offer him its best.

For this reason, partisans often achieve their greatest success at the very moment when the large-scale army is in a disadvantageous position and when, in one sense, Schiller's words given to Wallenstein are applicable: "It must be night, that Friedland's star may shine in all its splendor."

It is not easy to impart the waging of partisan warfare in all its fine points and variations. How can one prescribe to a genius what to invent in a given case or what resources to employ? How can one foresee and foreordain the means he should use to attain his purpose? It would be simpler to teach the way in which partisan war should not be fought.

Examples alone can serve as lessons here: not fictitious examples such as certain writers have attempted to invent but real ones drawn from the great book of experience. Therefore, we refer our readers to the history of war. Of the books written on partisan warfare, those of Ewald and Emmerich have interested us above all others. In truth, they do not possess the flowery, brilliant style brought from the universities by our modern writers; but they contain sound practical rules and unvarnished truths, and their simple language, speaking to the imagination as well as to good sense, owes its pleasing effect to this circumstance . . .

In the case of a special mission, it is the mission itself which should be paramount to the partisan above all other considerations. He ought never to deviate from his purpose, never, above all, at the expense of his mission, whatever inviting opportunities may tempt him. In short, the partisan should be a man of absolute reliability.

When he has no special mission, the partisan should take as his sole aim the infliction of appreciable losses on the enemy. Today, the taking of hundreds of prisoners counts for little; that would be but a trifle and, if information is to be obtained, there must not be too many.

The foremost enterprises that a partisan should carry out are:

1. To carry off or destroy munitions, weapons, and clothing;
2. To seize horse yards or supply columns;
3. To carry off or destroy vehicles of war, supply depots, and baggage trains (above all in sieges);
4. To seize provisions which the enemy must bring up from far in his rear and which he cannot find in the area of conflict;
5. To carry off military and other public coffers;
6. To destroy arms manufactories, powder factories, and other military establishments or to hinder the destruction of our own;
7. To carry off material for military construction, such as wood for bridges, tools to construct entrenchments, etc.;
8. To free prisoners;
9. To carry off enemy generals, high civil authorities, and hostages, and to levy ransoms;
10. To intercept enemy dispatches;
11. To pass on or seek out important information about an enemy corps, a fortress, etc. . . .

A partisan will avoid contact with the enemy insofar as the object of his expedition can be achieved without fighting if for no other reason than that he is not always his own master in providing for the needs of the wounded, nor can he count on anyone to replace his losses. However, if a free corps cannot avoid an engagement, each man must be inspired by the greatest bravery. No partisan should ever dream of laying down his arms, if only because he must consider himself and his men as outlaws. If a partisan band is scattered, each man must know the general meeting place and do his utmost to reach it.

On the failure of an undertaking, the locality must be left at once. This, however, holds good after a successful stroke too, for the enemy will certainly take steps to recoup his setback. Consequently, whether his operations fall out well or badly, the leader of a partisan band cannot stay long in the same spot or area. Nothing is more wretched for a partisan than to remain penned up in one district, to be fettered to the army, to commandeer its best provisions, and yet to be unable to furnish any scrap of information that could not be obtained much more cheaply and simply from the army's outposts. We recall one partisan (or so he called himself) who was obliged to retire at speed from a village because the army headquarters was due to arrive there that same day. This could hardly be called glorious.

To detail the conduct to be maintained in the eleven cases we have enumerated would scarcely be possible or useful. In such warfare, the permutations are infinite and each has its variants. Ruse, surprise, force, boldness, chance, and, above all, *luck*—these are the means that every intelligent partisan must know how to turn to advantage. Sometimes one, sometimes another will lead to his object. His salvation of today may destroy him tomorrow. Here all rules fall short and theory is of no avail.

Almost always, the partisan is weaker than the enemy he confronts; method, therefore, no longer applies, for all method is based on some equality of forces.

J. F. A. Lemière de Corvey

Un Peu du Fanatisme

During the three years I spent in Spain, I admired the courage of that nation. It was able to defend its independence against a formidable invasion with no other resources than ill-armed, ill-disciplined bands of partisans inspired by love of their country who were known under the name of guerrillas. I was astonished at the way they waged war; their devotion to the national cause, their courage, and their patience foiled the tactics of the French soldiers. These guerrillas worked on the principle of avoiding any engagement in line with our armies, and perseverance in this plan thwarted all our schemes. By attacking small detachments, under-strength escorts, or any isolated men they met, they beat us point by point, undermined us, and imperceptibly destroyed so many men that the Spanish War cost France more than five hundred thousand men throughout the seven years it lasted.

At the beginning of the revolution, I observed how the Vendéans organized their armies. I was struck by their new tactics and by their division of their territory into bishoprics, cantons, and parishes. But, in my opinion, they failed in their object for, although they had a central point for this or that general commanding the district of a bishopric, they had no such center for the whole countryside they occupied. Every general commanded over his district at his own pleasure, and although they did sometimes join forces, this was by arrangement among the generals. There was no one among them who was empowered to order an overall movement; they recognized no leader but the king or the French princes.

I have since compared their tactics with those of the Spaniards and have found many points of resemblance between the partisan

J. F. A. Lemière de Corvey, *Des partisans et des corps irréguliers* (Paris, 1823).

warfare of these two peoples. I shall only observe that the Vendéans, having several *départements* wholly enlisted in their cause, could have assembled together a larger body of men than could the Spaniards and could have fought battles. But if the Spaniards, whose principal towns we occupied, had been able to muster a national army headed by staunch leaders, then it is more likely that such an army, together with the corps of guerrillas, would have driven the enemy invaders from their territory than that Spain would have been subjected to the conqueror's yoke. In undertaking a national war to preserve independence and make a stand against a foreign invasion, a war of extermination must be waged and the enemy must perforce be driven away, otherwise the defending nation will be overrun, giving the victor the right to treat it as a conquered country. This has happened more than once. However, if the conquest is to be sustained, the vanquished must be treated gently: that is the way to win them over. Unfortunately, every war in which a mass rising occurs is nourished by some fanaticism, be it the spirit of faction, religion, etc.; otherwise, such wars of extermination with their fearful results would not exist.

The manner in which these two peoples marshaled their plan of defense has given rise to some interesting observations upon their organization and tactics. I have seen the advantage which bold and able leaders were able to make of irregular bands. I have thought therefore that if this manner of fighting could be brought under fixed rules, a great service would be rendered to all countries which, following an unsuccessful war, have found themselves exposed to invasion and subjection. No one has yet treated this subject thoroughly; writers on the art of war have mentioned partisans only very superficially. They have no doubt regarded these volunteer bands as unimportant auxiliaries. I myself, having a different viewpoint, have undertaken this work, believing it useful for all civilized nations, since, by providing rules for this means of defense on home ground, I prove to conquering peoples the folly of wishing to overrun a country when the nation threatened is disposed to make an impressive stand.

Energy is needed to repel an invasion and similarly to rise spontaneously in a body. It is necessary therefore that the motivating power should have so forceful an energy as to be able to communicate it to the entire nation. Otherwise a general council must be appointed.

. . . Provided this general council enjoys widespread confidence, it will have that energy and will perform miracles . . .

When earlier I discussed the manner of protecting an unfortified city against a surprise attack, I mentioned Berlin and Paris and based my example on the latter, since it is known to all. But neither Paris nor any great city will successfully defend itself against an army unless it is galvanized by some fanaticism. The reason is simple: in all great cities the property owners, merchants, or other established persons are not, or are no longer, military men. The cares of their business preoccupy them and, as to defending themselves, they say: "What need have I to match myself against professional soldiers? Who will back me up? Men who will perhaps abandon me at the first musket shot? I ought to stay at home to defend my family and property." If the enemy deals gently with these men, they will not stir. But if a bomb burns down the house of one of them or if a shellburst or a charge of grapeshot kills or dangerously wounds his wife or child, then he will take up arms and seek an opportunity to avenge himself. Almost all men allow themselves to be guided by private considerations. How many mediocre persons pass for great men because the motives behind their actions are unknown! . . .

This is the system Spain used against us. One hundred and fifty to two hundred guerrilla bodies throughout Spain each took a vow to kill thirty or forty Frenchmen a month, making six to eight thousand men a month for all the guerrilla bands. Unless possessing superior forces, they never attacked soldiers traveling in bodies. Instead they fired on all isolated men, attacked small escorts, and endeavored to make away with enemy resources, dispatch riders, and, above all, supply trains. Since all the inhabitants served as spies to their fellow citizens, the date of departure and the strength of escorts were known. Thus the bands could join together to be at least twice the enemy number. They knew the country well and attacked violently in the most favorable spot; success often crowned their undertaking, and, as many men were always killed, their object was fulfilled. As there are twelve months in a year, we lost at least seventy-two thousand men a year without any pitched battles. The Spanish War lasted seven years, so there were over five hundred thousand French soldiers killed, as I postulated in the preface. But I only speak of those killed by the guerrillas. If we add to the battles of Salamanca, Tallaveyra, Vittoria, and several others lost by our soldiers the sieges laid by Marshal

Suchet, the defense of Saragossa, the fruitless attack on Cadiz, and then subjoin the invasion and evacuation of Portugal and the fevers and various sicknesses inflicted by the climate upon our soldiers, you will see that three hundred thousand men over those seven years can assuredly be added to that number.

And who were these guerrilla leaders who defeated our worthy captains? No doubt they were distinguished retired officers, skilled in military tactics? Not at all; the principal leaders of those bands so audaciously resisting the French armies were a miller, doctor, shepherd, curate, some monks, a few deserters, but not a single man of mark before that time . . .

Their boldness in attack and perseverance often gave them the advantage in the war against our armies. They relied on local terrain and on their way of fighting; there was a touch of fanaticism too. To make a good defense of one's country in an invasion, one must decide on a war of extermination. Here a touch of fanaticism is essential, for enemy armies practice reprisals and are all the more severe in their judgment because they see no regular army confronting them. They deal with those who cannot otherwise be overcome as rebels and brigands, although if these were making regular war, they would be treated as soldiers. This is why wars of opinion, inspired by religious differences or for some cause which each party believes itself obliged to defend, are terrible wars: each faction, regarding its own side as a private cause to be avenged, often becomes cruel in victory. Even the leaders sometimes make use of this factional spirit to inspire their soldiers. In the Vendée, ill-armed peasants, quite undisciplined, were seen to rush at pieces of ordnance and carry them away. Afterward they turned them against the republican armies. Since artillery is useless to irregulars, they would dismount and spike them if the affair ended in their favor or, in the contrary case, they would cut the traces and take the horses with them.

This kind of warfare breeds terror. Regular soldiers think twice before pursuing an enemy in unfamiliar circumstances, for they do not know his strength and always fear an ambush.

Carlo Bianco

A Handbook
for Revolutionary Bands

General Rules for Insurrectionary Warfare

The rules of military tactics are designed to prevent any breakup of an army's forces and to provide against all occurrences that might lay the troops open to such a danger. Regular troops are trained to take up positions in line, column, and close formation, and to change front. This is done always with the aim of not losing contact with their military base such as a fortified town, an entrenched camp, or a locality protected by the nature of the ground itself where artillery, arms and ammunition, baggage, provisions, money, and stores of every kind necessary for the maintenance of an army obliged to stay in a compact body can be kept. War today no longer aims at driving the enemy from a given area but rather at occupying those places which contain the material elements of his power. Thus an advance is made only to a predetermined point: the enemy is expelled from a position and pursued to where it is judged advisable to stop; such a judgment is always made with the view of not running out of the army's means of supply, since in regular warfare these are held almost of more account than men. A general, therefore, has to limit his operations to his available material resources. This is the system we have to fight.

All individual effort, all the energies of the nation must come into play when a desperate war is undertaken against a tenacious and implacable enemy. All the rules of war cease to apply the moment that insurrection breaks out. All means are sacrosanct when their sole

Carlo Bianco, *Manuale pratico del rivoluzionario italiano* . . . (Italy, 1833).

aim is the annihilation of the country's enemies. *To obtain the liberation of Italy* is the only law.

Actions regarded as barbarous in regular warfare must be resorted to in order to terrorize, unnerve, and destroy the enemy. In this way Spain buried eight hundred thousand Frenchmen in the war against Napoleon Bonaparte.

Ardent patriotism, perspicacity, vigor, and stubborn determination are essential qualities for this war; also needed is energetic action combined with an understanding of the proper use of prudence.

The chief care of insurgent bands must be to thwart and render ineffectual the principles and rules of military tactics. Consequently, patriots will for the most part take up positions around the area where the enemy is stationed so that they can harass him with feints and forays and thus draw his forces away from their base. Such detachments, radiating out from their strategic center, their lines of communication weakening as they advance, will be exposed to attacks from the sides and rear by other bands who will cut them off from their base and overcome them.

The whole space between the enemy army and the periphery where the patriots are operating should be rendered of no possible use to the enemy.

The activities of the Italian combatants will thus be aimed at separating themselves from the enemy's base with land that they have laid waste by burning and flooding, so causing him serious shortages of fodder and provisions, indeed of everything needed by a regular army. In consequence, he will be obliged to send out frequent detachments of troops across this smoldering swamp to fight the bands beyond it and to obtain the necessities of life. Such units, cut off from contact with their base, will then easily be surrounded, attacked, and destroyed.

The flocks and herds together with stocks of grain and fruit having been withdrawn to the hills, the insurgents will leave the land around the enemy barren and devastated and will break up the roads by cutting deep ditches across them. They will lay mines in mountain passes and other narrow places through which the enemy has to go, timing the fuses to set off explosions when the troops are likely to be close to the spot; but even if one should go off before or after their passage, it will still do damage and have a useful effect in alarming the men and producing panic among them. Careful connections made between the dikes in the plain will cause the rivers and canals to overflow so that water near the part occupied by the army can be diverted to spread over the whole area. If the enemy persists in staying where he is, the army will suffer serious harm from the noxious air rising from this marshland which can result in pernicious fevers and consequent death. The north Italian plain, everywhere crossed by rivers and waterways, is well suited for such an operation. Bridges must be blown up, mills and bakeries destroyed, and wells and fountains poisoned; all crops not suitable to be taken away, trees, bushes, scattered houses in the plain, and finally the villages themselves, if within reach of the enemy, must be set on fire. In this way, deprived of everything around him, he will have to send for convoys of supplies from his headquarters; and because of his urgent need of food and stores, his lines of communication will be greatly extended, and his units, out of touch with their base and drawn farther and farther from it, will be open to attack from the flank and rear while the convoys will be endangered.

This is not a war between kings but a people's war, of insurgent masses formed into regular bodies of combatants against one or more professional armies. At such a time every Italian who loves his country and is brave of heart will pursue the barbarian oppressors with ardor, holding it a satisfying and indeed glorious occupation to bring about the death of the enemy.

The Volunteer

Very different from the unhappy young man torn by force from the bosom of his family to serve under the flag of the tyrant or from the contemptible wretch who, to gain his bread, blindly sells himself for a pittance and for a term of years for employment in shameful and brutal acts against his suffering compatriots: very different from these is the Italian citizen who, animated by a sacred enthusiasm, freely dedicates his life and possessions to his country and joins the patriot bands as a volunteer and takes up arms to serve Italy and play his part with all his strength in the sublime purpose of her regeneration.

The youth torn from the arms of his father, mother, and sisters and from a pleasant, quiet life among his dear ones will be morose, aloof, and unwilling when he suddenly finds himself, against his natural inclinations, among coarse and licentious companions and expected to obey harsh, stupid, and arrogant superiors who fill him with bitter hatred for his condition. His temper becomes violent and, carrying out his duty badly, he has no heart to learn how to do it better. If, however, he is by nature dissolute, evil-minded, or a bully, he will inevitably become a hired cutthroat forced to abandon himself to depravity and vice of every sort and to offenses against his companions, friends, relatives, and compatriots. It is the attribute of the patriotic volunteer to be imbued with the pure joy that gladdens the life of one devoted to a good cause; with the ardent and clear-sighted valor of a man who feels a love for humanity and for what is just and true; and with the disinterestedness by which virtuous souls hold it a duty to sacrifice everything to the realization of a sublime idea for the good of mankind.

Patience that is proof against all trials, unshakable constancy, decision and unlimited resolution, strength of body, the eyes of a lynx, and firmness of hand and agile limbs must necessarily be the distinctive qualities inherent in the volunteer fighter.

His life is all poetic ardor, continual emotions and transports of joy, fearful dangers, physical privations, and moral satisfaction. He moves from place to place in a group of loyal brothers; he finds that he belongs to an affectionate family, a gathering of fine and honorable young men all conspiring for the liberation of their country and the good of humanity. Strong as lions, swift as the mountain deer, they enjoy almost complete independence when charged with performing special operations. Always in movement, sometimes on mountain heights, at other times in the forests of the plain, they do not wait for sunrise in the place where they were at sunset, but turning this way and that, they take the enemy by surprise and always defeat him, owing to their own resourcefulness and conviction that a free man is always a match for a dozen serfs or slaves. The volunteer moves about at night and sleeps by day in the woods: with no tent, no bed, and no roof for shelter, he lies wrapped in a blanket on the bare ground with a stone for a pillow. On rare occasions he lodges in a peasant's hut, a house abandoned by its rich owner, old ruins, underground quarries, aqueducts, or caves. He eats frugally, contenting himself with water and any crust that may come his way; hunger will make the coarsest food palatable to him and the fatigues of the day will render hard ground as comfortable as any bed. His time is spent happily in contributing toward the great intention: he aids the wretched, consoles the afflicted, and helps those who have been misled to find the right way. Thus are the powerful opposed and kings discomfited.

Preliminary Operations and the Progressive Growth of the Insurgent Bands

In general, the smaller groups of insurgents are those first to be formed since it is easier for them to take the field before the government becomes aware of them.

These primary groups, and the flying columns that come already organized from beyond the frontiers or are set up as knowledge of their presence spreads, will not have to face such difficulties as the later ones. Those volunteers already expecting to take the field will either have or not have arms; in the latter case they must equip themselves by taking weapons from whomever has them. Supposing that twenty or thirty patriots have decided to start fighting yet are not armed, it is unlikely that none possess pistols, fowling-pieces, or other lethal weapons that they could use in raiding army stores for guns. Such volunteers will then decide individually but in agreement with their accepted leader on the safest and simplest way in which to arm themselves if, for instance, a detachment of troops, carabineers, or gendarmes is stationed in a volunteer's village or in one nearby and it would be possible to disarm them by a surprise attack. If this should appear too risky, each volunteer will lie in ambush not far from his own home (if possible) with a fowling-piece or pistol and wait for the daily or periodic passing of the troops or others who have to make contact with or take over from the police. When he sees one who has fallen out from the main unit, he will fire at him and kill him, then strip him of weapons and equipment of use in the field and disappear into the country to join his band. If he misfires, he must flee and discard his weapons in the scrub. If caught, he must protest that he is unarmed and was running away out of fear, in which case the authorities will face the alternative of exonerating an enemy or executing a man found without arms and apparently inoffensive. Public opinion will be on the side of the volunteer, and if the government decides to condemn him, the citizens' indignation will increase hostility toward the regime and produce other volunteers to replace him. A number of such cases will decide the government to send troops to reinforce the police guards; its opponents will grow in number and sufficient arms will be produced for one or more bands of insurgents. The troops will cause us casualties, but we shall kill many more of them in the way indicated above. Will they win the day? Since we are resolved to fight an unending war if necessary, reverses will only provoke us the more: if we are defeated, our daring will be redoubled.

In this way, and with the help of other groups and their established leaders, an insurrectionary force will begin by obtaining its equipment. But in this early phase the struggle must be purely defensive: the volunteer must not leave his home district; he must take advantage of his familiarity with the whole area and his personal relationship with his friends and family.

If the band, when formed, can already dispose of arms, it will not have to acquire them by the above methods. It will act in accordance with the situation obtaining in the town or village where it is located and will decide whether to continue with individual action or to move farther off to a more promising area.

The band must be in constant, secret movement, above all in the early part of the war when it must hide by day and march at night and follow little-known and unfrequented mountain paths. It must take cover during the day in a wood, chapel, some unoccupied house, or a cavern. Sometimes it must stay for two or three days or more in barren regions almost impossible of access; its movements must be swift, unaccountable, and unpredictable. Amid forests and mountain crags, in wooded valleys and plains, along rivers, on hidden, remote roads protected by thick hedges, and in isolated mountain ravines the group will find advantageous positions to occupy. To escape from enemy search-parties it will break up the roads and make them unusable. It will avail itself of walls, buildings, farmyards, fields, or gardens to serve as defenses against the regular troops sent out to attack them. The leader of the band will post lookouts along the ways of approach to keep watch for the enemy. They will be posted in places from where a safe line of retreat can be kept open and through which by day or at night mail vans, stagecoaches, traveling carriages, and carriers have necessarily to pass. All these the patriots must stop if they are not escorted by guards in superior strength. Government mail must be seized and travelers strictly interrogated. If among the latter any are recognized as hostile to Italy, they must be kept back and dealt with, the others being allowed to proceed should it appear unlikely that their talk might endanger the existence or subsequent operations of the insurgent band.

The patriots must move with lightning speed from one position to another, keeping always in mind the fact that their safety and success depend entirely on such activity. Fighting in country well known to them, they alone will possess the secrets of the winding turns in the labyrinthine mountain tracks, of the abysses and ravines, inaccessible crags and precipices, the hollowed-out paths in the rocks covered with thorny scrub and the ill-defined ways through widespread intricate woodland where, amid dark bogs and quagmires, it would be easy to hold up or destroy an enemy who can never have a perfect knowledge of the area. If despite such handicaps enemy troops should persist in trying to attack the patriots, unwisely pressing on into the depths of the forest, they will find it impossible to advance in closed order and the men will have to break ranks. Moving forward individually, they will at any moment find themselves encircled by the patriots, who from high ground will roll down rocks upon them if they have the temerity to attempt escape by climbing up the mountainsides. If this form of defense turns out to be ineffectual and the enemy with great courage reaches a summit and threatens the safety of the band, the volunteers will scatter to reunite in some better position and will have the satisfaction of slipping away in sight of the enemy, who will be unable to stop them. The expedition will therefore have proved a failure, and the troops will return tired out and disgusted with such service.

On another occasion, a shrewd insurgent leader, profiting from his own knowledge of the practicable places for traversing the swamp, will lure the imprudent troops into the midst of it, where, having carried out a skillful counter-march, the patriot forces will fall on them from the flank and rear. Unable to withstand the onslaught in

Mass Risings

such conditions, the enemy troops will unfailingly be left submerged in the mire.

The Italian people, encouraged by the successes of the insurgents, will everywhere determine on action for supporting them. They will decide on immediate measures of attack and defense and will not lay down their arms until liberty, equality, unity, and independence for their country are assured. The enemy will be assailed on every side by all classes and with every kind of weapon and will find no protection or security in any part of the peninsula.

Young and old, women and children will share in some way in the liberation and salvation of their country. The whole Italian population will rise against its oppressors.

The spirit of the people, everywhere in sympathy with this sacred cause, will hasten the success of the struggle; nor will threats or promises avail to induce our peasants to betray those who are fighting for them. Nothing will please them more than to see the citizens, armed with guns, pikes, spears, or axes seeking out the Austrians and their adherents. Indeed, they will feel it a duty to let the patriots know the whereabouts of the Austrians and their comrades, what road one or more Austrians may be expected to take, and where there is a safe hiding place from which to shoot them without risk. They will indicate the best way to escape pursuit by the enemy and the safest road or time for achieving their purpose. Sometimes, at the risk of their own lives, the peasants will save a few patriots by hiding them in their houses.

Those villages in no position to oppose the enemy, and whose inhabitants have not taken refuge in the hills or woods, will greet them in an amicable manner and let them pass. But as soon as the backs of the enemy troops are turned, the villagers will immediately block the roads, break up the bridges, cut off irrigation channels and ditches; arming themselves with stones, fishing spears, and guns, they will place themselves at doors, windows, and on roofs so that the troops on their return cannot pass through without serious damage to their artillery and baggage and injury to themselves. Finally, the villagers will succeed in instilling panic into the minds of the troops by random, unexpected assaults in places unfamiliar to them.

The whole nation will spontaneously take up arms with the one avowed intention of marching against the country's enemies. All fit men from the ages of sixteen to forty-five will join the insurgent bands or the Italian regular troops.

The youngest and oldest, despite their disabilities or lack of strength, will still be able to kill an enemy from the cover of a parapet, rock, door, or window. They will be enrolled in the national guard: in every village, township, or city the national flag will be raised, and round it the people will gather to pledge their support. Their accepted leaders, with help from the mayor, will draw up a general register of all the inhabitants that will be divided into groups and classified according to age and ability. All will be provided with such weapons as can be had in the circumstances. Each group, depending on its numerical strength and morale, will have an area assigned to it beforehand where it must assemble at the first stroke of the alarm bell, every man coming with victuals for several days. They will then divide into two parts: one for the defense of the houses, streets, and churches of the city or village, which they will be expected not to leave; the second will issue forth into the countryside to collaborate with and support the insurgent bands and the patriotic troops operating in the area.

In the towns and fortified cities the inhabitants themselves will defend the ramparts, thus enabling the garrisons to be reduced and more fighting forces to be made available for the country districts. In the streets and town centers the patriot troops will be sustained and encouraged by the sight of the whole populace, well or badly armed and without distinction of class or sex, joining in manning the defenses, unsparing of themselves and performing prodigies of valor. Monks and priests will carry guns and cartridge belts over their cassocks as the volunteers and simple artisans carry them over their belted blouses.

None will be indifferent to the crisis facing the nation. All, young and old, will have their share in achieving success for the great purpose.

Women

This more delicate and attractive part of the nation will be called upon to assume important and interesting duties both in the early stages of this war and at the moment of mass rising at the height of the revolution. The women must set an example of more than manly strength of mind inspired by ardent love for their Italian fatherland. In those places where revolution has not yet broken out or which unfortunately are occupied by the enemy, they will not take it ill—indeed they will be proud—to be dubbed rebel women. Instead of attending social festivities they will gather at the prisons where their friends and relatives are confined. They will console them and encourage them not to yield to the fury of the tyrant but to remain firm, preferring imprisonment to infamy and death to servitude. They will persuade them that the evils they suffer will bear fruit in winning the inestimable blessing of liberty, which is man's birthright. Women will meet secretly in some friendly house to lament the misfortunes of their country and to discuss how best to deliver it from the anguish of foreign oppression; also they will exhort and beseech their fathers, husbands, sons, and brothers to be firm of purpose in not yielding to ill-fortune and in not letting their love for their families be so strong that they forget what they owe to their country. The women will keep contact with the patriots in the field, letting them know what happens in their home town and what people are saying, hoping, or fearing. They will themselves prepare and coordinate the collection of materials and the enlistment of helpers in disposing of stores. In short, they will pave the way for a planned uprising and will find ways to entrap the enemy. In towns where revolutionary warfare is active, great use will be made of the powerful influence they can exert in rousing young men's enthusiasm so that they will throw themselves on the enemy and overcome him, even if he is superior in numbers, arms, and tactical training. They will stir up the populace against the foreign troops and urge it to defend itself by barricading or mining the streets and by incendiarism too, if the moment is opportune. They will bring the wounded into their houses and give them care and comfort. In fortified places they will help by going up to the breaches and even to the advanced posts, in fact to wherever there is need of support for the hard-pressed defenders. Some will tend the fallen;

others will do their utmost to bring them water, wine, and provisions of all kinds; altogether, they will share in all the operations of the patriot bands and their allied forces in defending their homes.

Old Men and Boys

At the glad moment when the Italian revolution breaks out, there will be heard on every hand the noise of arms and the sound of trumpets and drums. Everywhere men will be seen drilling and learning the use of weapons; old and young, fathers and sons and women, too, will all be intent on working for their country, some to learn and others to encourage and give comfort to the rest.

The old and feeble and those not fit for any active form of service must be aided by the young in collecting the ingredients necessary for making gunpowder and the means for supplying it to the combatants; they must melt lead and use some of it to make bullets and keep the rest to pour on the enemy when, held up by the barricades in the streets, some may stop beneath their windows. Other old people will sharpen daggers, clean and repair guns, sabers, swords, and knives; others will make spears, pikes, hayforks, and iron-bound clubs. Old women, boys no more than twelve years old, and young girls can help by collecting victuals and taking them to the fighting men; they can prepare medicaments, dressings, and bandages for the wounded and watch beside them to relieve their needs. Finally, as their chief occupation by day and by night, they will make thousands of cartridges.

General Cooperation

When enthusiasm has become general, then every day and every moment will be marked by some great enterprise impossible in times of peace. Indispensable services of every sort will be rendered to the great advantage of the nation by general cooperation in the country districts. The inhabitants will join in procuring gunpowder and making all kinds of weapons and munitions; working in isolated buildings, they will hide them skillfully to escape the enemy's vigilance. They will help to transport cannon and carry bullets and other instruments of war past enemy outposts in carts laden with dung and they will carry gunpowder in baskets of fruit, sacks of grain, or other farm produce. Those going to market will hide cartridges in packing cases of candles, and so on.

The peasant, plowing or hoeing his fields, will keep his loaded gun near at hand, covered with straw. When an army unit passes by, he will take no notice or else humbly salute the display of force. But once it is gone, if, owing to an accident or to fatigue or from a wish for diversion, one of the men falls out and stays behind, sure that he can make his way alone, as often happens in armies, the peasant-patriot will cautiously take out his gun and noiselessly move to a wall or hedge where he can lie in ambush until the straggler is within reach and then shoot him. Stripping the body of its equipment, he will hide his booty in one place and the corpse in another and then recharge his gun and calmly return to work.

Giuseppe Mazzini

Rules for the Conduct of Guerrilla Bands

Guerrilla warfare may be considered as the first stage of a national war. Guerrilla bands should therefore be so organized as to prepare the way for, and facilitate by their action, the formation of a national army.

The general method of organization, the authorization of leaders, the moral and political precepts regulating the conduct of the bands with regard to the country and to individuals should be under the superintendence of a Center of Action, whose duty it will be to ensure

Life and Writings of Mazzini, Vol. I (London, 1864).

the greatest possible amount of uniformity even in their apparently most unconnected movements.

The political mission of the bands is to constitute the armed apostolate of the insurrection. Every band should be a living program of the morality of the party. The most rigorous discipline is at once a duty and a necessity among them. It is a sacred duty toward their country, and a necessity for the bands themselves, which could not long exist if their conduct were such as to deprive them of the sympathy of the people.

Respect for women, for property, for the rights of individuals, and for the crops, should be their motto.

Guerrilla bands are the precursors of the nation, and endeavor to rouse the nation to insurrection. They have no right to substitute themselves for the nation.

To the nation alone belongs the right of declaring its intentions and belief.

Toleration, a consequence of liberty of conscience, is among the first virtues of the republican. The bands are therefore bound to show respect for the churches and symbols of Catholicism, and to the priests, so long as they maintain their neutrality.

The right of compelling expiation, or executing justice upon those guilty in the past, belongs to the nation alone. The bands may not usurp this right. The vengeance of the country must not be entrusted to individuals, be they whom they may.

A commission, elected by the soldiers, and presided over by the captain, will be chosen to watch over and maintain the inviolability of these rules. The names of those soldiers who have either been punished or expelled for disobedience to any of them will be forwarded by the captain to the Center of Action for publication at the proper time.

The captain of each band is responsible to the Center of Action for the conduct of his men.

Any captain guilty of dishonorable conduct will be deprived of his commission by the Center of Action, and, if necessary, punished by publicity.

When repeated complaints have been made of the collective misconduct of any band, proving it to be unworthy to represent the national cause, it will be immediately disbanded by the Center of Action. Should it disobey the command of the Center of Action, it will be regarded from that time forward as a mere horde of men without flag or mission.

Every band has the right of taking measures for its own safety and preservation, and of promoting the national insurrection. All acts of aggression or resistance, all information given to the enemy by the country people, and all acts of hostility shown to individual Italians will be speedily and severely punished by the bands.

The bands have a right to live, and it is their duty to increase the forces of the insurrection by adding to the means of the party.

The bands will subsist upon the booty taken from the enemy, treasure seized from the government, forced contributions imposed upon those of the wealthy notoriously adverse to the national cause, and supplies demanded from the provinces through which they pass.

All booty seized is the collective property of the band. It will be distributed either in value or substance, as equally as circumstances permit, among the officers and soldiers, according to the regulations voted by the bands themselves.

All governmental funds seized are the property of the national party. The captain will be responsible for them. He will leave a document with the official in custody of those funds, stating the amount. With regard to forced contributions, the captain will obey the orders of the Center of Action.

Demands and requisitions of victuals should be made as seldom as possible, and they are to be paid for whenever the band possesses the means of paying. When they have no such means, the captain or officer in command making such requisition will sign an acknowledgment of the amount of food received and leave it with the civil authorities of the place. By this means the nation will be enabled, when the war is ended, to note the contributions of each locality.

Whatever monies the captain can dispense with without injury to his band, he will forward to the Center of Action.

The captain will keep an exact account of all the pecuniary transactions of his band. A copy of this account will be audited by the civil commissioner to be employed in all possible cases by the Center of Action, whose duty it will be to watch over the observance of the rules above mentioned.

The bands will make it a general rule to seek to compromise all large cities and avert the vengeance of the enemy from all small localities.

In passing through small and unarmed localities, the captain will rather seek to repress than promote any revolutionary demonstration on the part of the inhabitants. Those patriots who are able to join the bands will enroll themselves as simple individuals and quit the locality.

It will be the aim of every band to increase its numbers, by admitting every possible element into its ranks. But so soon as the band shall have reached the maximum cipher indicated by the Center of Action as constituting a company in the future army, all fresh recruits will be regarded as forming the nucleus of a new band.

The captains of the first bands will naturally be either chosen or recognized by the Center of Action. The blanks caused among the officers by war will be filled up upon the principle of universal suffrage, exercised progressively, from the ranks up to the captain. The captain of the new band, formed out of the superabundance of recruits joining the former band, will thus be chosen by the captain and officers next in rank belonging to the first band. The organization of each separate band, with a view to the formation of a company in the future army, will in no way interfere with the practical character of their operations as guerrilla bands.

In order to increase the facilities of obtaining subsistence without serious inconvenience to the country, and to enable them more rapidly to disband or conceal themselves, the bands will be divided into small bodies of from twenty-five to fifty men, acting as detachments under the orders of a single commander, and within the territory assigned to his operations.

The uniform of the bands will be a shirt or *blouse*. In the first period of the war it is perhaps better to avoid all uniform, and content themselves with the national cockade, which can be easily thrown away or hidden in cases where it is necessary abruptly to disband or disappear. A ribbon, or other distinctive mark, not visible at a distance, will be worn by the officers during action. If the blouse be adopted, the color should be the same both for the officers and the men.

The essential weapons are a musket or rifle with a bayonet and a dagger. Each soldier will carry his cartouche box, a case containing bread and spirits, a thin but strong cord, a few nails, and, if possible, a light axe. The clothes worn by the soldiers should be so made as to allow of rapidity of movement, and of a shape not calculated to betray them in case of dispersion.

The signals and commands will be sounded by a horn or trumpet. The following are the most important movements, and therefore those the bands must first be taught to distinguish: (1) assault in the front; (2) on the right; (3) on the left; (4) combined; (5) assault of riflemen; (6) reassembling; (7) retreat.

The noncommissioned officers will employ all leisure moments in drilling the men in the few movements most necessary in guerrilla warfare, teaching them to acquire rapidity in loading and firing, and in dispersing and reassembling.

The principal aim of the bands will be constantly to damage and molest the enemy with the least possible exposure or danger to themselves, to destroy their ammunition and supplies, shake their confidence and discipline, and reduce them to such a condition as will secure their defeat, so soon as the regular army or the united bands are able to give them battle.

The means by which to attain this aim are—to attack the enemy as frequently as possible in the flank or rear; to surprise small detachments, escorts, vedettes, outposts, and stragglers; to seize upon their convoys of provisions, ammunition, or money; to interrupt their communications and correspondence by lying in wait for their couriers, destroying the roads, bridges, fords, etc.; to continually break in upon their hours of refreshment and sleep, and seize their generals and superior officers, and so on.

Guerrilla war is a war of judicious daring and audacity, active legs, and *espionage*.

The captain of a guerrilla band must be able to calculate and plan coolly, execute boldly, march unweariedly, retire rapidly, and keep himself thoroughly informed about the enemy's movements.

In this, as in regular warfare, the great secret is to preserve the means of communication. The possibility of contact and communication between the various detachments of each band, and between the different bands acting in the same province, must be jealously maintained, so as to insure simultaneous action at the decisive moment.

The greatest merit in the commander of regular troops is to know when to fight and conquer; the greatest merit of the guerrilla chief is to contrive constantly to attack, do mischief, and retire.

A band that is surrounded is lost. The retreat must always be left open. The captain will never command an assault without first assigning a point of reunion for his men in case of dispersion.

The best time for attacking the enemy is at night, during refreshment, or after a long march.

Unless circumstances compel the adoption of a different method, the best mode of attack is for the bands to spread their forces like sharpshooters. The greater the extension of the ground they occupy, the less dangerous will be the enemy's fire.

Country abounding in hedges, forests, or broken ground, affords natural entrenchments for guerrilla bands. The mountains are their fortresses . . .

Wojciech Chrzanowski

The Polish Experience

Here is a brief summary of the main principles of this type of warfare. A partisan war can of course be waged to great advantage in hilly country, but it can be waged in flatter terrain too. It can always be employed with profit in one's country, provided the inhabitants possess at least sufficient courage to wish to defend themselves and resist the insults, plundering, and, ultimately, the yoke of their enemy. In inaccessible, difficult terrain where there are woods, marshes, dikes, gullies, and ditches, the war can be fought by detachments on foot, just as in mountainous regions. In open, flat country, however, detachments of horse should be used, the only difference being that entailed by the type of arms used in each case.

Partisan warfare can succeed in destroying the enemy and forcing him to quit the country he has invaded only when the size of his army is incommensurate with the area of land he is occupying. Since this is rarely the case, partisan warfare is most frequently waged in

Wojciech Chrzanowski: *Über den Parteigänger-Krieg* (Berlin, 1846).

conjunction with the regular army. Great benefit may be expected from it when it is waged against the enemy's flanks and rear. Any strongholds in the area still in the hands of the national troops are of the greatest value for this type of warfare because hard-pressed partisans can find refuge there to rest after strenuous marches and replenish their supplies of ammunition. Furthermore, should a corps of the national army be located in the vicinity of such a stronghold, then the detachments of partisans can undertake bolder and more decisive actions from the very beginning. Finally, partisans are of two kinds: they consist of detachments selected from the main army or of irregular, independent detachments formed for this one specific purpose . . .

Each man in a company of partisans receives a number from a consecutive series and a special name (nom de guerre) under which he is entered in the log book and by which he is known thereafter. The partisan must be sober and cool-headed and no good-for-nothing. The man on foot must be a good marcher and a crack shot; the man on horseback must be a good rider and possess great stamina. The selection of partisans must be carried out as carefully and rigorously as possible: quality not quantity is important; the flower of the nation should not be set alongside its dregs. The selection of officers naturally requires even greater care. They must enjoy a good reputation in the area in which the partisan detachment is being formed. Inquiries into their past conduct are not out of place in time of war. Above all one should guard against accepting officers who have been relieved of their duties at some earlier date because of poor leadership: true courage is grounded in morality. As a last point, it is by no means obligatory to select old soldiers to serve as officers; among those who led the bands of guerrillas in Spain were doctors and provosts. They were brave, circumspect, and energetic people.

Clothing—the dress of the local people is the best and simplest clothing for the partisans. Broad leggings and no more than a cockade worn in the hat should serve as an insignia. Officers ought to wear the same dress as their men, with woolen belts denoting their rank; officers of lower rank can wear woolen braid to make themselves noticed. In a word, each man must be clothed in such a way that if he is forced to scatter, he can readily (hide his weapons and) dispose of his insignia . . .

Partisan war is of use only if it is of long duration. The two qualities needed for it more than any others are patience and stamina. The chances for the success of partisan war increase with time, for the longer a nation wages this kind of war, the better it grows at it. The longer an enemy army is involved in such a war, the weaker and more disorganized it becomes until it is eventually destroyed. The greatest evil, however, that can befall a nation is its enslavement.

The first exploits of an organized body of partisan troops are decisive for its later success. For this reason, partisans should initially avoid any direct engagement of the enemy and should restrict themselves to such smaller actions as disrupting postal communications in the enemy's rear, ambushing couriers, capturing generals and officials traveling without a proper guard, and picking off individual soldiers. Tactics of this sort force the enemy to protect his communications with numerous garrisons, place all his transports and couriers under escort, and constantly send out large numbers of moving columns (large patrols). This in turn offers the partisans a variety of opportunities for attacking the enemy and provides them with plenty of scope for action. Even if the detachments of partisans are not strong enough to launch direct attacks on enemy positions, they will nevertheless have sufficient men to give such positions a fight and to creep up on vedettes and sentries and kill them. Although seemingly insignificant, small losses of this nature will, if inflicted a hundred times a day, every day, finally be the ruin of any army, no matter how big it is. . . .

Initially partisan groups should attack only isolated enemy soldiers. Success in their activities, however, will soon permit them to undertake actions against single enemy detachments. If later the number of companies in a particular province considerably increases and if both leaders and soldiers have grown accustomed to skirmishing and are sufficiently experienced, then they may even tackle enemy corps of a thousand men. They will still retain their idiosyncratic tactics, seeking as far as possible to destroy the enemy piecemeal. From this tactical principle it follows that partisans must never face an enemy corps en bloc, even when there is equality of numbers; they must spread themselves out in mile-long lines. If the enemy follows suit and divides into lines of similar length, then a few partisan detachments should gather on one flank in order to make an attack on one section of the line with superior forces. . . .

Karol Stolzman

"Terrifying for the Strongest Enemy"

The method considered here is guerrilla warfare. The Italians waged it in the Middle Ages. They did not appreciate either its power or its subtleties, as the national concept had not yet come into existence. Later the French became acquainted with guerrilla warfare in Calabria. Yet the Italians did not make immediate use of what they had acquired. Subsequent events were conditioned by the considerable cowardice displayed by their great revolutionary leaders, by obsolete prejudices, the envy displayed by the military aristocracy, and a naïve trust in treaties.

Guerrilla war is truly a people's war; it uses means which are terrifying even for the strongest enemy. From time immemorial it was left exclusively to bandits, who used it for vile purposes. They taught, nevertheless, that it could be used against governments to good effect. The same Italians who took to shameful flight as a result of waging war by orthodox methods later gained renown in Spain as brave guerrilla fighters.

The efficacy of guerrilla warfare lies in the fact that it satisfies simultaneously both material and moral needs—two things which ought never be separated if good results are to be reaped from one's endeavor.

With regard to the material aspect, the people who rise in arms contribute maximum resources into the fight against the enemy. Thus, from their point of view this is the very best type of warfare because it makes the best use of these resources in a way most suited to their nature. The most advantageous war is the one which can be reinforced by the greatest amount of resources while forcing the enemy

Karol Stolzman, *Partyzanka czyli wojna dla ludow powstajacych najwlasciwza* (Paris, 1844).

to use the maximum of his own forces. In such a war the result of a defeat is less decisive, but victories do not lose importance.

These are the conditions which are suited for guerrilla warfare. It is a war which points a way to activity and glory to anyone who feels he is strong enough, making him a creator and king in his realm. This kind of war gives rise to countless reasons for solidarity between one province and another, one district and another, and one man and another. It leaves room for personal talent, arouses the nation from its lethargy, and both cultivates and channels a feeling of independence so prejudicial to action in orthodox warfare. Yet such a war does not in the least hinder anyone who prefers the orthodox method and wants to join the national army. It helps, however, to bring out the most talented among the masses, those who desire to throw off as soon as possible their shameful shackles and who do not possess the knowledge of the art of war but are uneasy only because they want to move. Yet without steering, they will inevitably become a turbulent gang highly dangerous to the cause. Everyone will be glad to be of use whenever offered the chance if he is certain that his deeds, not mixed with the deeds of thousands, will bring him glory and profit. As far as the aim is concerned, the only choice that remains is that between the banner of tyranny or a bandit's disgusting name and the national flag seized by brave men who gladly rally under the latter in order to satisfy their inborn instinct of freedom. The people are craving for action; let us provide them with a purpose. If we open a path toward it, the people will go on this path. In Spain, after the word was given, many people whose torpor infected the whole country and who were arms smugglers by trade became the terror of the French. Now they are included among the most ardent protagonists of the holy cause.

Our last uprising, designed to wage war the way it is being waged among great powers, has left inactive forces which have succumbed to lethargy, one from which a single word could wake them. They have renounced their intrinsic nature and have faded. Sentiments of hatred and vengeance were doomed to be eroded by the maledictions and inaction of the cold, diplomatic, and vague language of a government which only derisively could be called a revolutionary government. How advantageous could be the use of these sentiments so common in our country had they been used in the war? But this government did the the very opposite; it rejected those sentiments and gave orders to calm them down. How different would have been the results of the people's general enthusiasm which at that time was doomed to inaction because there was no room for it in the regular army. If only the then leaders had made the nation aware of its own power, acquainted it with war, which, instead of drill, study, military equipment, and slavish submissiveness, requires only enthusiasm, strong hands and feet, knowledge of localities, cunning, and sharpness of wit. Had they disseminated in all the appropriate places proclamations and general outlines of guerrilla warfare, had only a certain number of military veterans put themselves at the head of the youth which was ready to respond to any sign from them, had the banner of insurrection fluttered in the villages and been struck on the towers of the parish churches, matters would have been different.

Let us not seek examples from among other nations. Let us consider the Confederation of Bar.[1] It succeeded in maintaining its action for six years because it fought its battles according to the system of guerrilla warfare. But for the important fact that it was conducted solely by the gentry (*szlachta*), who did not call on the mass of population for support, it would have undoubtedly blocked, perhaps forever, the frontiers of Poland to the invader. The Russians used to compare this confederation to a hydra whose head was growing incessantly.

The Circassians, who to this very day fight successfully against the Muscovite army, are further proof that even the smallest nation can successfully resist the strongest enemy if guerrilla warfare is chosen as the basis of its resistance. The glorious deeds of Ziska, that great hero of the Czechs, and the fight of the Serbs for independence which was waged from 1804 until 1813 are the strongest arguments in favor of guerrilla warfare. They are proof that it is the only war for the people.

Indeed, guerrilla warfare, whose center is everywhere and whose range of activity is unlimited, is the most appropriate and effective war for a people rising in arms. It is for this reason that we can call it a popular war. There is no treason which could instantly extinguish it, as so often—almost always—happens in the case of orthodox warfare. The conquest of the capital by the enemy does not decide

---

[1] "Confederation of Bar" was a patriotic Polish uprising against the Russians to prevent the partition of Poland.

the fate of the uprising. No military action can thus ensure a decisive victory for the enemy. A regular army is rarely capable of resisting an enemy invasion—as our history teaches us; and the converse is also true: what invasion would be powerful enough against a whole nation? There is no organization of the army of old which could prevent it dispersing its forces in order to lay siege to numerous guerrilla strong points. How can one reach an adversary and fight him when the adversary suddenly divides his forces into small mobile columns, scatters his forces in all directions, amidst natural obstacles, for instance, and slips away in small groups within the compass of the range of action taking place? More concretely, how can one reach a detachment operating within a mountain range or situated between numerous rivers, lakes, and swamps in which Poland abounds or located in such extensive forests, like the forest of Biaowieza? How can one cut off their lines of communication when the number of points through which the rebel units could slip is countless?

What army would have to be used by the enemy to lie in wait for all of them? A regular army against which the rebels are waging war would have to advance on a two-pronged front and would either have to disperse its forces or concentrate them in order to occupy a certain area of the country. It is in this area, there and then, that the guerrillas would sting them by frontal attacks as well as by attacks from the rear and flanks. Or the enemy might have to disperse his forces so widely as to be incapable of manning every one of the thousands of positions suitable for offensive actions. It is there that the enemy might be attacked by forces stronger than his own. Thus the regular forces would be forced into both defensive and offensive actions.

The impending revolution in Poland must be, in accordance with the spirit and strivings of this age, a people's revolution, not a revolution of privileged factions, military or civil. Therefore, the banner which has to lead the Polish insurrection ought to be dedicated to the people. Then the people will reveal itself in its greatness.

But in order to achieve this, the people has to be emanicipated. It has to be enlisted. One has to entrust the fate of the homeland to its hands. One also has to make the people aware of its own might and to convince it that no power in the world will be capable of crushing this might against its will.

This might has to be instructed in the methods of military activities. It has to become the embodiment of revolutionary thought. Thus, the people will be ordered to buy with their own blood both the right and independence of free men. This sacrifice will teach the people to live it and to keep it pure. This war will give birth to strength, trust, and free education for the people because struggle tempers nations and rebellion wipes out the stigma of bondage from the rebels' brows. Guerrilla warfare causes minds to adapt themselves to independence and to an active and heroic life; it makes nations great.

When every Pole has a heritage to defend and to pass on to his descendants when every inch of Polish soil becomes famed for heroic deeds and when our cornfields become consecrated with the bones of our brave men mingled with the bones of the invaders, who will dare to foul and violate this consecrated space? Which hated home or foreign power will venture to establish compounds of oppression or usurper camps on those fields on which the great deed of liberation has created a truly free nation which by means of an experience both sublime and triumphant has gained the knowledge of its own strength and of its right, not lost by prescription but given to it by the Creator? . . .

We say once again to our fellow countrymen: do not look at the French because they have no need as urgent and as sacred as ours to rise in arms. It would, however, be a deadly sin to wait with folded arms for foreign help when our own strength is sufficient. To do so would mean that we were unable to appreciate our strength and that we sinned against the sacred mission Providence has imposed on every nation as part of mankind. Anyone who causes the sacred deed of liberation to depend on either chance or circumstance offends the sanctity of this deed and impresses the stigma of shame on his brow.

Let us not await events. Let the nobleman and the peasant join hands since all are Poles created by the same God and in His image. Above all, do not stand idly by and await with folded arms the fulfillment of the prophecy that the Turks will water their horses in the Vistula in order to achieve our redemption. Instead, make the greatest possible effort to ensure that our own cavalry horses should be able to taste the waters of our Polish rivers—the Niemen, the Dnieper, the Dniester, the estuary of the Warta, and the sources of the Vistula.

To arms, then, brothers. The future is ours.

A. Gingins-La Sarraz

Partisans and the Defense of Switzerland

The phrase "partisan warfare" is applied to a war of piecemeal actions, surprises, and ambushes carried out by small irregular bodies of volunteers.

Its primary object is to contest the enemy's free and unhindered subordination of the country he occupies or passes through, and its methods are to scatter obstacles in his path, impede his operations and communications, and tire and weaken him.

Partisan warfare is an active means of resisting foreign invasion; when fulfilling this purpose, its nature is undeniably highly patriotic and popular.

Considered from this purely defensive point of view, it also bequeathes valuable traditions and arouses and revives national sentiment. History transmits to future generations the tales of honorable and often glorious struggles; the acts of courage and devotion performed by partisans, unpretentious yet serviceable defenders of their country, are graven in the memories of their families and villages and give an enduring example for the future. In short, a people which has reconquered or only helped to reconquer its independence and national liberties by a partisan war will acquire so great an awareness of its power and the sanctity of its rights that new aggressors will henceforth find it invincible . . .

Defensive partisan warfare must necessarily be a spontaneous act of the populace against a foreign invader.

Patriotism, love of independence, and bravery are virtues which

A. Gingins-La Sarraz, *Les partisans et la défense de la Suisse* (Lausanne, 1861).

cannot be improvised or made to order. Citizens of any state either have them or they do not; in the first case, those whose circumstances allow them to do so rise spontaneously and of their own free will against foreign usurpation and violence; in the second case, they docilely bend their necks to conquest or the humiliation of subjection imposed by force . . .

A defensive partisan war has as its final aim the expulsion of the invader and to that end his extermination and the destruction of everything contributing directly or indirectly to his power.

It is not simply a question of killing the enemy's soldiers or representatives; they must also be harassed by exhaustion and misery. Not only must the invading power be made to suffer the greatest possible loss of men, it must also undergo pecuniary damage and be deprived of material resources.

Partisans are therefore ever on the alert to harm the invader as much as possible by destroying or spoiling any of his possessions which are within their reach or grasp and whose appropriation would be imprudent or unprofitable.

No opportunity is lost to spike pieces of ordnance, dismount them, and throw them into rivers or ravines; to break and buckle firearms and side arms; to break, burn, or overturn wagons; to scatter, sink, or burn victuals and ammunition; and to kill or maim horses, mules, and livestock.

As for animals, they are killed or maimed either by shooting them as they pass by or when they are in encampment or at their grazing and watering places; or by freely strewing nails and broken glass at some point in their path; or else by tackling them at close range with side arms . . .

The invader will neither voluntarily practice any moderation toward partisans whom he may capture nor grant any quarter to them as adversaries. Thus partisans for their part are fully justified in making the harsh results of war weigh heavily upon the enemy.

If a partisan falls into enemy hands and the free corps has a prisoner available, they will suggest an exchange. Where the enemy refuses this and the captive partisan suffers a violent death, the prisoner should be shot as a reprisal.

In any event, the invader has only a very small hold over skillful and resolute partisans; they easily evade his pursuit and only engage in fighting in conditions favorable to personal safety and success.

However, the enemy may try to shield himself behind what he calls the responsibility for the region's peaceful inhabitants.

The French armies at the turn of the last century covered themselves with ineradicable shame by their cruelty toward the innocuous inhabitants of Germany, Spain, Italy, and several parts of Switzerland.

Indeed, at that time Piedmontese troops shamelessly committed every horror imaginable in various parts of Italy in cowardly revenge against the people's repulse of foreign intrusion and its fight for independence and nationhood.

Such iniquitous methods, unworthy of humane and civilized men, have never yet achieved their end nor will they ever succeed against peoples endowed with any spark of energy and patriotism. Their only effect is to increase popular hostility until the invader is driven out or destroyed. These methods leave in their train an undying sense of justified repugnance toward the nations whose armies have committed these excesses and crimes.

Nevertheless, it does not follow from these moral truths that the reenaction of such abuses of power is out of the question. Suppose a sovereign and army, driven by an ambition to conquer or a desire for supremacy, invade a peaceful, inoffensive neighboring state on some dubious pretext, trampling its rights and independence underfoot. Their conduct of war may well not be affected by scruples about humanity, justice, or honor.

To avert this danger, the enemy must be shown the futility of violence against the inhabitants and, should he attempt it, he must be made to feel the full extent of his own danger.

The partisans' role in such preventive measures is to react immediately to even the smallest attempt at violent acts against the harmless population with the most terrifying reprisals. Far from abandoning warfare wherever the enemy would like to deal with a heavy hand, the partisans carry it on even more stubbornly there; they redouble their hostile acts; they abandon all previous considerations dictated or inspired by humanity; they take prisoners and shoot or hang them; they call in for aid neighboring free companies with less in hand; they incite the population to rise and resist in defense of their families and homes. In short, they work in such a way that the enemy's attempt at repression, far from giving him more security, causes him greater ruin, crueler losses, and more adversaries.

Thus, in his own interests and quite apart from any generous or humane feeling, the invader is induced to abandon coercive measures against the inhabitants not directly participating in free corps actions. On the contrary, he endeavors to quieten and pacify; he rejects violent means as useless and dangerous and limits himself to hunting down partisans only. It is incumbent on the latter to continue the struggle and care for their own safety.

Antoine-Fortuné de Brack

A Hazardous Profession

Q.   What is the meaning of partisan?

A.   A detachment is in partisan, when it operates detached and isolated from the army, and under the genius of its leader, which is not controlled except by orders given in a general manner, and by the indications of the combined movements of the army.

A partisan is sent to raise a province; to harass the flanks and rear of the enemy's army; to carry off, or destroy depots, convoys, etc.; to make prisoners; and sometimes to deceive the enemy as to the movements of our army.

Q.   What is the first care of an officer directed to carry on partisan warfare?

A.   It is to be scrupulously careful that the detachment which he commands is composed of bold and well-mounted troopers.

Q.   And the second?

A.   To receive from his general an accurate map of the country in which the scene of his operations is, and as correct information as is procurable regarding the dispositions of the enemy, and the plans which he is supposed to have formed; and further to have an eye upon the present and future movements of our different *corps d' armée.*

Antoine-Fortuné de Brack, *Advanced Posts of Light Cavalry* (London, 1850).

Q. Why should he care about this last, when he is acting independently?

A. In order to know whither he should send his reports, and to find a support to his retreat, should he find himself hard-pressed.

The profession of a partisan is a hazardous one. It can only be properly followed out by a skillful, rapid, and bold leader, and by a body of men resembling him. No more rest for the partisan; he ought always to have his eyes open, and if fatigue compels him to snatch a momentary slumber, it is necessary that an advanced line of spies should watch over and warn him.

The war, which he carries on, is piratical. The strength of his warfare lies in surprise. The kite unperceived, which makes a sudden swoop at its prey, bears it off, and vanishes, is the image of the partisan! Let him then inflict a decided, prompt, and, if necessary, even terrible, blow, and let no traces point out his retreat.

Every stratagem of war is at the disposal of the partisan. Let him combine his attack so judiciously, and fling his lasso so accurately around the enemy, whom he surprises, that not an individual can escape to give the alarm.

Such a one in an enemy's country maneuvers with the enemy, levies in his name contributions of clothing and horses, and fresh clothes, and remounts his detachment at the expense of the King of Prussia.

Such another strips his prisoners, clothes his men in their uniforms, enters the unsuspecting bivouacs of the enemy, whom he surprises and cuts to pieces.

Another one, at twenty leagues in rear of the Russian army, recaptures our prisoners, whom he mounts upon the horses of their escort, and thus doubles his force.

Such another carries off a park of artillery. The enemy, informed of it, hastens up two hours afterward, and, by the time that he reaches the smoldering remains of his blown-up wagons, the partisan deals a blow equally severe three leagues in his rear.

The enemy, utterly ignorant of the numerical force of this daring band, halts, takes up a position, and forms those detachments in mass, which would have been a splendid reinforcement to his own army, and ours profits by the delay.

Such another, lastly, like the brave and illustrious Pole Uminski, at the head of a few squadrons, penetrates through the enemy's army, raises a province, makes a powerful diversion, and, after several victories, when compelled to retreat, rejoins the national army with his forces trebled.

The partisan, owing to the isolation in which he is placed, and owing to his not being compelled to march immediately in such or such a direction, or to retire upon a certain point, is not trammeled or fettered in any way: he is master of the whole country which his eye takes in; let him survey it with no ordinary intelligence, and let him conceive it in his imagination, not so much as viewed from the spot where he stands, as from the point of view of the enemy. Thus, let him calculate the hollows, the heights, the natural screens, in their connection with this point of view, and let him always post himself in such a manner as to intercept by these screens the visual ray which the enemy might direct toward him.

If he descend by this path, the rising ground on his right will conceal his movements. If he traverse the plain in that direction, the little wood, which is to be seen on his left, will mask his march for the next ten minutes, and these ten minutes will be sufficient to enable him to gain the ravine, in which he may conceal himself.

The partisan, acting only by surprise, the offensive positions which he takes up are invariably ambuscades. The closer they are to the point of attack, the better; but it is requisite that this proximity should always be calculated with reference to the greater or less confidence and vigilance of the enemy.

The partisan, after having boldly swept off a convoy, commences his retreat. It is necessary that this retreat should be prompt, for the enemy may receive intelligence and pursue with superior forces. He therefore compares the importance and the possibility of preserving the prize, which he has captured, with that of the attack which he may have to sustain, and of the rapidity with which he is obliged to make his retreat. This rapid comparison will cause him to destroy everything which would dangerously retard him, and he retreats, not by the road, which he has followed in gaining the spot, but by that which contracts the distance that he will have to travel over in order to gain a place of safety. The undulations of the ground, the woods, the ravines, mask his retreat, and he does not halt until after he has been some hours on the road, because he is aware that the pursuit of the enemy is never pushed beyond a certain distance, and that the farther it is carried, the more languid and less dangerous it becomes, especially if the pursuers are led by the pursued over a difficult and intersected country, causing apprehensions of ambuscades.

If, however, the pursuing enemy appears at some distance and threatens to attack briskly and powerfully, the partisan does not hesitate to put him on a wrong scent. He makes the convoy file off under an officer, whom he enjoins to proceed rapidly, and, in the case of being attacked, to abandon everything which he deems it impossible to save. Then, with the bulk of his body, he proceeds either to the right or left, draws the misled enemy in that direction, whom he thus carries to a distance from his object.

A partisan, knocked out with long-continued duties, and who needs repose, ought either to gain one of our posts, situated in rear of the enemy, and which is not invested by the enemy, or to throw himself suddenly beyond the line of his operations. In general, this line, in rear of the enemy's dispositions, is confined to some roads, held by detachments on their way to rejoin, and patrolled to very short distances.

The partisan has, then, only a few leagues to traverse to place himself in safety; nevertheless, in order to render this security more complete, he frequently changes his position.

If the partisan have some sick and wounded, he carries them along with him, and is lavish of his care of them. If the diseases or wounds are too severe to admit of the men laboring under them keeping up with him without retarding his rapid marches, he places them in the villages and entrusts them to men of mark upon their personal responsibility.

If the partisan have made prisoners, in order not to weaken his strength, he confides the care of them, in a friendly country, to the care of the national rural guards, who take them to our army by roundabout ways.

If the partisan have captured guns and cannot convey them in safety to our army, he buries them privately, and especially out of view of his prisoners, in a wood seldom frequented, and marks the spot where they are concealed. He then carries off the limbers with him, which he destroys at some leagues farther off; thus the place of their concealment is entirely unknown.

As a general rule, as the partisans ought to be in the highest state of mobility, he should retain nothing with him that can retard or encumber his march.

PART III

Partisan Warfare
1860–1938

Introductory Note

This section covers the period between the American Civil War and the outbreak of the Second World War. During that time the study of guerrilla war was not part of the curriculum of the military academies despite the fact that European armies were engaged in many colonial wars and that partisans frequently played a role of some importance in major wars too. This qualification refers, for instance, to the Civil War, Franco-Prussian War, Boer War, and also, to a lesser degree, the First World War. But it is also true that victory in all these wars went to the stronger battalions, the decision being determined in massive battles between vast armies. Military thinkers were almost exclusively concerned with issues such as *Vernichtungsschlacht, Blitzkrieg,* and, later with tank warfare and airpower. The new weapons seemed to tip the balance even further against guerrilla warfare. Political theory and military doctrine, "bourgeois" and Leninist alike, accorded to guerrilla warfare only a limited role. Guerrilla warfare, almost by definition, could succeed only if the internal or external enemy was weak and if it was conducted within the framework of a prolonged general war. The guerrillas could hope to challenge regular armies only in certain exceptional conditions which rarely existed during the period under review. Propitious conditions arose only upon the collapse of the colonial powers in World War II. Neither was there pronounced interest in guerrilla war among revolutionary leaders; indeed, guerrilla tactics were used more frequently by the extreme right than the left in the Russian civil war and elsewhere in Europe after the First World War.

There were, nevertheless, some military experts who believed that it was premature to write off guerrilla warfare altogether. Among these was Friedrich Wilhelm Rüstow (1821–1878), one of the most original and prolific (as well as controversial) German military writers of the period. A radical democrat, he left Germany after the defeat of the revolution of 1848, served as Garibaldi's chief of staff, and settled in Switzerland where he was the first professor of military science at the Zurich Polytechnic. His *Die Lehre vom kleinen Krieg* was published in Zurich in 1864.

Francis Lieber (1800–1872) was another political emigré from Germany. Arrested as a liberal in his native country, he volunteered to fight in the Greek War of Independence and subsequently emigrated to the United States. He was editor of the *Encyclopaedia Americana* and in 1835 became professor of history and political economy at South Carolina College. In 1856 he accepted an appointment at the Columbia Law School. During the Civil War he was asked by the United States government to provide legal advice. One of his papers, "Guerrilla Parties, Considered with Reference to the Laws and Usages of War," is quoted in the present volume. Albrecht von Boguslawski (1834–1905) was a colonel (subsequently lieutenant-general) in the German army when his *Der kleine Krieg und seine Bedeutung für die Gegenwart* (Berlin, 1881) was published. He was also the author of a history of the war in the Vendée which is of considerable interest in the guerrilla context. Karl Hron was an officer in the Austro-Hungarian army and later became a newspaper editor and writer on European and Oriental politics.

Charles Callwell (1859–1928) is the author of *Small Wars* (London, 1899). An artillery captain by training, he had been seconded to intelligence. He saw action in Afghanistan and South Africa but resigned from the army when he was passed over for promotion— apparently as the result of the publication of his indiscreet literary "Sketches from Military Life." He was recalled to duty in 1914, became chief of operations in the War Office, and was promoted to major-general and knighted. T. Miller Maguire (1849–1920) was a barrister and a successful army "coach" who lectured and wrote about strategy and great campaigns. Among his students were Allenby and Gough. He is the author of *Guerrilla or Partisan Warfare* (London, 1904).

Thomas Edward Lawrence (1888–1935) needs no introduction. The present excerpt is reprinted by permission, © *Encyclopaedia Britannica*, 14th edition (1929).

Arthur Ehrhardt (1895–1971) was one of the very few German authors of the twentieth century to comment on guerrilla war. He was a lieutenant in the First World War and a captain with the *Abwehr* in World War II. A publisher in civilian life with apparently no pronounced political views before 1945, he became editor in chief of *Nation-Europa,* a monthly journal of the extreme right.

"Notes on Guerrilla Warfare" by Lieutenant T. H. C. Frankland of the Royal Dublin Fusiliers was published in the *United Service Magazine,* Vol. 33 (1912); Major Harold H. Utley's "An Introduction to the Tactics and Techniques of Small Wars" appeared in the *Marine Corps Gazette* of May, 1931. They are reprinted here with the permission of the publishers. These articles are of interest because early on they drew attention to certain aspects of guerrilla warfare which became common knowledge only several decades later. Thus Frankland noted that the absence of civilization afforded great facilities to guerrilla warfare.

B. C. Dening stressed that modern guerrilla war would aim at draining the financial rather than the military resources of the Great Powers. The American Utley emphasized the importance of Congress and domestic public opinion: "In small wars we are at peace no matter how thickly the bullets are flying . . ." In short, in guerrilla wars the hands of the military would be tied.

Francis Lieber

Guerrillas in International Law

The term "guerrilla" is the diminutive of the Spanish word *"guerra,"* war, and means petty war, that is, war carried on by detached parties generally in the mountains. Further it means the party of men united under one chief engaged in petty war, which, in eastern Europe and the Levant is called a capitainry, a band under one *"capitano."* The term "guerrilla," however, is not applied in Spain to individual members of the party. Each is called a *"guerrillero,"* or, more frequently, a *"partida,"* which means partisan. Thus Napier, in speaking of the

Francis Lieber, "Guerrilla Parties, Considered with Reference to the Laws and Usages of War" (New York, 1862).

guerrilla in his *History of the Peninsular War,* uses with rare exception the term *"partidas"* for the chiefs and men engaged in the petty war against the French. The dictionary of the Spanish academy gives as the first meaning of the word guerrilla—"A party of light troops for reconnaissance, and opening the first skirmishes." I translate from an edition of 1826, published long after the Peninsular War, since which the term "guerrilla" has passed into many other European languages. Self-constitution is not a necessary element of the meaning given by the Spaniards or by many writers of other nations to the word "guerrilla," although it is true that the guerrilla parties in the Peninsular War were nearly all self-constituted, since the old government had been destroyed, and the forces which had been called into existence by the provisional government were no more acknowledged by the French as regular troops than were the self-constituted bands under leading priests, lawyers, smugglers, or peasants because the French did not acknowledge the provisional Junta or Cortes. Many of the *guerrilleros* were shot when made prisoners, and the guerrilla chiefs executed French prisoners in turn. It is the state of things the existence of these bands almost always leads to, due to their inherent character. Yet, when the *partidas* of Mina and Empecinado had swelled to the imposing number of twenty thousand and more, which fact of itself implies a degree of discipline, Mina made a regular treaty with the French for the passage of certain French goods through the lines. On these the partisan leader levied regular duties according to a tariff agreed upon by the belligerents.

What, then, do we in the present time understand by the word "guerrilla"? In order to ascertain the law or to settle it according to elements already existing, it will be necessary ultimately to give a distinct definition. Whatever may be our final definition, it is universally understood in this country that a guerrilla party means an irregular band of armed men carrying on an irregular war which is not able, according to its character as a guerrilla party, to carry on what the law terms a regular war. The irregularity of the guerrilla party consists in its origin, for it is either self-constituted or constituted by the call of a single individual, and not according to the general law of levy, conscription, or volunteering. It consists in its disconnection from the army as to its pay, provision, and movements; and it is irregular as to its permanency: it may be dismissed and called together again at any time. These are the constituent ideas of the term "guerrilla" as now used. Other ideas are associated with the term differently by different persons. Thus many persons associate the idea of pillage with the guerrilla band because, not being connected with the regular army, the men cannot provide for themselves except by pillage, even in their own country—acts of violence with which the Spanish *guerrilleros* sorely afflicted their own countrymen in the Peninsular War. Others connect with it the idea of intentional destruction for the sake of destruction because the guerrilla chief cannot aim at any strategic advantages or any regular fruits of victory. Others, again, associate with it the idea of danger with which the spy surrounds us because he that today passes you in the garb and mien of a peaceful citizen may tomorrow, as a guerrilla man, fire your house or murder you from behind a hedge. Others connect with the *guerrillero* the idea of necessitated murder because guerrilla bands cannot encumber themselves with prisoners of war; they have, therefore, frequently, perhaps generally, killed their prisoners and of course have been killed in turn when made prisoners, thus introducing a system of barbarity which becomes intenser in its demoralization as it spreads and is prolonged. Others, again, connect the ideas of general and heinous criminality, robbery, and lust with the term because, the organization of the party being but slight and the leader being utterly dependent upon the band, little discipline can be enforced. And where no discipline is enforced in war, a state of things results which resembles far more the wars recorded in Froissart or Comines, the Thirty Years' War, or the Religious War in France than the regular wars of modern times. And such a state of things results speedily too; for all growth, progress, and rearing, moral or material, is slow; all destruction, relapse, and degeneracy, fearfully rapid.

It does not seem that, in the case of a rising en masse, the absence of a uniform can constitute a difference. There are cases, indeed, in which the absence of a uniform may be taken as very serious prima facie evidence against an armed prowler or marauder, but it must be remembered that a uniform dress is a matter of impossibility in a levy en masse; and in some cases regulars have not had uniforms for at least a considerable time. The Southern prisoners at Fort Donelson had no uniform. They were indeed dressed very much alike, but theirs was the uniform dress of the countryman in that region. Yet they were treated by us as prisoners of war, and well treated too.

Nor would it be difficult to adopt something of a badge, easily put
on and off, and to call it a uniform. It makes a great difference,
however, whether the absence of a uniform is used for the purpose of
concealment or disguise in order to get by stealth within the lines
of the invader for destruction of life and property or for pillage and
whether the parties have no organization at all and are so small that
they cannot act otherwise than by stealth. Nor can it be maintained
in good faith, or with any respect for sound sense and judgment, that
an individual—an armed prowler (now frequently called a bushwhacker)—shall be entitled to the protection of the law of war simply because he says that he has taken up his gun in defense of his
country or because his government or his chief has issued a proclama-
tion by which he calls upon the people to infest the bushes and commit homicides which every civilized nation will consider murders.
Indeed, the importance of writing on this subject is much diminished
by the fact that the soldier generally decides these cases for himself.
The most disciplined soldiers will execute on the spot an armed and
murderous prowler found where he could have no business as a
peaceful citizen. Even an enemy in the uniform of the hostile army
would stand little chance of protection if found prowling near the
opposing army, separate from his own troops at a greater than picket
distance and under generally suspicious circumstances. The chance
would, of course, be far less if the prowler was in the common dress
worn by the countrymen of the district. It may be added here that
a person proved to be a regular soldier of the enemy's army and
found in citizens' dress within the lines of the captor is universally
dealt with as a spy.

It has been stated that the word "guerrilla" is not only used for
individuals engaged in petty war but frequently for an equivalent of
the partisan. General Halleck, in his *International Law, or Rules
Regulating the Intercourse of States in Peace and War* (San Francisco, 1861), page 386 and seq., seems to consider partisan troops
and guerrilla troops as the same and seems to consider "self-constitution" a characteristic of the partisan. Other legal and military writers
define partisan as I have stated, namely, as a soldier belonging to a
corps which operates in the manner given above.

If the term "partisan" is used in the sense in which I have defined
it, it is not necessary to treat of it specially. The partisan, in this
sense, is, of course, answerable for the commission of those acts for

which the law of war grants no protection and by which the soldier forfeits being treated as a prisoner of war, if captured.

It is different if we understand by guerrilla parties self-constituted sets of armed men in times of war who form no integral part of the organized army, do not stand on the regular payroll of the army, or are not paid at all, who take up arms and lay them down at intervals and carry on petty war (guerrilla) chiefly by raids, extortion, destruction, and massacre, and who cannot encumber themselves with many prisoners and will therefore generally give no quarter.

They are peculiarly dangerous because they easily evade pursuit and by laying down their arms become insidious enemies and because they cannot otherwise subsist than by rapine and almost always degenerate into simple robbers or brigands. The Spanish guerrilla bands against Napoleon proved a scourge to their own countrymen and became efficient for their own cause only in the same degree in which they gradually became disciplined.

But when guerrilla parties aid the main army of a belligerent, it will be difficult for the captor of guerrilla men to decide at once whether they are regular partisans distinctly authorized by their own government; and it would seem that we are borne out by the conduct of the most humane belligerents in recent times and by many of the modern writers if the rule be laid down that guerrilla men, when captured in a fair fight and open warfare, should be treated as the regular partisan is until special crimes such as murder, the killing of prisoners, or the sacking of places are proved upon them, leaving the question of self-constitution unexamined.

The law of war, however, would not extend a similar favor to small bodies of armed country people near the lines whose very smallness shows that they must resort to occasional fighting, the occasional assuming of peaceful habits, and to brigandage. The law of war would still less favor them when they trespass within hostile lines to commit devastation, rapine, or destruction. Every European army has treated such persons and, it seems to me, would continue, even in the improved state of the present usages of war, to treat them as brigands, whatever prudential mercy might be decided upon in single cases. This latter consideration cannot be discussed here because it does not pertain to the law of war.

It has been stated already that the armed prowler, the so-called bushwhacker, is a simple assassin and will thus always be considered by soldier and citizen; and we have likewise seen that the armed bands that rise in a district fairly occupied by military force or in the rear of an army are universally considered, if captured, brigands, and not prisoners of war. They unite the fourfold character of the spy, brigand, assassin, and rebel, and cannot—indeed, it must be supposed, will not—expect to be treated as a fair enemy of the regular war. They know what a hazardous career they enter upon when they take up arms and that, were the case reversed, they would surely not grant the privileges of regular warfare to persons who should thus rise in their rear.

Albrecht von Boguslawski

Guerrilla War–A Prussian View

A war to the knife of this kind, in which not only the residue of the male population but also, as happened in Spain and the Tyrol, women and children sometimes take part, will occur only rarely because the great mass of any population does not consist of heroes.

Nevertheless, it is wrong to dismiss a popular rebellion and popular participation in the war as meaningless and unimportant in theoretical and general terms.

Now that wars have become national wars, we shall in the future have to expect more people's wars, especially when the mass of the people have suffered some great provocation and can fight where the land is favorable.

One should prepare oneself as well as possible for all eventualities. Therefore we must know not only how to crush a popular rebellion with speed and severity but also how to use one in furtherance of our own operations on our own and allied territory.

Here it is necessary to consider in some detail the legal aspects of

Albrecht von Boguslawski, *Der kleine Krieg und seine Bedeutung für die Gegenwart* (Berlin, 1881).

the matter, which have been so much discussed in recent years. Those convinced of the uselessness of supportive action by the local population have commonly held that such action is thoroughly reprehensible in international law.

On several occasions, attempts have been made to set up internationally binding rules and laws governing both the conduct of armies and the participation of the civil population in a war. In the latter case the rules concerned when and in what circumstances the populace be allowed or forbidden to take part in the fighting. For example, at the Brussels Conference in 1874 it was proposed that as soon as the *occupatio bellicosa* was completed, the inhabitants should be obliged to obey the foreign power and that a subsequent uprising should be regarded as rebellion.

But when is such an occupation to be regarded complete? How many troops are needed for it to be considered so? Is it enough for a patrol of three men to occupy a village, or must there be five hundred men? In his *Modern Military Law*, Bluntschli says (page 50) that a popular uprising is legal when it is carried out in defense of the country; those taking part in it are to be treated as soldiers. If, however, the inhabitants stage an uprising in land occupied by the enemy, they could also be prosecuted in law by the hostile military power after their suppression. In other words, they could be treated as rebels. Bluntschli then says: "This also applies to uprisings in the rear of the enemy army. However, it can be that a popular uprising reaches such proportions that it can no longer be regarded as such but rather as constituting a new warring power." It is clear how shaky and easily blurred are those lines of demarcation by which the law has tried to stake out its province here.

It is wasted effort to attempt to codify such matters by means of mutual agreement. No hardened and courageous people that *wants* to defend its home weapon in hand or that rises up in open insurrection in the rear of an enemy army will be kept from doing so by the stipulations of international law. The introduction in almost every state of general conscription as the system by which new men are drafted into the army has likewise in no way affected the legal aspects of the question. The native population will thus continue to lend the home troops the support it considers appropriate to the situation and to which its patriotic feelings move it or, for reasons of expediency, it will abandon all resistance. To see the matter in any other light and, for example, to recognize an *obligation* of obedience to foreign troops and power would mean literally to encourage in the native population a cowardly and unpatriotic frame of mind.

For its part the occupying army will demand obedience from the local population. Solely on its own authority, and without reference to any international code, it will declare martial law in the occupied areas and deal harshly with any examples of disobedience or resistance.

Out of necessity and in the interests of its own security, it will violently suppress any attempt at an uprising in areas it has already occupied. International efforts of the kind suggested to codify the behavior of occupying armies in the interests of lessening the sufferings of war at the Brussels Conference will remain powerless in practice in view of the obligation a commanding officer must have to protect the safety and honor of the detachments under him. What prevents acts of barbarity and offensive behavior is not externally imposed laws but the moral sensibility that flows naturally from the cultural life of a people and from the sense of decency of the individual, of which that cultural life is a guarantee.

There are numerous examples of such moral achievements. Among them, we may number: respecting the persons of members of parliaments, sparing the lives of prisoners-of-war and giving them food and shelter, respecting private property if it is not needed for military purposes, and respecting civil law. All these moral injunctions are already recognized, however, by civilized nations. There is little question of their observance, and should they be infringed or should fear, weakness, or anger unleash the wild beast in a soldier or the troops, then a particular case can only be prosecuted under the laws of the warring army. To draw up an international code would only put the screw on the individual soldier's resolve; it would not influence the conduct of a military leader beyond what he himself perceives as his duty and obligation according to the law.

Further, to wish to remove all legality from any participation in the fighting by a native population seems as misguided as to try to codify the conduct of an invading army.

Certainly the laws of morality and honor have to be satisfied as much in such fighting as in that between regular armies.

In this domain it will rarely be possible to draw clear lines between what is and is not permitted. For example, an uprising somewhere in the rear of an invading army and the overpowering of any troops that happen to be there can by no means be branded an immoral action. Yet during the course of such an uprising, a number of incidents may take place that are indeed immoral and criminal, for instance, the assassination during their sleep of quartered troops by their landlord. The punishment for such a crime should be the same as that meted out to robbers and arsonists.

An attack on resting troops by an armed band, even if the band is dressed in civilian clothes, is in itself certainly not immoral. On the other hand, our sense of international law and the morality that is supposed to live within us should be shocked by a peasant who shoots down an officer, throws his gun into a hedge, and returns to his plowing. Thus we can see how vague these things are and how frequently it becomes almost impossible to distinguish between good and bad in such matters.

Karl Hron

Partisans in the Austrian Mirror

It would be unjust to accuse present-day writings on military science of a poverty of ideas, but it is certainly fair to say that they are monotonous: they treat only of masses and the use of masses. And not without reason, for with the advent of vast armies military leadership has become not only a duller but also a weightier matter. In the scales of the final outcome, isolated exploits are as light as a feather when balanced against such weight. Furthermore, if one considers the rapid development of those branches of technology such as railways, the telegraph (and, in future, the air-balloon) which military science has appropriated for its own uses and which help shorten wars, then it seems natural that the small war should be disappearing under the shadow of its big brother. Yet it has not entirely

Karl Hron, *Der Parteigänger-Krieg* (Vienna, 1885).

withered away, and it may be longer in dying than one might otherwise think.

In times gone by, the small war was a highly respected branch of warfare and the subject of a sizable number of military treatises. There was scarcely a campaign that was not planned in close conjunction with an intensive "small war" waged by one's "light troops" who hung doggedly at the enemy's heels and harried him with needlepricks and stabs of the dagger until the sword of actual battle was drawn. The tasks carried out nowadays by our autonomous advanced cavalry divisions—reconnoitering, preventing the enemy from gaining information about one's circumstances, and covering areas removed from the main theater of operations—fell at that time to the light troops and was part of the small war. Indeed, they did more; they roved about in the enemy's rear, harassed his communications, threatened his depots, captured his supplies, and overpowered important positions in daring surprise attacks.

The golden age of the small war was in the days when armies were still small but had to cover theaters of operations the same size as those the mighty columns of our armies fill today. To avoid the nucleus of the army, the striking force proper, being dissipated over large areas and to protect it against surprise enemy raids, the general command unleashed the pack of light troops to encircle the enemy on all sides and to ensure that the main force was left in peace.

Nowadays we are presented with a somewhat different picture. A half million soldiers concentrated in a small space sleeps peacefully wherever it is. Larger disturbances than pistol shots are needed to wake them up and unsettle them today. The value of the light troops and their activities has therefore suffered some depreciation over the years as far as army movements over large areas are concerned. But as I said, their death knell has not yet sounded, least of all here in Austria, for in the occupied areas and farther south, and likewise in the Tyrol and the Siebenburg Carpathians, we shall never be able to wage anything but a small war. Moreover, our Russian neighbors also set great store by the small war, as is sufficiently proved by the way they arm and train their cavalry. This cavalry is developing into a partisan troop par excellence.

The waging of partisan warfare comprises an infinite variety of tasks. Generally speaking, the partisans are to the main body of the army what the hounds are to the hunter. They smell out the enemy and stick to his trail; whenever possible, they get their teeth into him and tug at him. They drop back if he really shows his teeth, only to move up on him again at the next favorable opportunity. They surround the enemy's troops on every side and watch his every move; they hamper his freedom of movement as much as their strength allows and at the same time conceal their own forces' movements. They never recklessly risk their own necks, and while they do not refuse a fight, they are extremely careful not to deliver themselves into the enemy's hands.

They must pester and unsettle the enemy, wear him down and drive him to distraction with a continuous succession of tricks and ruses so that, without any decisive battle being fought, he is actually weakened for the decisive battle to come. By making a great clamor at a spot far removed from the scene of the main action, they will often be able to lure him into sending off detachments of troops, thus weakening his main striking force. Conversely, because of their mobility, they will be able to slow down the enemy's advance to distant areas of operations and relieve their side's main force of the responsibility for the security of these areas and thus keep that force intact.

The partisans will dog the heels of a defeated enemy and harry him as long as possible until he can be routed completely. In the case of a victorious enemy, on the other hand, they will do everything they can to slow down or halt his advance. They will set traps and threaten him on his flanks or in his rear so that their own defeated forces can gain time to recover. It may well be that at times when the military situation is going against their own forces they will prove themselves most invaluable, for, in Schiller's words: "All around must be night when Friedland's star is shining." The same is true of the partisan's star of honor.

General R.v.L. says in one of his books that when partisan warfare truly lives up to its name, it is the finest flower of all the departments of the small war. In his view, the lot of the partisan is an enviable one, as indeed it is when the partisan stands at the head of fine, courageous troops prepared to undertake anything and when his general bestows upon him a trust that allows him complete freedom and even some latitude for personal caprice. The partisan must be in part a born military genius, and genius needs freedom if it is to stretch its wings to the full.

"That which is exceptional in life acknowledges no rules, submits to no coercion; it knows no law or virtue but its own; it cannot be measured by an earthly measure nor bound by earthly limitations," as Körner says.

Friedrich Wilhelm Rüstow

People's War and Mobile Warfare

Let us now turn to the question of the particular ways in which those resources characteristic of small war are to be exploited. The paucity of resources available will often lead to the use of naked force customary in large-scale warfare being replaced—or at least supplemented—by *cunning, deception,* and *surprise,* for which small war offers much greater opportunity. As mobile troops enjoy much greater scope for the application of such methods than do stationary troops and as mobility enhances one's strength of arms, small wars will tend to involve more movement than large-scale wars, even when the fighting is restricted to a very small area.

As we might expect, the deliberate confrontation with the enemy characteristic of large wars are more seldom sought here. Should circumstances be especially favorable, then the fighting should take the form of a violent charge, preceded by a surprise attack or ambush. But just as often it will be delaying tactics that are required, particularly in small wars involving security troops which are, after all, primarily intended as preparation for larger engagements and battles. Partly because they always try to turn the particular terrain to their advantage, partly because the fighting in small wars only ever involves small numbers, the troops waging such wars will always seek to engage the enemy in places where they can impose their own character on the fighting.

A troop dispatched to a secondary theater of war to carry out this

Friedrich Wilhelm Rüstow, *Die Lehre vom kleinen Krieg* (Zurich, 1864).

or that task may, circumstances permitting, regard itself as nothing more than the nucleus of a fighting force to be drawn from among the local population if this secondary theater is located on the troops' own soil or in allied territory. These local reinforcements may be organized in one of two ways. The first alternative is to create by voluntary recruitment or conscription new *mobile* battalions and squadrons from among the local inhabitants which then are welded onto the nucleus of regular troops. The second is to have the local population remain in their homes ready, when the moment arrives, to rise up as a local militia and wreak all manner of destruction on the enemy without, however, remaining continually under arms and without following the movements of the mobile nucleus of troops. This second alternative represents a true people's war, a type of war which has always proven ruinous to conquering armies when they have encountered freedom-loving peoples and which, for this reason, has been so heartily cursed by such armies and their allies who have coined a variety of terms, all equally unpleasant, for this kind of war and those who wage it . . .

In general one should create small tactical units, for this enables one to keep a greater number of units in the field at any one time and also to mislead the enemy about the true strength of one's forces. Moreover, untrained officers, without whom it is almost impossible to get by in such circumstances, will not have too great a responsibility thrust upon them. There is a further consideration. It may be possible to supplement one's forces from among the inhabitants of the country in which the small war is to be waged.

If the situation allows, it is a great help if the new recruits can be integrated into already existing units, for there they will develop more rapidly into soldiers than if each time separate new tactical units were to be formed. If the units were very large from the outset, the addition of any new recruits would render them unmanageable.

On occasions, it is true, this policy of integrating local recruits into old units may meet with special difficulties. In 1860, for instance, when Garibaldi was advancing through Sicily and Calabria, there appeared wherever the Neapolitan troops had retreated individuals of standing in their particular area who—often before a nucleus of Garibaldi's troops had arrived—began to assemble bands of partisans who themselves, however, were only interested in serving under these leaders. These partisans then had to be placed alongside the nucleus as *special* battalions. This arrangement did not benefit the cause as a whole, for, as soon as the fighting or the advance had passed beyond their part of the country, these new battalions shrank dramatically. Nor did they, due to the rapidity with which the campaign developed, ever attain the standard of discipline of the old battalions and those from northern Italy, in which ranks the forces which had been recruited (where circumstances allowed) from among the local population quickly became accustomed to military organization and discipline. . . .

Charles Callwell

The Dangers
of Guerrilla Warfare—1900

It may be accepted as a general rule that guerrilla warfare is the most unfavorable shape which a campaign can take for the regular troops. At surprises and ambushes, at petty skirmishes, at attacks on detached parties, and at cutting off stragglers, the enemy is usually an adept. Intimate acquaintance with the terrain, natural agility, cunning, and the warlike instinct which is natural in races where security of life and property does not exist, all combine to make antagonists of this kind formidable when hostilities are confined to operations of a guerrilla character. In most small wars the enemy inclines to this mode of carrying on the campaign and shirks more regular engagements. It becomes necessary, therefore, to force him into decisive action. During the French campaigns against Abd el Kader it was found almost impossible to get the wary Emir to fight. The British troops have experienced the same difficulty in recent times in Burma, and also in the Kaffir wars. It is a feature of most insurrectionary wars on a small scale, as for instance in Montenegro in 1876–77. The great Circassian leader Schamyl kept the Russians at bay for years

Charles Callwell, *Small Wars: Their Principles and Practice* (London, 1899).

with guerrilla tactics; his cause declined when he formed his followers into armies and weighed them down with guns. The Poles in 1863 committed the fatal error of assembling in formed bodies; had they confined themselves to desultory warfare their overthrow would have been more difficult. But circumstances often are such that the enemy cannot be tempted into battle and adheres entirely to the guerrilla form of making war . . .

Guerrilla warfare is what the regular armies always have to dread. And when this is directed by a leader with a genius for war an effective campaign becomes well-nigh impossible. The guerrilla has ever been a thorn in the side of the organized force. It was so in the Peninsular War, where the Spanish partisans proved a formidable foe to the French invaders. Fra Diavolo and his brigand bands were almost a match for the veterans of Massena in Calabria. The Turks before the last Russian intervention in the Balkans found the Montenegrins far more difficult to subdue than the organized Serbian armies. Therefore it is that the art of combating this method of conducting operations deserves especial attention when small wars are in question. Moreover, even when there have been at the outset armies in the field to beat, the campaign often drifts on in desultory fashion long after these have been overthrown.

The terrain has much to say to effective conduct of partisan warfare. Montenegro and Brittany, Castille and Trans-Caucasia present theaters of operations eminently suited to operations of this class. New Zealand, the kloofs and bushland of Kaffraria, Burma, and Achin suited to a nicety the guerrilla tactics of opponents designed by nature to pursue this form of war. Hilly and broken ground, or districts clothed in jungle growth and thickets are requisite. On the prairie and the steppes guerrilla warfare is confined to mounted men whose mobility compensates for the want of cover.

Surprise is the essence of such operations—surprise, with retreat ere the opponent can recover as a sequel. And in consequence the combinations are of necessity framed on a small scale. Surprises with large forces are difficult to carry out; the withdrawal of these when once committed to action is most risky. Guerrilla warfare therefore means petty annoyance and not operations of a dramatic kind. But such capricious methods are best met by a resolute plan of campaign, and by an organization favoring rapid and energetic counterstrokes. Surprise can to a certain extent be guarded against by measures taken for security. But the escape of the enemy can only be frustrated by having troops ready to follow up at once and to follow up effectively. . . .

The guerrilla mode of war must in fact be met by an abnormal system of strategy and tactics. The great principle which forms the basis of the art of war remains—the combination of initiative with energy. But this is applied in a special form. The vigor and decision must be displayed in harassing the enemy and in giving him no rest. The hostile bands may elude the regular detachments, but their villages and flocks remain. The theater of war must be subdivided into sections, each to be dealt with by a given force or by a given aggregate of separate detachments. Defensive posts must be established where supplies can be collected, whither raided cattle can be brought, and which form independent bases. To each such base are attached one or more mobile or "flying" columns, organized to be ready to move out at a moment's notice, and equipped so as to penetrate to any part of the district told off to it and to return, certain of supplies for the task.

This question of flying columns deserves some further notice. The system which General Bugeaud introduced in Algeria was not new. General Hoche had worked on similar lines against the Chouans in Brittany with brilliant success. The principle of flying columns has since been used with great success in the Western States against the Red Indians, in Afghanistan, and recently in Burma.

The troops forming such columns must be thoroughly equipped and must be able to travel light. Mobility is the first essential; for the guerrilla trusts to sudden strokes, and it is of the utmost importance that the marauding party should not have time to disperse, and that it should be attacked before it can withdraw and dissolve. Hoche urged the leaders of mobile columns to accustom their men to fatigue and hardships, and to keep them in condition. The strength of such columns depends upon the circumstances of the case. In Burma they seldom numbered more than three hundred men, with one or two guns. In Algeria where the enemy was brave and resolute small bodies would have been unsuitable, and General Bugeaud recommended three or four battalions with cavalry and two guns as a proper strength. Practically they should be as small as possible consistent with safety. Their composition, of course, depends upon the conditions of the campaign and upon the terrain. On open ground a large part of the force would often consist of mounted men. In the bush infantry alone can be used. In Abd el Kader's days portable artillery scarcely existed, and it was wheeled guns to which General Bugeaud so much objected. Guns on mules are not out of place in a flying column of dismounted troops, and they may be very useful. Where it is proposed to raid livestock some mounted troops are indispensable to bring the booty in. . . .

But, although the columns should be as small as possible they must not be too small. If there is any fear of the enemy combining his forces to attack columns in detail, or of acting on interior lines as it is called, there must be troops enough to deal with whatever hostile forces can be assembled. In the early days of La Vendée separation proved fatal to the Republican forces. The peasants assembled from time to time in great force and overwhelmed the detachments of regulars. The system of small columns introduced later by General Hoche was adapted to different conditions, to a more purely guerrilla warfare than when the insurrection was at its height. In Mexico small columns of French and of Imperial troops suffered very severely when the troubles first broke out against Maximilian's rule; the enemy was able to bring considerable forces against them. In Upper Burma where very small columns were adopted during the prolonged period of pacification no serious disaster occurred; and this, considering the great number of columns operating in a vast extent of almost unexplored country for many months, is remarkable. But on one or two occasions it would have been advantageous had they been stronger. Sir F. Roberts' instructions were that "the troops should make their presence felt everywhere." And in view of the enormous area to be overrun the columns had to be reduced to a minimum strength. . . .

In no class of warfare is a well-organized and well-served intelligence department more essential than in that against guerrillas. Hoche instituted an elaborate system of espionage in Brittany, paying especial attention to this very important subject. Guerrillas trust to secret and to sudden strokes, and if the secret is discovered, their plan miscarries. On the other hand all movements intended against them must be concealed. Guerrilla warfare means that the regular troops are spread about a hostile country where all their movements can be watched by the enemy and where their camps are full of spies. Partisan leaders seldom can be trusted, and in all dealings with them,

great circumspection is essential. Hoche discouraged parleying with
the rebels by subordinate officers, distrusting their chiefs. *"Parle
comme si tu avais confiance en tout le monde"* was the motto of
General Bugeaud *"et agis comme si tu ne pouvais t'en rapporter à
personne."*

T. Miller Maguire

Differences Between Guerrilla and Regular Warfare

Advantages of Savage and Semicivilized Races

The natural man—the dweller in the hills and plains as distinguished
from the product of the factory or large towns—has other qualifica-
tions besides eyesight and woodcraft which make him an ideal recruit. He can usually do with less food than his more civilized
brother; he will exercise greater frugality and economy with regard
to what he obtains; he is an adept at cooking or preparing an im-
promptu meal; he knows where and how to obtain food if there is
any to be had in the country; and he can usually manage to carry
it with him in a small compass. He is comparatively little affected
by heat or cold; he can sleep as soundly on the ground as in bed;
he is not often ill and, when he has slight ailments *or* has met with
minor accidents, knows how to treat himself and requires no medical
advice. In a word, he is tougher, harder, more enduring than his
more civilized brother, just as it is natural his mode of life should
render him. In everything except discipline and armament he is, as
a rule, superior to the man he has to fight.

But now the growth of trade routes and facilities of communication are rapidly taking away from us and the other civilized powers

T. Miller Maguire, *Guerrilla or Partisan Warfare* (London, 1904).

the privileges of better armaments. The possession of the very newest and most perfect weapons is simply a matter of money, and the firms which turn them out will sell as freely to a savage as to the most enlightened of the world's rulers.

Nor have the minor powers and half-civilized, or wholly savage, tribes of the world failed to avail themselves of their chances . . .

Well-Armed Savages or Moslems

An Abyssinian or Afghan war would now mean for us that we should have to face foemen individually superior to the vast majority of our men in all the qualities that go to make a good soldier, and no longer wielding swords and spears, but rifles equal in every respect to our own. In a few years it may well be that a similar state of things will be seen in China, while the distribution of modern weapons all over the globe will make it often probable that when we send an expedition against savages, it will not follow that we shall find primitive weapons in their hands.

If Fuzzy-wuzzy be, as he often is, as good a man as Tommy Atkins, or Fritz, or Jacques, and is even approximately as well armed, numerical superiority, knowledge of the country, and better health will go a long way to redress the balance in our favor, which experience and discipline in these days of loosened fighting may produce. Both sides—nature and civilization—being once more on an equality, the scale must be turned by better generalship in the future, as it has been in the past.

A careful study of the military art and the selection of the most competent men for leaders will become as requisite in the future when a "little war" is undertaken, as when a struggle with a great power is inevitable. . . .

Differences Between Regular and Guerrilla Warfare

The mere initiative does not make so much difference as in regular European warfare.

The strategical conditions are not reciprocal, and are against the regular invader, as the savage or irregular is not troubled about his lines of communication.

Observe the swelling or contracting of savage forces, according to failure or success of invader.

Reverses, even at first, must be avoided at all costs. The motto: "Don't begin till you are ready," applies even more to these wars than to great wars; as even a stategical defensive must be combined with a tactical offensive for moral reasons.

Prolonged operations are to be avoided; hence prefer tactics to strategy.

Complete enveloping movements like those of the Germans at Sedan are to be avoided; if driven to bay the savage will, in his fear of massacre, fight *à outrance*.

Leave the enemy an avenue of escape and hit him hard in the flank as he is trying to escape.

The army must be split up into several unconnected columns; the inner line principle is not so effective against invaders as it has been in France, Bohemia, or the United States, as the savage has no idea of strategy.

The situation as to flying columns, and long lines of communications and transport columns, unless very carefully managed, soon becomes hazardous.

Terrible embarrassment if many men are wounded, as they must not be allowed to fall into the hands of the enemy.

Most serious dangers accompany the resort to guerrilla warfare by the enemy—therefore the necessity to strike them hard and demoralize them.

The subaltern officers were formerly of a higher standard of efficiency relatively than in regular warfare, but this condition is rapidly changing with the growing importance of individual efficiency in all wars.

Still, there is much more freedom and latitude of movement for subordinates.

Lack of maps—difficulty of obtaining information—while the natives gain information with an almost incredible speed and accuracy.

Savages are masters of surprises, and yet are taken aback by ambuscades and surprises applied to themselves. The individual savage is a far better tactician than the individual European—and his armament is daily improving.

Turning movements surprise savages, but may do more harm than good. Get the irregular to stand and crush him, keep him in his position; don't frighten him away from it. Don't drive him to stand at bay.

Press the pursuit hard; the enemy does not pursue ably and does not understand persistent pursuit.

Reserves are not very much required for battles, but the flanks and rear are in constant danger on the march and in the battle.

Attack early; savages and irregulars are not vigilant at dawn.

When the enemy pushes his attack with fanatic swordsmen, or spearmen, it is sink or swim, and counterstrokes are impossible till the crisis is over; then use them.

Squares and defense works are far more important than in regular warfare. The study of rigid and of elastic squares is needful.

Guns and cavalry produce an enormous moral effect in these wars —lancers are of great moral value.

The outpost systems are quite different. Dangers of isolation of advanced and rear guards, dangers from lateral valleys and from even the semblance of retreat and from "sniping."

Regulars in small wars must frequently adopt retrograde movements, but these must be very deliberate, as they always encourage the enemy.

Always get close to the enemy and insist on his being roughly handled.

The principles on which outposts, patrols, vedettes, advanced guards, and rear guards are arranged are quite different.

The extraordinary rapidity of movement by savages must be borne in mind.

Races who live in the tropics, and in countries full of jungle and bush, are timid as compared with hill men and the nomad wanderers of the desert.

There is a danger of rushes by day and by night.

The more irregular and desultory the campaign the more important is the service of security.

As to defensive works:—attack and not defense is the first principle for regulars in small and irregular wars; but all isolated forces must be well protected and have clear fields of fire with flanking positions and obstacles.

T. H. C. Frankland

Efficacy and Difficulties

Country and Character

We are told that the objects of a regular army engaged in regular warfare are, firstly, the destruction of the enemy's organized forces, and, secondly, if the terms demanded by the conqueror are not already acceded, the seizure of the capital, chief centers, and therefore the resources of the enemy's country.

In a civilized country the dislocation of trade and government that results brings about inevitable surrender. Sometimes, as was the case in 1871, hastily levied armies of untrained inhabitants are placed between the invader and his second object. But the doom of these is foregone. To prevent the enemy reaching certain objectives, his masses must be opposed by masses, and where masses are contending, organization, trained leaders, and a trained staff are more important than the individual qualities of the rank and file; so that however brave, however patriotic, the untrained levies may be, the very necessity of forming them into large armies dooms them to defeat. It is when fighting in masses that the untrained combatant becomes an amateur indeed.

We have arrived at this, then: that where it is necessary to bar the conqueror's way to a certain objective, untrained men are useless. In other words, in civilized countries, where the loss of capital and chief towns paralyzes all action, the destruction of its organized forces must be followed by surrender.

In less civilized countries, however, where the inhabitants are self-contained and dependent on the soil rather than the town, the loss

T. H. C. Frankland, "Notes on Guerrilla Warfare" in *United Service Magazine*, Vol. 33 (1912).

of capital by no means entails loss of resources, and frequently has no effect on their resisting power, and the very fact of their offering no stationary vitals as an object to the enemy's armies gives them a great advantage. It relieves them of the necessity of opposing the march of the enemy's masses; it relieves them of the necessity of concentrating; it relieves them of the necessity of being beaten. In an only partially civilized country roads are generally bad and railways few, and the movements of large bodies of troops with their cumbrous supply columns is a matter of greater difficulty than in more developed countries.

Where, then, civilization precludes resistance to an invader except by organized forces, the absence of civilization affords great facilities for guerrilla warfare. As regards the nature of country most suitable for irregular fighting, one of two conditions is necessary—either a wild surface or great space. In the one the difficulties of transport, of the movement of troops and guns, and of reconnaissance obstruct the path of the invader, while inaccessible fastness and facilities of ambush favor the defenders. In the other, the guerrilla has plenty of room to deliver his blow and get away. The mobility of mounted bands has its full scope, and the number of troops required by the enemy is out of all proportion to the numbers of its adversary. It is natural that countries most suitable to guerrilla fighting should breed the best guerrilla fighters. Where civilization from the point of luxury and comfort is absent, the inhabitants, hardened to exposure and accustomed to irregular and primitive feeding, find in the hardships of campaigning but the ordinary routine of their daily life. Possessing practically no capital, they have generally little to lose and much to gain, for it is more congenial to reap by plunder and capture what others have sown than to toil all day for a bare living. Beyond this the inhabitants of a wild or extended country, where self-reliance, keen eyesight, knowledge of country, and other qualities are daily acquired, becomes naturally and almost unconsciously excellent scouts and skirmishers.

Difficulties of Guerrilla Warfare

Generally speaking, guerrilla warfare has as its object the exhaustion of the invader, for the primary aim of driving him away can only be brought about in this way; unable to bar his progress to any part of their country, or to prevent his occupation of what territory he chooses, the guerrilla can at least dog his steps, delay his progress, and sap his strength until exhaustion or intervention causes the invader to withdraw. As has already been remarked, the guerrillas start with a great advantage, namely, their invulnerability. Only by actually capturing or killing each individual can the prospective conqueror, so long as the patriotism of the inhabitants remains firm, hope to terminate the struggle. The guerrillas have no accessible vitals, and receding, like the tide, before their organized foe, they close in again behind him unharmed. On the other hand, their "regular" opponent is always open to serious wounds. The necessary appendage of a line of communication, the essential small posts, lie a perpetual prey to the swoop of the moving bands.

Again, the guerrillas derive an advantage from their very want of organization. Untrammeled by detailed orders, they move hither and thither till, each band reported in several places at the same time, the veriest paragon of an intelligence officer is puzzled to distraction. For themselves, served by their friends and families, whom, in hopes of pacification, the invader has left on the land, their intelligence is of the surest. And their scouts are in turn aided in their work by the very organization and methodical movements of their opponents. For the comparatively slow-moving columns of a regular army, with their train of transport and artillery, betrayed by their regularly formed advanced guards, are easily located; the direction of their march is obvious, and their arrival at any particular spot readily calculated. Ambushes are, hence, easily laid for flank or rear guards, and convoys, always moving on the same routes, and protected in the same way, are easily held up.

On the other hand, the want of organization has its disadvantages —in the consequent difficulty of cooperation. For, though a common object and a common instinct, namely, to harm the enemy in every possible way, brings of its own accord some semblance of unity of action, yet cooperation on a large scale has been often proved to be almost impossible, and big results therefore unattainable. . . .

Efficacy of This Class of Warfare: A Comparison

As to the efficacy of unaided guerrilla warfare, Napier speaks in no uncertain terms: "They (the Spanish partidas) never occupied half their own numbers of French at the same time, never absolutely defeated a single division, never prevented any considerable enterprise."

Our experience in South Africa was very different to this, and this difference may be partly traced to the stamp of leader in each case. With a few exceptions, such as Mina, the leaders of the Spanish bands failed to grasp the essentials of guerrilla warfare. Full of arrogance and a false notion of their military abilities, they assumed the dignity of generals, tried to form armies out of their irregular bands, and with their inextinguishable self-confidence constantly sought pitched battles.

Wellington, seeing that their true role was to avoid encounters in large bodies, and to concentrate their attentions on the less glorious but more certain operations of harassing the enemy's communications, was ever trying to persuade his allies so to act. But his advice was constantly rejected, and defeat as constantly followed. The Boer leaders, on the contrary, recognized their true *role* from the beginning, and the almost systematic way in which they worked, each in their own districts, concentrating suddenly on weak points and dispersing as rapidly before relieving columns, ensured such success as is possible in this method of warfare.

But the greater difficulties experienced by the British in South Africa find, perhaps, a better explanation in the modern rifle; in the hands of the Boers it proved a very formidable weapon. The difficulties of reconnaissance in guerrilla warfare, already remarked on, were greatly increased. Rapidity of fire, accuracy, smokeless powder, and long range added to the irregular's power of harassing, while a few guerrillas could easily impose on large columns. In the Peninsula the Spaniards, even when well armed, could only attack French columns at close ranges, when a charge of the regular troops would always route them, and the escape of the intruders was a matter of difficulty.

In South Africa a few men with rifles could force a column to deploy at fourteen hundred yards, and could withdraw after doing considerable damage, while their opponents were still half a mile distant.

The modern rifle, however, gave also advantages to the invaders. Posts could be held by fewer men, and the blockhouses on the lines of communication could be separated by wider distances. It was on account of the modern rifle that the "drives" in South Africa were possible, for with the Brown Bess of the Peninsula the number of men that would have been necessary to hold the blockhouse lines efficiently would have been prohibitive.

Still, the advantages rest rather with the guerrilla, and the fact that, armed and led as they were, the Boers succumbed at last to the relentless pressure of a regular army, proves that guerrillas alone, even under the most favorable circumstances, cannot even hope for incessant war as a reward to their exertions.

Thomas Edward Lawrence

The Lessons of Arabia

The Arab Revolt of 1916–18

The Arab revolt began in June, 1916, with an attack by the half-armed and inexperienced tribesmen upon the Turkish garrisons in Medina and about Mecca. They met with no success, and after a few days' effort withdrew out of range and began a blockade. This method forced the early surrender of Mecca, the more remote of the two centers. Medina, however, was linked by railway to the Turkish main

Reprinted from the *Encyclopaedia Britannica*, 14th ed. (1929).

army in Syria, and the Turks were able to reinforce the garrison there. The Arab forces which had attacked it then fell back gradually and took up a position across the main road to Mecca.

At this point the campaign stood still for many weeks. The Turks prepared to send an expeditionary force to Mecca, to crush the revolt at its source, and accordingly moved an army corps to Medina by rail. Thence they began to advance down the main western road from Medina to Mecca, a distance of about two hundred fifty miles. The first fifty miles were easy, then came a belt of hills twenty miles wide, in which were Feisal's Arab tribesmen standing on the defensive: next a level stretch, for seventy miles along the coastal plain to Rabegh, rather more than halfway. Rabegh is a little port on the Red Sea, with good anchorage for ships, and because of its situation was regarded as the key to Mecca. There lay Sherif Ali, Feisal's eldest brother, with more tribal forces, and the beginning of an Arab regular army, formed from officers and men of Arab blood who had served in the Turkish army. As was almost inevitable in view of the general course of military thinking since Napoleon, the soldiers of all countries looked only to the regulars to win the war. Military opinion was obsessed by the dictum of Foch that the ethic of modern war is to seek for the enemy's army, his center of power, and destroy it in battle. Irregulars would not attack positions and so they were regarded as incapable of forcing a decision.

While these Arab regulars were still being trained, the Turks suddenly began their advance on Mecca. They broke through the hills in twenty-four hours, and so proved the second theorem of irregular war—namely, that irregular troops are as unable to defend a point or line as they are to attack it. This lesson was received without gratitude, for the Turkish success put the Rabegh force in a critical position, and it was not capable of repelling the attack of a single battalion, much less a corps.

In the emergency it occurred to the author that perhaps the virtue of irregulars lay in depth, not in face, and that it had been the threat of attack by them upon the Turkish northern flank which had made the enemy hesitate for so long. The actual Turkish flank ran from their front line to Medina, a distance of about fifty miles; but, if the Arab force moved toward the Hejaz railway behind Medina, it might stretch its threat (and, accordingly, the enemy's flank) as far, potentially, as Damascus, eight hundred miles away to the north. Such a move would force the Turks to the defensive, and the Arab force might regain the initiative. Anyhow, it seemed the only chance, and so, in January, 1917, Feisal's tribesmen turned their backs on Mecca, Rabegh and the Turks, and marched away north two hundred miles to Wejh.

This eccentric movement acted like a charm. The Arabs did nothing concrete, but their march recalled the Turks (who were almost into Rabegh) all the way back to Medina. There, one half of the Turkish force took up the entrenched position about the city, which it held until after the Armistice. The other half was distributed along the railway to defend it against the Arab threat. For the rest of the war the Turks stood on the defensive and the Arab tribesmen won advantage over advantage till, when peace came, they had taken 35,000 prisoners, killed and wounded and worn out about as many, and occupied 100,000 square miles of the enemy's territory, at little loss to themselves. However, although Wejh was the turning point, its significance was not yet realized. For the moment the move thither was regarded merely as a preliminary to cutting the railway in order to take Medina, the Turkish headquarters and main garrison.

Strategy and Tactics

The author was unfortunately as much in charge of the campaign as he pleased, and lacking a training in command sought to find an immediate equation between past study of military theory and the present movements—as a guide to, and an intellectual basis for, future action. The textbooks gave the aim in war as "the destruction of the organized forces of the enemy" by "the one process battle." Victory could only be purchased by blood. This was a hard saying, as the Arabs had no organized forces, and so a Turkish Foch would have no aim: and the Arabs would not endure casualties, so that an Arab Clausewitz could not buy his victory. These wise men must be talking metaphors, for the Arabs were indubitably winning their war . . . and further reflection pointed to the deduction that they had actually won it. They were in occupation of 99 percent of the Hejaz. The Turks were welcome to the other fraction till peace or doomsday showed them the futility of clinging to the windowpane. This part of the war was over, so why bother about Medina? The Turks sat in it on the defensive, immobile, eating for food the transport animals which were to have moved them to Mecca, but for which there was no pasture in their now restricted lines. They were harmless sitting there; if taken prisoner, they would entail the cost of food and guards in Egypt; if driven out northward into Syria, they would join the main army blocking the British in Sinai. On all counts they were best where they were, and they valued Medina and wanted to keep it. Let them!

This seemed unlike the ritual of war of which Foch had been priest, and so it seemed that there was a difference of kind. Foch called his modern war "absolute." In it two nations professing incompatible philosophies set out to try them in the light of force. A struggle of two immaterial principles would only end when the supporters of one had no more means of resistance. An opinion can be argued with: a conviction is best shot. The logical end of a war of creeds is the final destruction of one, and Salammbô the classical textbook instance. These were the lines of the struggle between France and Germany, but not, perhaps, between Germany and England, for all efforts to make the British soldier hate the enemy simply made him hate war. Thus the "absolute war" seemed only a variety of war; and beside it other sorts could be discerned as Clausewitz had numbered them, personal wars for dynastic reasons, expulsive wars for party reasons, commercial wars for trading reasons.

Now the Arab aim was unmistakably geographical, to occupy all Arabic-speaking lands in Asia. In the doing of it Turks might be killed, yet "killing Turks" would never be an excuse or aim. If they would go quietly, the war would end. If not, they must be driven out: but at the cheapest possible price, since the Arabs were fighting for freedom, a pleasure only to be tasted by a man alive. The next task was to analyze the process, both from the point of view of strategy, the aim in war, the synoptic regard which sees everything by the standard of the whole, and from the point of view called tactics, the means toward the strategic end, the steps of its staircase. In each were found the same elements, one algebraical, one biological, a third psychological. The first seemed a pure science, subject to the laws of mathematics, without humanity. It dealt with known invariables, fixed conditions, space and time, inorganic things such as hills and climates and railways, with mankind in type masses too great for individual variety, with all artificial aids, and the extensions given our faculties by mechanical invention. It was essentially formulable.

In the Arab case the algebraic factor would take first account of the area to be conquered. A casual calculation indicated perhaps 140,000 square miles. How would the Turks defend all that—no doubt by a trench line across the bottom, if the Arabs were an army attacking with banners displayed . . . but suppose they were an influence, a thing invulnerable, intangible, without front or back, drifting about like a gas? Armies were like plants, immobile as a whole, firm-rooted, nourished through long stems to the head. The Arabs might be a vapor, blowing where they listed. It seemed that a regular soldier might be helpless without a target. He would own the ground he sat on, and what he could poke his rifle at. The next step was to estimate how many posts they would need to contain this attack in depth, sedition putting up her head in every unoccupied one of these 100,000 square miles. They would have need of a fortified post every four square miles, and a post could not be less than 20 men. The Turks would need 600,000 men to meet the combined ill wills of all the local Arab people. They had 100,000 men available. It seemed that the assets in this sphere were with the Arabs, and climate, railways, deserts, technical weapons could also be attached to their interests. The Turk was stupid and would believe that rebellion was absolute, like war, and deal with it on the analogy of absolute warfare.

Humanity in Battle

So much for the mathematical element; the second factor was biological, the breaking point, life and death, or better, wear and tear. Bionomics seemed a good name for it. The war philosophers had properly made it an art, and had elevated one item in it, "effusion of blood," to the height of a principle. It became humanity in battle, an art touching every side of our corporal being. There was a line of variability (man) running through all its estimates. Its components were sensitive and illogical, and generals guarded themselves by the device of a reserve, the significant medium of their art. Colmar von der Goltz had said that when you know the enemy's strength, and he is fully deployed, then you know enough to dispense with a reserve. But this is never. There is always the possibility of accident, of some flaw in materials, present in the general's mind, and the reserve is unconsciously held to meet it. There is a "felt" element in troops, not expressible in figures, and the greatest commander is he whose intuitions most nearly happen. Nine-tenths of tactics are certain, and taught in books; but the irrational tenth is like the kingfisher flashing across the pool and that is the test of generals. It can only be ensued by instinct, sharpened by thought practicing the stroke so often that at the crisis it is as natural as a reflex.

Yet to limit the art to humanity seemed an undue narrowing down. It must apply to materials as much as to organisms. In the Turkish army materials were scarce and precious, men more plentiful than equipment. Consequently the cue should be to destroy not the army but the materials. The death of a Turkish bridge or rail, machine or gun, or high explosive was more profitable than the death of a Turk. The Arab army just then was equally chary of men and materials: of men because they being irregulars were not units, but individuals, and an individual casualty is like a pebble dropped in water: each may make only a brief hole, but rings of sorrow widen out from them. The Arab army could not afford casualties. Materials were easier to deal with. Hence its obvious duty to make itself superior in some one branch, guncotton or machine guns, or whatever could be most decisive. Foch had laid down the maxim, applying it to men, of being superior at the critical point and moment of attack. The Arab army might apply it to materials and be superior in equipment in one dominant moment or respect.

For both men and things it might try to give Foch's doctrine a negative twisted side, for cheapness' sake, and be weaker than the enemy everywhere except in one point or matter. Most wars are wars of contact, both forces striving to keep in touch to avoid tactical surprise. The Arab war should be a war of detachment: to contain the enemy by the silent threat of a vast unknown desert, not disclosing themselves till the moment of attack. This attack need be only nominal, directed not against his men, but against his materials, so it should not seek for his main strength or his weaknesses, but for his most accessible material. In railway cutting this would be usually an empty stretch of rail. This was a tactical success. From this theory came to be developed ultimately an unconscious habit of never engaging the enemy at all. This chimed with the numerical plea of never giving the enemy's soldier a target. Many Turks on the Arab front had no chance all the war to fire a shot, and correspondingly the Arabs were never on the defensive, except by rare accident. The corollary of such a rule was perfect "intelligence," so that plans could be made in complete certainty. The chief agent had to be the general's head (Antoine de Pas de Feuquière said this first), and his knowledge had to be faultless, leaving no room for chance. The headquarters of the Arab army probably took more pains in this service than any other staff.

The Crowd in Action

The third factor in command seemed to be the psychological, that science (Xenophon called it diathetic) of which our propaganda is a stained and ignoble part. It concerns the crowd, the adjustment of spirit to the point where it becomes fit to exploit in action. It considers the capacity for mood of the men, their complexities and mutability, and the cultivation of what in them profits the intention. The command of the Arab army had to arrange their men's minds in order of battle, just as carefully and as formally as other officers arranged their bodies: and not only their own men's minds, though them first; the minds of the enemy, so far as it could reach them; and thirdly, the mind of the nation supporting it behind the firing line, and the mind of the hostile nation waiting the verdict, and the neutrals looking on.

It was the ethical in war, and the process on which the command mainly depended for victory on the Arab front. The printing press is the greatest weapon in the armory of the modern commander, and the commanders of the Arab army being amateurs in the art, began their war in the atmosphere of the twentieth century, and thought of their weapons without prejudice, not distinguishing one from another socially. The regular officer has the tradition of forty generations of serving soldiers behind him, and to him the old weapons are the most honored. The Arab command had seldom to concern itself with what its men did, but much with what they thought, and to it the diathetic was more than half command. In Europe it was set a little aside and entrusted to men outside the general staff. But the Arab army was so weak physically that it could not let the metaphysical weapon rust unused. It had won a province when the civilians in it had been taught to die for the ideal of freedom; the presence or absence of the enemy was a secondary matter.

These reasonings showed that the idea of assaulting Medina, or even of starving it quickly into surrender, was not in accord with the best strategy. Rather, let the enemy stay in Medina, and in every other harmless place, in the largest numbers. If he showed a disposition to evacuate too soon, as a step to concentrating in the small area which his numbers could dominate effectively, then the Arab army would have to try and restore his confidence, not harshly, but by reducing its enterprises against him. The ideal was to keep his railway just working, but only just, with the maximum of loss and discomfort to him.

The Turkish army was an accident, not a target. Our true strategic aim was to seek its weakest link, and bear only on that till time made the mass of it fall. The Arab army must impose the longest possible passive defense on the Turks (this being the most materially expensive form of war) by extending its own front to the maximum. Tactically it must develop a highly mobile, highly equipped type of force, of the smallest size, and use it successively at distributed points of the Turkish line, to make the Turks reinforce their occupying posts beyond the economic minimum of twenty men. The power of this striking force would not be reckoned merely by its strength. The ratio between number and area determined the character of the war, and by having five times the mobility of the Turks the Arabs could be on terms with them with one fifth their number.

Range over Force

Success was certain, to be proved by paper and pencil as soon as the proportion of space and number had been learned. The contest was not physical, but moral, and so battles were a mistake. All that could be won in a battle was the ammunition the enemy fired off. Napoleon had said it was rare to find generals willing to fight battles. The curse of this war was that so few could do anything else. Napoleon had spoken in angry reaction against the excessive finesse of the eighteenth century, when men almost forgot that war gave license to murder. Military thought had been swinging out on his dictum for one hundred years, and it was time to go back a bit again. Battles are impositions on the side which believes itself weaker, made unavoidable either by lack of land room, or by the need to defend a material property dearer than the lives of soldiers. The Arabs had nothing material to lose, so they were to defend nothing and to shoot nothing. Their cards were speed and time, not hitting power, and these gave them strategical rather than tactical strength. Range is more to strategy than force. The invention of bully beef had modified land war more profoundly than the invention of gunpowder.

The British military authorities did not follow all these arguments, but gave leave for their practical application to be tried. Accordingly the Arab forces went off first to Aqaba and took it easily. Then they took Tafile and the Dead Sea; then Azraq and Dera'a, and finally Damascus, all in successive stages worked out consciously on these theories. The process was to set up ladders of tribes, which should provide a safe and comfortable route from the sea bases (Yenbo, Wejh, or Aqaba) to the advanced bases of operation. These were sometimes three hundred miles away, a long distance in lands without railways or roads, but made short for the Arab army by an assiduous cultivation of desert power, control by camel parties of the desolate and unmapped wilderness which fills up all the center of Arabia, from Mecca to Aleppo and Baghdad.

The Desert and the Sea

In character these operations were like naval warfare, in their mobility, their ubiquity, their independence of bases and communications, in their ignoring of ground features, of strategic areas, of fixed directions, of fixed points. "He who commands the sea is at great liberty, and may take as much or as little of the war as he will": he who commands the desert is equally fortunate. Camel raiding-parties, self-contained like ships, could cruise securely along the enemy's land frontier, just out of sight of his posts along the edge of cultivation, and tap or raid into his lines where it seemed fittest or easiest or most profitable, with a sure retreat always behind them into an element which the Turks could not enter.

Discrimination of what point of the enemy organism to disarrange came with practice. The tactics were always tip and run; not pushes, but strokes. The Arab army never tried to maintain or improve an advantage, but to move off and strike again somewhere else. It used the smallest force in the quickest time at the farthest place. To continue the action till the enemy had changed his dispositions to resist it would have been to break the spirit of the fundamental rule of denying him targets.

The necessary speed and range were attained by the frugality of the desert men, and their efficiency on camels. In the heat of summer Arabian camels will do about two hundred fifty miles comfortably between drinks, and this represented three days' vigorous marching. This radius was always more than was needed, for wells are seldom more than one hundred miles apart. The equipment of the raiding parties aimed at simplicity, with nevertheless a technical superiority over the Turks in the critical department. Quantities of light machine guns were obtained from Egypt for use not as machine guns, but as automatic rifles, snipers' tools, by men kept deliberately in ignorance of their mechanism, so that the speed of action would not be hampered by attempts at repair. Another special feature was high explosives, and nearly every one in the revolt was qualified by rule-of-thumb experience in demolition work.

Armored Cars

On some occasions tribal raids were strengthened by armored cars, manned by Englishmen. Armored cars, once they have found a possible track, can keep up with a camel party. On the march to Damascus, when nearly four hundred miles off their base, they were first maintained by a baggage train of gasoline-laden camels, and afterward from the air. Cars are magnificent fighting machines, and decisive whenever they can come into action on their own conditions. But though each has for its main principle that of "fire in movement," yet the tactical employments of cars and camel corps are so different that their use in joint operations is difficult. It was found demoralizing to both to use armored and unarmored cavalry together.

The distribution of the raiding parties was unorthodox. It was impossible to mix or combine tribes, since they dislike or distrusted one another. Likewise the men of one tribe could not be used in the territory of another. In consequence, another canon of orthodox strategy was broken by following the principle of the widest distribution of force, in order to have the greatest number of raids on hand at once, and fluidity was added to speed by using one district on Monday, another on Tuesday, a third on Wednesday. This much reinforced the natural mobility of the Arab army, giving it priceless advantages in pursuit, for the force renewed itself with fresh men in every new tribal area, and so maintained its pristine energy.

An Undisciplined Army

The internal economy of the raiding parties was equally curious. Maximum irregularity and articulation were the aims. Diversity threw the enemy intelligence off the track. By the regular organization in identical battalions and divisions information builds itself up, until the presence of a corps can be inferred on corpses from three companies. The Arabs, again, were serving a common ideal, without tribal emulation, and so could not hope for any *esprit de corps*. Soldiers are made a caste either by being given great pay and rewards in money, uniform or political privileges; or, as in England, by being made outcasts, cut off from the mass of their fellow citizens. There have been many armies enlisted voluntarily; there have been few armies serving voluntarily under such trying conditions for so long a war as the Arab revolt. Any of the Arabs could go home whenever the conviction failed him. Their only contract was honor.

Consequently the Arab army had no discipline, in the sense in which it is restrictive, submergent of individuality, the lowest common denominator of men. In regular armies in peace it means the limit of energy attainable by everybody present; it is the hunt not of an average, but of an absolute, a 100 percent standard, in which the ninety-nine stronger men are played down to the level of the worst. The aim is to render the unit a unit, and the man a type, in order that their effort shall be calculable, their collective output even in grain and in bulk. The deeper the discipline, the lower the individual efficiency, and the more sure the performance. It is a deliberate sacrifice of capacity in order to reduce the uncertain element, the bionomic factor, in enlisted humanity, and its accompaniment is compound or social war, that form in which the fighting man has to be the product of the multiplied exertions of long hierarchy, from workshop to supply unit, which maintains him in the field.

The Arab war, reacting against this, was simple and individual. Every enrolled man served in the line of battle, and was self-contained. There were no lines of communication or labor troops. It seemed that in this articulated warfare, the sum yielded by single men would be at least equal to the product of a compound system of the same strength, and it was certainly easier to adjust to tribal life and manners, given elasticity and understanding on the part of the commanding officers. Fortunately for its chances nearly every young Englishman has the roots of eccentricity in him. Only a sprinkling were employed, not more than one per one thousand of the Arab troops. A larger proportion would have created friction, just because they were foreign bodies (pearls if you please) in the oyster; and those who were present controlled by influence and advice, by their superior knowledge, not by an extraneous authority.

The practice was, however, not to employ in the firing line the greater numbers which the adoption of a "simple" system made available theoretically. Instead, they were used in relay; otherwise the attack would have become too extended. Guerrillas must be allowed liberal work room. In irregular war if two men are together, one is being wasted. The moral strain of isolated action makes this simple form of war very hard on the individual soldier, and exacts from him special initiative, endurance, and enthusiasm. Here the ideal was to make action a series of single combats to make the ranks a happy alliance of commanders in chief. The value of the Arab army depended entirely on quality, not on quantity. The members had to keep always cool, for the excitement of a blood lust would impair their science, and their victory depended on a just use of speed, concealment, and accuracy of fire. Guerrilla war is far more intellectual than a bayonet charge.

The Exact Science of Guerrilla Warfare

By careful persistence, kept strictly within its strength and following the spirit of these theories, the Arab army was able eventually to reduce the Turks to helplessness, and complete victory seemed to be almost within sight when General Edmund Allenby by his immense stroke in Palestine threw the enemy's main forces into hopeless confusion and put an immediate end to the Turkish war. He deprived the Arab revolt of the opportunity of following to the end the dictum of Maurice Saxe that a war might be won without fighting battles. But it can at least be said that its leaders worked by his light for two years, and the work stood. This is a pragmatic argument that cannot be wholly derided. The experiment, although not complete, strengthened the belief that irregular war or rebellion could be proved to be an exact science, and an inevitable success, granted certain factors and if pursued along certain lines.

Here is the thesis: Rebellion must have an unassailable base, something guarded not merely from attack, but from the fear of it: such a base as the Arab revolt had in the Red Sea ports, the desert, or in the minds of men converted to its creed. It must have a sophisticated alien enemy, in the form of a disciplined army of occupation too small to fulfill the doctrine of acreage: too few to adjust number to space, in order to dominate the whole area effectively from fortified posts. It must have a friendly population, not actively friendly, but sympathetic to the point of not betraying rebel movements to the enemy. Rebellions can be made by 2 percent active in a striking force, and 98 percent passively sympathetic. The few active rebels must have the qualities of speed and endurance, ubiquity and independence of arteries of supply. They must have the technical equipment to destroy or paralyze the enemy's organized communications, for irregular war is fairly Wilhelm von Willisen's definition of strategy, "the study of communication," in its extreme degree, of attack where the enemy is not. In fifty words: Granted mobility, security (in the form of denying targets to the enemy), time and doctrine (the idea to convert every subject to friendliness), victory will rest with the insurgents, for the algebraical factors are in the end decisive, and against them perfections of means and spirit struggle quite in vain.

B. C. Dening

Guerrillas and
Political Propaganda

In studying the guerrilla wars of the past, it is remarkable how little the characteristics of this type of fighting have altered with the passage of time. Thus the cause of such warfare has inevitably been an actual or imaginary suppression of the national aspirations of a smaller race by the force of a larger one. Such wars have always been carried out with the utmost ferocity on both sides. Tactics have varied only in detail from century to century. Mobility, good intelligence, surprise and cunning, and the nature of the country have continued to play their part time after time. What is more—far more so than has been possible in the case of greater wars—with the facts of history available, it has been feasible nearly always to forecast the inevitable result of guerrilla wars. This latter fact being so, it is remarkable how often one side has embarked on the struggle, knowing well what its end was likely to be. While discussing this aspect of the question, it is interesting to go back over the principal guerrilla wars of comparatively modern history and to note the results of these struggles and how such results were obtained.

The ten principal guerrilla wars which have taken place since 1792 are summarized in the table at the end of this article. In five of them, the victory rested with the Great Power, though in two of them only after a most protracted struggle. In two cases the result was indecisive, and in the remaining three the guerrilla forces were victorious. If the causes which led to these results are examined, it is abundantly clear that where the Great Power had the means and the will to exert itself, where it employed the right tactics, unless outside intervention entered as a factor, it invariably won, and that only where the reverse was the case could the guerrillas hope to win.

B. C. Dening, "Modern Problems of Guerrilla Warfare" in *Army Quarterly*, Vol. 13, No. 2 (1927).

Where outside factors, such as the remoteness, or other entanglements, of the Great Power have come in to balance the scales, at least temporarily, in a guerrilla struggle, the decision has rested to some extent upon the tactics employed by the combatants.

For the Great Power, it has been sound tactics in all cases to employ strong mobile columns. In confined territories these have worked in conjunction with fixed lines intended progressively to envelop the disaffected areas. These methods were employed by Hoche in La Vendée in 1796, and by Kitchener in South Africa in 1901–1902. In more extensive or very inaccessible territories, such as Algiers and the Caucasus, successive envelopment of the whole country has been impracticable and results have taken longer to achieve. In such cases it has been necessary to wait for the guerrillas to provide an objective and then to strike with the nearest mobile column.

For the guerrillas, the right tactics have consisted in concentrating for the attack of suitable objectives and dispersing immediately afterward in order not to give the regular forces an objective. Where guerrillas have so often failed is in not adhering to this primary principle. Success in minor actions has led them to believe themselves capable of fighting large battles, and attempts to do so have usually proved disastrous to themselves. This was the case in Spain in 1811. Again in the Caucasus, the Circassians, in the latter part of their long struggle, made the fatal mistake of acquiring artillery and attempting to fight as permanently formed bodies.

It is now for consideration whether the problems of guerrilla warfare have changed, and, if so, whether the principles which have been applied to their solution in the long past still hold good today.

It is certain that the conditions in which guerrilla warfare is likely to be fought today have altered. To begin with, modern methods of communication and publicity, combined with the progress which has been recorded in the civilization of most of the Great Powers, it is inconceivable that the forces of the Great Power will be able to display that ferocity in their conduct of the struggle, whatever the guerrillas may do, which has been such a potent ally in the past in the task of putting down an insurrection. The methods of the Great Power will of necessity, if not by inclination, have to be cleaner and more above board than was the case in bygone years. Otherwise such an outcry would arise as would be certain to bring about either the fall of the government responsible or the intervention of an interested outside power. This change is definitely a loss to Great Powers and a gain to the fomenters of guerrilla troubles, for by barbarous acts guerrillas can possibly compel the forces of the Great Power into reprisals and thereby weaken the case of the Great Power. Guerrillas have in fact, today, a new weapon, political propaganda, which draws blood upon the home front of the Great Power.

Further, methods by the guerrillas of conducting warfare have advanced. In former days, the object of the guerrilla was to incapacitate, permanently, as many of the soldiers of the Great Power as was possible, hoping that the accumulation of pinpricks would cause the Great Power to give way. Today the policy of pinpricks continues, but the nature of the prick has changed. Guerrillas aim, where possible (and today every Great Power, except perhaps the U.S.A., is sensitive where expenditure is concerned), at draining the financial rather than the military resources of the Great Power. This method may be said to have been started with the Cuban insurrection of 1895, where the guerrillas, realizing that Spain was very greatly dependent upon the revenue obtained from their island, concentrated their strategy and tactics upon the destruction of the chief crop of the island, the sugar crop. In this objective the guerrillas were successful, and it is on record that Spain had given way to them before the threat of American intervention became real. This same object underlay the majority of de Wet's exploits in South Africa where the burning of trains, bridges, and supplies was a feature of the later guerrilla operations. In Ireland in 1921 the Republicans were pursuing the same ends and instructions to that effect were issued to their forces and were being carried out up to the time of the truce, as the burning of the Customs House, the main Army M.T. workshops, and other government property in Dublin at the time testify. This new line of attack may well again be a source of weakness to Great Powers, where vulnerable and valuable property is readily accessible to the civil population, for it is impossible to abandon such property and face the losses that may be entailed, and at the same time their protection ties up in guards incalculable numbers of troops or police.

In addition, the invention of bombs, automatic pistols, and high explosive mines as effective weapons of attack has increased the difficulties of stopping guerrilla warfare, particularly in large centers of population. These weapons are readily concealed on the person in a crowd or in endless hiding places in a city. They lend themselves to the first principle of guerrilla fighting, the rapid concentration of armed force for an operation, combined with its equally rapid dispersion upon the completion of the task.

Against these advantages which guerrillas now have, Great Powers have also certain advantages compared to former days. The advent of mechanical transport has added greatly to the mobility of troops in most countries, though in Ireland it was shown what could be done to reduce this mobility by systematic road cutting and destruction. The invention of wireless enables news to travel very quickly, and in future will greatly facilitate the rapid concentric advance of scattered columns when an objective has been located. The increased firepower of small arms also enables small detachments to be more effective than was formerly the case.

On the whole, however, it must be admitted that by modern developments, guerrilla forces have gained more than the forces of Great Power. This being so, it behooves Great Powers to have a clear doctrine as to the action required if and when a guerrilla trouble breaks out.

Harold H. Utley

War at a Time of Peace

The rules of land warfare for the guidance of the combatants in small wars, or "wars that are not wars," have not been, and probably never will be written. When a situation arises not contemplated by the instructions issued, the only sound guide to action is a thorough knowledge of the mission of the whole force coupled with knowledge of the methods that have been used in the past by civilized nations in like situations. These comprise:

The killing or wounding or capture of those opposed to us and the destruction of their property;

Harold H. Utley, "An Introduction to the Tactics and Techniques of Small Wars," *Marine Corps Gazette*, Vol. 15, No. 5 (1931).

The destruction of the property of those who aid or abet those hostile to us;

The laying waste of entire sections inhabited by people generally supporting those hostile to us;

The removal and dispersion of all of the inhabitants of an area of unrest.

The great disadvantage in the application of these measures, excepting the first, lies in the fact that their application will probably exasperate the people as a whole against us, and tend to forfeit their friendship permanently, as well as stir up more or less trouble for us among neighboring nations and at home . . .

The late Lieutenant Colonel Ellis in his article on the subject lays down this sound doctrine:

"That the friendship of the people of any occupied nation should be forfeited by the adoption of any unnecessarily harsh measures, is avowedly contrary to the policy of the United States."

When Uncle Sam occupies the territory of a small nation he wants to enforce his will, but he does not want any trouble, that is, anything that will cause undue comment among his own or foreign people. Such comments may not only cause countless "investigations" at a more or less later date (there have been seven in Haiti in the fourteen years of occupation), but what is more important from our point of view, such comments in the Halls of Congress and in the press of our own and nearby countries are interpreted by the natives as having far greater weight than they really possess, are taken indeed as an indication of strong support for the forces arrayed against us, and thus serve to intensify and prolong the opposition we must overcome. Of course the leaders know better, but they are skilled in the use of propaganda for their own ends, and there will always be found so-called Americans who under one pretext or another will assist in originating and spreading tales of alleged "atrocities" said to have been committed by our troops. If we were at war, if the laws of war applied, we could justly charge them—the originators and the publishers—with giving aid and comfort to the enemy. But in small wars we are at peace no matter how thickly the bullets are flying.

We must never in our zeal for the perfection of plans for a small war, overlook the fact that behind and over us is that force known as "public opinion in the United States. . . ." Measures justifiable in a regular war, tactically sound, and probably the most efficient available, must frequently be eliminated from the plan of campaign as not being in accord with public policy in the existing situation. . . .

Some writers have held that in small wars only a limited number of the principles of war apply. The implication is that the remainder may be disregarded. With such a doctrine we cannot agree, although of course in each situation arising in small wars, as in every other situation, whether in the map problem room or in the field, some of the principles will predominate. It is believed that a careful analysis of those occasions where it is alleged that the principles were disregarded will show that the principles as a whole were not violated with success. The fact that due to difference in weapons, terrain, hostile methods of fighting, etc., the manner of applying the principles —the tactics—will sometimes vary from the accepted doctrine for major warfare must not be confused with the nonapplication of the principles of war.

Arthur Ehrhardt

In Praise of Bold Attack

Attack remains the best policy in small war, despite the development of automatic weapons. Nor have progressive motorization and mechanization . . . altered this principle in any way. On the contrary, the increasing use of motorized units, tanks, and aircraft tends to disperse the fighting over much larger areas, thus positively encouraging guerrilla activity. Nowadays, strikes against the enemy's supply lines, the Achilles' heel of every tank army, or on his flanks or even in his own territory are much easier to carry out than they used to be. The transportation of troops and arms by air is no longer a pipe dream, and even tank and motorized units can be used to support the aggressive tactics of the guerrillas. Nor do the thrusts against the enemy's flanks and rear so typical of the new mobile units have to be satisfied

Arthur Ehrhardt, *Kleinkrieg* (Potsdam, 1935).

with short-lived tactical gains. Provided the terrain in question is suitable for small war, motorized units, by setting down partisans in the vicinity of strategically important points in the enemy hinterland to which they have broken through, not only cut gashes in the body of the enemy's forces but also introduce noxious foreign bodies, so to speak, into the vulnerable tissue of his supply system, the effects of which will with time become increasingly annoying and, in critical situations, may even prove highly dangerous. Motorized units on the ground and the aircraft above it break up the rigid lines of the old fronts. One effect of this is to greatly extend the area open to guerrilla warfare. In the First World War we got used to advancing deep into the field of battle and seeing coherent firing lines completely disintegrate. In the coming war the fronts will in all probability be entirely dissolved and far deeper battle areas created; the theater of operations will stretch at least as far as motor vehicles can travel—and possibly as far as the effect of propaganda and financial support can reach. This extension of the theater of operations is literally an invitation to guerrilla activity. What this means is a return to the style of campaign not seen for many years and certainly never even dreamed of during the First World War, at least on the Western Front. . . .

The air force is particularly effective in countering partisan activity. The years after the First World War have provided us with several illustrations of how useful a weapon it is for modern troops fighting against partisans and guerrilla bands. There can be no doubt that its use has severely diminished the chances of successful small wars. On the other hand, it is true that there are considerable problems attached to sending out modern fighter- and bomber-squadrons against partisans. One drawback is that high flying-speeds make it almost impossible to observe enemy bands if they are quick and clever at taking cover. It is also hard to distinguish enemy bands from one's own partisans. . . .

It follows from the significant role tanks and airplanes have to play in fighting partisans that out-of-date airplanes and motor vehicles are a by no means insignificant part of an enemy's strength. They can be used to great effect to protect one's hinterland, supply lines, bases, camps, and airfields, thereby freeing more valuable units for operational use.

Such reinforcements in the form of motor vehicles and tanks will be very welcome to the troops guarding the supply lines in the rear, for, as I have already mentioned, the supply lines of a highly motorized army are literally an invitation to ambushes and sudden attacks. To keep the tanks and motorized units on the move and the squadrons of aircraft in the air there must be a continuous stream of fuel flowing down the supply lines. If partisan warfare were to flare up along this highly inflammable stream or even near important depots, this would constitute a grave threat to the efficacy of the decisive weaponry. The deeper the steel prongs of the tank and motorized units thrust their way into the enemy, the longer the supply lines become and the harder it will be to ensure that the huge fuel requirement is satisfied. . . .

The most important principle of small war, then, remains unchanged: in partisan and guerrilla warfare, bold attack is the best strategy. From this it follows that the forces fighting against such partisans must themselves be mobile. They should always be looking to attack and always be trying to strike at the opposing forces, even if they occasionally misfire. For a troop to try to fight a group of partisans purely defensively would be like a boxer fighting in the dark, defending himself against his opponent just by parrying his blows: such a troop would suffer one blow after another. As history shows us, surprise attacks and lightning descents upon the enemy are of greater importance than force of arms in such warfare. *Anyone who relies purely upon defensive tactics in a small war is lost.* No advances in weapons technology will alter this fact. . . .

Now to the last, but by no means least, principle: it is impossible to wage a protracted small war without either support from a troop of regular soldiers or help from the population! This rule has lost nothing of its validity. To be sure, the development of the motor vehicle has considerably increased the possibility of providing support for partisans. For one thing, partisans may well be able to carry out their exploits from motor vehicles in many cases. One instance would be a sudden declaration of war when the enemy has not had time to take even the most rudimentary defensive measures and poorly guarded frontiers are open to deep forward thrusts by guerrillas. The longer the war goes on, the less chance improvized motorized units will have to score any successes in the hostile environment of the enemy's hinterland. However, in a country where the tolerance and support of the large mass of the population may be reckoned with, the use of motor vehicles can be of inestimable value to guerrilla bands, even in the later stages of a war. Motorized support makes it far easier for them to practice their characteristic methods, namely, sudden appearance, lightning attack, and rapid disappearance. It therefore goes without saying that on their own territory, partisans should make general use of motor vehicles for as long as possible—provided, of course, that they have sufficient fuel.

Small war shock troops in enemy territory, however, will have to forego the advantages of motor vehicles as soon as they meet serious opposition. They can be flown far behind enemy lines to within a short distance of their target and dropped there by parachute; in favorable circumstances, they may possibly be escorted there by tanks that have broken through enemy lines; in each case, the long and dangerous march to their destination is avoided and the area of guerrilla warfare in enemy territory is greatly extended. Necessarily, the regions involved will be sparsely populated and offer sufficient cover. Only seldom, however, will the return to the guerrillas' own lines be facilitated by tanks or planes. After completing their mission, the guerrillas will as in the past have to find their way back to their base without outside help. They must realize that their withdrawal will require a maximum of caution, quick thinking, and toughness. There will always be fighters prepared to court even such dangers as these. However, the commanding officers must be clear in their own minds that even successful operations undertaken deep inside enemy territory frequently end in the obliteration of the shock troops involved. To put it metaphorically, the command fires the supremely valuable missile of the shock troops at the target in the enemy hinterland, and only in a few rare cases will it return, boomerang-like, to the hand of him who launched it. In other words, the "firing" of such commandos is only justified if the results of the undertaking outweigh the sacrifice of such prized troops.

In the case of weak guerrillas, although it is more or less inevitable that they will eventually be destroyed if they make forward thrusts into territory inhabited by a predominantly hostile or ill-disposed populace, their thrusts may be successful if they find support among the population. One of the aims of propaganda, therefore, must be to create and sustain a state of mind among the populace favorable to the guerrillas, assuring them a stratum of sympathy to fall back on; and, on home ground, one of its aims must be to rouse the people to resistance against enemy guerrilla bands. It will further direct itself toward undermining the will to fight of the inhabitants of the enemy hinterland. Often, a daring raid is all that is needed to spark off a smoldering uprising which will tie down considerable enemy forces, endanger the army's supplies, and even, in a critical situation, present incalculable strategic consequences. We can expect, then, to see partisan warfare and propaganda working hand in glove in areas where the populace is undecided in its loyalties. In many cases, skillful propaganda will be able to create nests of unrest in the enemy's home territory or in the vicinity of his supply lines where the partisans will meet with a favorable attitude among the people. We saw time and time again when we were studying the history of small war how valuable, vital even, such support among the local inhabitants, or groups of them at least, is for partisans. *Small war has always been and will continue to be supported and nurtured from among the ranks of the people* . . .

PART IV

Socialism and the
Armed Struggle

Introductory Note

Insurrection as an idea played a central role in European revolutionary doctrine of the nineteenth century, but insurrection as a technique was neglected. It was discussed in the writings of Mazzini and Carlo Bianco, and there was preeminently the example of Auguste Blanqui (1805–1881), the arch revolutionary about whom Trotsky said that he did not know the difference between revolution and insurrection. This hardly did him justice. Trotsky could not possibly have been familiar with Blanqui's writings on the subject because *Instructions pour une prise des armes* was published only in the 1930s. Far from being a blind believer in violent action, Blanqui wrote after 1848 that conspiracy, which had been a virtue under the monarchy, was a public offense under the republic.

Marx and Engels wrote much on military affairs, but guerrilla warfare rarely preoccupied them. They thought it had only limited applicability. And Engels doubted whether guerrilla warfare, effective under specific conditions in the preceeding fifty years, had much of a future. This conclusion emerges, for instance, from his writings on the French colonial experience in North Africa. For a few weeks in late 1870 he thought that the spirit of popular resistance had been reawakened in France and that a people's war would keep the Prussians at bay. But soon he sadly concluded that such fanaticism and enthusiasm were no longer customary among civilized nations and that they could only be found among Turks and Mexicans. Engels thought that guerrilla warfare in Europe could succeed only in certain mountainous regions and in conjunction with regular army operations. Outside Europe the conditions for it were more propitious. While not belittling the importance of colonial wars, he would have had difficulty accepting that the fate of the world would be decided in the jungles of Asia and Africa. The excerpts published here are from Marx's article in the *New York Tribune* of October 30, 1854 (on

Spain) and from Engels's article in the London *Pall Mall Gazette* of October and November, 1870.

Marx and Engels, who showed little enthusiasm about the prospects of guerrilla warfare, became the idols of a subsequent generation of guerrillas. On the other hand, John Most (1846–1906), who first provided an elaborate strategy for "urban guerrillas," has virtually been forgotten. One of the first German Social Democrats to be elected to the Reichstag, he had to leave Germany under Bismarck's antisocialist emergency laws. Having been expelled from the party for anarchist deviations, he settled in the United States where, as editor of *Freiheit*, he had a considerable following for a time. His *Revolutionäre Kriegswissenschaft* was published in German in New York in 1884.

James Connolly (1868–1916), vice-president of the provisional government and commander of the Irish forces in Dublin, was one of the heroes of the Dublin Easter uprising of 1916. A lifelong socialist, he organized many Irish republican clubs and edited left-wing republican journals. He emigrated to the United States in 1903, became a member of the IWW, and returned to Ireland seven years later. A convert to Marxism, he still remained a Catholic and tried to provide an ideological synthesis of the two in his writings. Connolly published several articles on the technique of revolutionary warfare; the article presented below was published in the *Workers' Republic* of July 24, 1915.

Lenin, like Trotsky and Marx and Engels, seldom commented on guerrilla warfare. He regarded it as merely one rather unimportant aspect of revolutionary war since he was primarily concerned with European politics. Lenin's article on guerrilla warfare in *Proletary*, No. 5 (1906) points to the experiences gained in the abortive Russian revolution 1905–6. Lenin's late references to guerrilla warfare and "guerrillaism" concern the post-revolutionary situation and are without exception negative in character. Marshal Mikhail Nikolayevich Tukhachevsky (1893–1937) wrote three articles on how to fight counterrevolutionary guerrillas; these were published in three installments in *Voina i Revolutsia, VII-IX* (1926) and are of particular interest as an early outline of counter-guerrilla operations from unexpected quarters. Tukhachevski was Deputy Minister of War before he was executed as a spy in the great "purge" of the 1930s. He was rehabilitated in 1956.

Auguste Blanqui

A Blueprint for Insurrection

This program is purely military, and the political and social question, which is out of place here, is entirely set aside. In any case, it goes without saying that the revolution should [be made for the benefit of labor against the tyranny of capital and] reconstitute society on the basis of justice.

Today, a Parisian insurrection along the mistaken old lines has lost all chance of success. In 1830, the people's impulse alone was enough to overthrow an authority surprised and terrified by a show of armed force, something unheard-of and far from anticipated. It was successful, but only once. The government, which was still monarchic and counterrevolutionary, even though it had sprung from a revolution, profited by the lesson. It embarked upon a study of street warfare and soon recovered the natural superiority of skill and discipline over inexperience and confusion.

Yet, you may say, in 1848 the people gained the upper hand by the methods of 1830. Very well. But have no illusions! The victory of February was only a fluke. If Louis-Philippe had made a stout defense, power would have rested with the uniforms. The days of June are proof of this. On that occasion, it was revealed how fatal were the insurrection's tactics, or rather, how totally wanting were its tactics. Never had its chances been so splendid: the odds were ten to one in its favor. On the one hand, the government was in total disarray and the troops demoralized; on the other, all the workers were roused and almost sure of success. How were they beaten? By their lack of organization. To understand their defeat, we need only analyze their strategy.

Auguste Blanqui, *Instructions pour une prise des armes*, ca. 1850, published posthumously.

The rising erupts. In the working class districts, barricades are at once set up, here and there, randomly, at many points. Five, ten, twenty, thirty, fifty men, assembled by chance, mostly unarmed, begin to overturn carts and carriages and pile up paving stones to bar the road, sometimes in the middle of streets, more often where roads join. Many of these barriers would present little hindrance to the passage of cavalry. Sometimes, after making a rough attempt at an entrenchment, the builders go in search of guns and ammunition.

Over six hundred barricades might have been counted in June; some thirty, at most, bore the brunt of the battle. At the others, nineteen out of every twenty, not a shot was fired. Hence those vainglorious bulletins which rapped out reports of fifty barricades—where not a soul was present—being removed.

While some men are thus taking up paving stones, other small bands go off to disarm the guard rooms or to seize powder and weapons at the gunsmiths. All this is done without concert or direction and at the whim of the individual.

Little by little, however, a certain number of barricades, higher, stronger, better built, prove more attractive to defenders, who concentrate around them. Not calculation, but chance determines the emplacement of these main fortifications. Only a few of them, by some not inconceivable kind of military inspiration, are at major street openings.

During this first stage of the insurrection, the soldiers have assembled. The generals receive and study the police reports. They take care not to imperil their detachments without sure and certain information and not to risk a setback which would demoralize the soldiery. As soon as they are thoroughly familiar with the insurgents' position, they mass their regiments at definite points which are henceforward to constitute the base of operations.

The armies are face to face. Watch their maneuvers. This is where the flaw of the people's tactics will show itself and be the infallible cause of disaster.

There is neither overall control nor general command, nor even agreement between the fighters. (No general command, hence no control.) Each barricade has its particular group which varies in number; it is always isolated. Whether its force is ten men or a hundred, it maintains no communication with the other posts. Often there is no leader to direct the defense, and where there is one, his influence counts for little. The soldiers simply follow their own way. They stay; they leave; they return as the fancy takes them. At night they go to bed.

Because of these continual comings and goings, the number of citizens changes rapidly, now down to a third, now a half, sometimes three quarters of the total. None can rely on any other. Consequently, there is no confidence in success and so discouragement reigns.

No one knows or cares about what is happening elsewhere. Rumors fly, some gloomy, some cheerful. Drinking at the bar, the men placidly listen to the cannons and rifle fire. There is not the least notion of bringing help to the positions under attack. "Let each man defend his post," say the staunchest, "and all will go well." This peculiar reasoning is based on the fact that most insurgents are fighting in their own district. This is a fatal error with disastrous consequences, notably denunciation by neighbors after the defeat.

With such a system, defeat is a foregone conclusion. In the end, it takes the shape of two or three regiments which fall upon the barricade and crush its few defenders. The entire battle is nothing but the monotonous repetition of this unvarying maneuver. While the insurgents smoke their pipes behind the pile of paving stones, the enemy successively brings all his forces to bear on one point, then on a second, a third, a fourth, and so wipes out the insurrection piecemeal.

The people do nothing to thwart this easy task. Each group philosophically waits its turn and never takes it into its head to go to the help of an imperiled neighbor. No: "He defends his post; he cannot abandon his post."

See how men die of absurdity!

If, owing to such a gross error, the great Paris revolt of 1848 was broken like glass by the paltriest of governments, what a catastrophe might not be apprehended if the same folly were embarked upon again in the face of a cruel army? An army which can now exploit the latest achievements of science and artifice—railways, the electric telegraph, rifled cannon, and the Chassepot rifle.

Take, for example, something which should not be regarded as an advantage to the enemy—the strategic roads now scoring the city in all directions. They are feared, but wrongly so. They should cause no anxiety. Far from having created an additional danger for the insurrection, as is believed, on the contrary they offer mixed drawbacks and advantages to both parties. The soldiers, it is true, can move about them more easily; on the other hand, they are in a very exposed and unprotected position on them.

Such streets are impassable under fire. Moreover, unlike ordinary streets, their windows, balconies, and miniature bastions furnish opportunities for flanking shots. In short, these long, straight avenues are quite properly called bulwarks or boulevards, as they have been named. They really are bulwarks constituting the natural front of a very great force.

The preeminent weapon for street warfare is the gun. The cannon has more bark than bite. The only way in which artillery can be really effective is by starting fires. However, such an atrocity systematically employed on a large scale would soon rebound on its perpetrators and bring about their destruction. The grenade—people have improperly taken to calling it a bomb—is an auxiliary only and, moreover, subject to many disadvantages; it uses a great deal of powder to little effect, is highly dangerous to handle, has a negligible range, and can only be thrown out of windows to be of use. Flagstones do nearly as much damage and are cheaper. Workmen have no money to waste. For the interior of houses, the revolver and side arms, bayonets, swords, sabers, and daggers are useful. In hand-to-hand fighting, a pike or an eight-foot halberd would always master the bayonet.

The army has only two great advantages over the people, the Chassepot rifle and organization. The latter, above all, is an immense and irresistible advantage. Fortunately, the army can be dispossessed of it and then the ascendancy passes over to the insurrection.

In civil conflicts the soldiers, with rare exceptions, march reluctantly and under the influence of constraint and liquor. They wish themselves elsewhere and are readier to look behind than before them. But an iron hand holds them slaves and victims of a ruthless discipline: with no love of authority, they obey only through fear and are incapable of the slightest initiative. A detachment cut off is a detachment lost. Aware of this, their leaders make it their first care to maintain communications between all their corps. The need for this cancels out part of their effective forces.

In the ranks of the people there is nothing like this. There an idea is fought for. There are found only volunteers motivated not by fear but by enthusiasm. Superior to their adversaries in devotion, they are far more so in their intelligence. They rise above them on the moral and even on the physical scale by their conviction, vigor, resourcefulness, and agility of body and mind; both head and heart are theirs. No troops in the world equal these picked men.

What, then, do they lack to give them mastery? They lack that unity and cohesion which, by making them combine to one and the same end, quickens all those qualities made impotent by isolation. They lack organization. Without it they have no chance. Organization is victory: dispersion is death.

June, 1848, has shown this truth to be incontrovertible. What would happen today? If they followed the old procedures, the entire populace would succumb, provided the troops were willing to hold out; and they will hold out as long as they see only irregular and uncontrolled forces confronting them. On the other hand, the sight of a Parisian army in good order, maneuvering according to the rules of tactics, will dumbfound the soldiers and overthrow their resistance.

A military organization, above all when it has to be improvized on the battlefield, is no slight thing for our party. It presupposes a high command and, to some extent, the customary chain of offices of all ranks. Where is this staff to be found? Revolutionaries and socialists of the middle class are rare, and the few that exist wage war only with the pen. These gentlemen imagine that they will turn the world upside down with their books and newspapers. For sixteen years they have been daubing paper as far as the eye can see and untiringly accepting rebuffs. With horselike patience, they have borne the bit, saddle, and whip and not once have lashed out. For shame! Return a blow? That is only fit for oafs.

These desk heroes profess the same scorn for the sword as the military do for their screeds. It does not seem to have occurred to them that force is the only guarantee of liberty and that a country is enslaved when the citizens know nothing of the craft of arms and surrender that privilege to a caste or public body.

In the republics of the ancient world everyone knew and practiced the art of war. The professional soldier was unknown. Cicero was a general and Caesar a lawyer. In putting off the toga for the uniform, the first comer found himself colonel or captain and knew his subject thoroughly. For as long as this does not apply to France, we remain civilians cut down at will by the swaggering soldiery.

Thousands of informed young men, workers, and bourgeois tremble under a detested yoke. Do they dream of taking up the sword to break it? No! the pen, always the pen, nothing but the pen. But why not both, as duty demands of a republican? In times of tyranny, to write is good; to fight is better when the enslaved pen still lacks all power. Not at all! A newspaper is issued, a prison sentence passed, and no one dreams of opening a book on maneuvers to learn in twenty-four hours that trade which constitutes the whole might of our oppressors and which would put into our hands our revenge and their punishment.

But what do such complaints avail? It is the foolish custom of our age to bewail our lot instead of acting. Jeremiads are the fashion. Jeremiah strikes every attitude; he weeps, he flogs himself, he dogmatizes, he domineers, he thunders, himself a plague among all the other plagues. Let us turn from these elegaic buffoons, the grave-diggers of liberty! The duty of a revolutionary is unending strife, despite all, strife to the death.

Is there no framework round which an army can be formed? Very well, one must be improvised in the field itself during the action. The people of Paris will provide the basic elements—old soldiers and former National Guards. Their scarcity will oblige us to reduce the number of officers and noncommissioned officers to a minimum. No matter. The zeal, ardor, and intelligence of the volunteers will make up the deficit.

It is essential to get organized (at whatever cost). No more tumultuous uprisings with ten thousand isolated men acting at random, in disorder and with no thought of cohesion, each in his own little spot at his own fancy! No more of these barricades without rhyme or reason that waste time, block the streets, and hinder free passage as necessary to one party as to the other. The republicans as well as the troops must have freedom of movement.

No more useless running about, hurly-burly, and outcry. Minutes and steps are equally precious. Above all, no sticking tight to your own neighborhood as the insurgents, to their great disadvantage, have never failed to do in the past. This craze, having brought about defeat, has made proscription easier. It must be remedied on pain of disaster.

Karl Marx and Friedrich Engels

Guerrillas in Spain

When the disasters of the standing army became regular, the rising of the guerrillas became general, and the body of the people, hardly thinking of the national defeats, exulted in the local success of their heroes. In this point at least the central junta shared the popular delusion. "Fuller accounts were given in the *Gaceta* of an affair of guerrillas than of the battle of Ocaña."

As Don Quixote had protested with his lance against gunpowder, so the guerrillas protested against Napoleon, only with different success. "These guerrillas," says the *Austrian Military Journal*, (Vol. 1, 1821), "carried their basis in themselves, as it were, and every operation against them terminated in the disappearance of its object."

There are three periods to be distinguished in the history of the guerrilla warfare. In the first period the population of whole provinces took up arms and made partisan warfare, as in Galicia and Asturias. In the second period, guerrilla bands formed of the wrecks of the Spanish armies, of Spanish deserters from the French armies, of smugglers, etc., carried on the war as their own cause, independently of all foreign influence and agreeable to their immediate interest. Fortunate events and circumstances frequently brought whole districts under their colors. As long as the guerrillas were thus constituted, they made no formidable appearance as a body, but were nevertheless extremely dangerous to the French. They formed the basis of an actual armament of the people. As soon as an opportunity for a capture offered itself, or a combined enterprise was meditated, the most active and daring among the people came out and joined the guerrillas. They rushed with the utmost rapidity upon their booty, or placed themselves in order of battle, according to the object of

Karl Marx and Friedrich Engels, "Revolution in Spain" in *New York Tribune* (October 30, 1854).

their undertaking. It was not uncommon to see them standing out a whole day in sight of a vigilant enemy, in order to intercept a courier or to capture supplies. It was in this way that the younger Mina captured the Viceroy of Navarra, appointed by Joseph Bonaparte, and that Julian made a prisoner of the Commandante of Ciudad Rodrigo. As soon as the enterprise was completed, everybody went his own way, and armed men were soon scattering in all directions; but the associated peasants quietly returned to their common occupation without "as much as their absence having been noticed." Thus the communication on all the roads was closed. Thousands of enemies were on the spot, though not one could be discovered. No courier could be dispatched without being taken; no supplies could set out without being intercepted; in short, no movement could be effected without being observed by a hundred eyes. At the same time, there existed no means of striking at the root of a combination of this kind. The French were obliged to be constantly armed against an enemy who, continually flying, always reappeared, and was everywhere without being actually seen, the mountains serving as so many curtains. "It was," says the Abbé de Pradt, "neither battles nor engagements which exhausted the French forces, but the incessant molestations of an invisible enemy, who, if pursued, became lost among the people, out of which he reappeared immediately afterward with renewed strength. The lion in the fable tormented to death by a gnat gives a true picture of the French army." In their third period, the guerrillas aped the regularity of the standing army, swelled their corps to the number of from three thousand to six thousand men, ceased to be the concern of whole districts, and fell into the hands of a few leaders, who made such use of them as best suited their own purposes. This change in the system of the guerrillas gave the French, in their contests with them, considerable advantage. Rendered incapable by their great numbers to conceal themselves, and to suddenly disappear without being forced into battle, as they had formerly done, the *guerrilleros* were now frequently overtaken, defeated, dispersed, and disabled for a length of time from offering any further molestation.

By comparing the three periods of guerrilla warfare with the political history of Spain, it is found that they represent the respective degrees into which the counterrevolutionary spirit of the government had succeeded in cooling the spirit of the people. Beginning with the rise of whole populations, the partisan war was next carried on by guerrilla bands, of which whole districts formed the reserve and terminated in *corps francs* (commandos) continually on the point of dwindling into *banditti,* or sinking down to the level of standing regiments.

Estrangement from the supreme government, relaxed discipline, continual disasters, constant formation, decomposition, and recomposition during six years of the *cadrez* must have necessarily stamped upon the body of the Spanish army the character of praetorianism, making them equally ready to become the tools or the scourges of their chiefs. The generals themselves had necessarily participated in, quarreled with, or conspired against the central government, and always thrown the weight of their sword into the political balance. Thus Cuesta, who afterward seemed to win the confidence of the central junta at the same rate that he lost the battles of the country, had begun by conspiring with the *Consejo Real* (Royal Council) and by arresting the Leonese deputies to the central junta. General Morla himself, a member of the central junta, went over to the Bonapartist camp, after he had surrendered Madrid to the French. The coxcombical Marquis de las Romerias, also a member of the junta, conspired with the vainglorious Francisco Palafox, the wretch Montijo, and the turbulent junta of Seville against it. The Generals Castaños, Blake, La Bisbal (an O'Donnell) figured and intrigued successively at the times of the Cortes as regents, and the Captain-General of Valencia, Don Xavier, Elio, surrendered Spain finally to the mercies of Ferdinand VII. The praetorian element was certainly more developed with the generals than with their troops.

On the other hand, the army and *guerrilleros*—which received during the war part of their chiefs, like Porlier, Lacy, Eroles and Villacampa, from the ranks of distinguished officers of the line, while the line in its turn afterward received guerrilla chiefs, like Mina, Empecinado, etc.—were the most revolutionized portion of Spanish society, recruited as they were from all ranks, including the whole of the fiery, aspiring, and patriotic youth, inaccessible to the soporific influence of the central government; emancipated from the shackles of the ancient regime; part of them, like Riego, returning after some years' captivity in France. We are, then, not to be surprised at the influence exercised by the Spanish army in subsequent commotions; neither when taking the revolutionary initiative, nor when spoiling the revolution by praetorianism.

As to the guerrillas, it is evident that, having for some years figured upon the theater of sanguinary contests, taken to roving habits, freely indulged all their passions of hatred, revenge, and love of plunder, they must, in times of peace, form a most dangerous mob, always ready at a nod in the name of any party or principle, to step forward for him who is able to give them good pay or to afford them a pretext for plundering excursions.

Friedrich Engels

Franc-Tireurs 1870

In the course of the last six weeks, the character of the [Franco-Prussian] war has markedly changed. The regular armies of France have disappeared. The struggle is being carried on by recently mobilized troops whose inexperience makes them more or less irregular. Wherever they attempt to mass and fight in the open, they are easily defeated; but when they fight under the cover of villages and towns equipped with barricades and embrasures, it becomes evident that they are capable of offering serious resistance. They are encouraged to carry on this type of struggle, with night surprise attacks and other methods of guerrilla warfare, by proclamations and orders from the government, which also advises the population of the district in which they operate to give them every possible assistance.

If the enemy possessed sufficient troops to occupy the whole of the country, this resistance could be easily broken. But for this, up to the surrender of Metz, he has not had the strength. The ubiquitous "four Uhlans" are no longer able to ride into a village or town outside their own lines, demanding absolute subjection to their orders, without incurring the risk of captivity or death. Requisitioning detachments have to be accompanied by escorting troops, and single companies or squadrons quartering in a village must guard against night

Friedrich Engels in *Pall Mall Gazette*, November 11, 1870.

attacks, and also, when they are on the march, against attacks from the rear. The German positions are surrounded by a belt of disputed territory, and it is just here that popular resistance makes itself felt most seriously.

In order to break this popular resistance, the Germans are resorting to a type of martial law that is as obsolete as it is barbaric. They act on the principle that any town or village in the defense of which one or more inhabitants have taken part, have fired on German troops or generally assisted the French—any such town or village is to be burnt down. Further, any man found carrying weapons, and not in their eyes a regular soldier, is to be summarily shot. When there is any suspicion that a considerable section of a town has been guilty of such a misdeed, all men capable of bearing arms are to be massacred forthwith. For the past six weeks this policy has been pitilessly carried out, and is still at this moment in full sway. One cannot open a single German newspaper without coming on half a dozen reports of such military executions; these are made to appear as a matter of course, as a simple process of military justice, carried out with salutary firmness by "honest soldiers against cowardly assassins and robbers." There is, of course, no disorder, no looting, no raping of women, no irregularity. Indeed no. Everything is done systematically, and by order. The condemned village is surrounded, the inhabitants driven out, the provisions confiscated, the houses set alight. The real or imaginary culprits are brought before a court martial, where a brief, final confession and half a dozen bullets are their certain lot.

It is no exaggeration to say that wherever the German flying colums march into the heart of France, their path is all too often marked with fire and blood. It is hardly sufficient, in this year of 1870, to claim others, not immediately recognizable as soldiers are the equivalent of banditry, and must be put down with fire and sword. Such an argument might have been valid in the day of Louis XIV or Frederick II, when there was no kind of fighting other than that of regular armies. But ever since the American War of Independence and up to the American War of Secession, it has been the rule rather than the exception for the people to take part in war. Wherever a people has allowed itself to be subjected for no other reason than that its armies have been incapable of offering resistance, it has earned general contempt as a nation of cowards; and wherever a people has energetically waged such irregular warfare, the invader

soon found it impossible to carry through the obsolete law of blood
and fire. The English in America, the French under Napoleon in
Spain, and in 1848, the Austrians in Italy and Hungary, were very
soon compelled to treat popular resistance as an entirely legitimate
form of warfare. They were compelled to do so from the fear of
reprisals against their own prisoners . . .

Of all the armies in the world, the Prussian army should have been
the last to revive these practices. In 1806, Prussia collapsed solely
because nowhere in the country was there any sign of such a national
spirit of resistance. After 1807, the reorganizers and the administra-
tors of the army did everything in their power to resurrect this spirit.
It was at this time that Spain furnished a glorious example of how a
nation can resist an invading army. The military leaders of Prussia
all pointed to it as an example worthy of the emulation of their
compatriots. Scharnhorst, Gneisenau, Clausewitz—all were of the
same opinion. Gneisenau even went to Spain himself to take part in
the struggle against Napoleon. The whole military system that was
subsequently introduced in Prussia was an attempt to mobilize popular resistance against the enemy, insofar as this was possible at all in
an absolute monarchy. Not only had every fit man to join the army
and serve in the reserves (*Landwehr*) up to his fortieth year; boys
between seventeen and twenty and men between forty and sixty-five
were also included in the *levée en masse,* or mass conscription, in
the final reserves (*Landsturm*) whose function it was to rise in the
rear and on the flanks of the enemy, to interfere with his movements,
and to cut off his supplies and his couriers; they were expected to
use any weapon they could lay their hands on and to employ without
distinction all available measures to harry the invader—"the more
effective the measure the better"; nor was "any kind of uniform to
be worn," so that the men of the *Landsturm* might at any moment
resume their character of civilians, thus remaining unrecognizable to
the enemy.

The Landsturm Order of 1813, as the document in question was
called—its author being no other than Scharnhorst, the organizer of
the Prussian army—was drawn up in this spirit of irreconcilable
national resistance, according to which all means are valid, and the
most effective the best. At that time, however, all this was to be done
by the Prussians against the French; when the French chose to behave
in precisely the same manner toward the Prussians, it was quite

another matter. What had become patriotism in one case became banditry and assassination in the other.

The fact is that the present Prussian government is ashamed of this old semirevolutionary Landsturm Order, and by its actions in France seeks to erase it from memory. But the deliberate atrocities they themselves have committed in France will, instead, call it all the more to mind. The argument brought forward in favor of so despicable a method of waging war serves only as proof that, if the Prussian army has immeasurably improved since Jena, the Prussian government, on the other hand, is ripening for the conditions that made Jena possible.

John Most

The Case for Dynamite

The importance of modern explosives for social revolution need hardly be stressed nowadays. They are going to be the decisive factor in the next period of world history.

Naturally, therefore, revolutionaries throughout the world are increasingly trying to acquire them and learn how to use them. . . .

It is of course out of the question that revolutionaries should try to procure a dynamite gun (cumbersome things over forty feet long), but they can certainly make bombs of the type described above. These bombs either have to be planted or be flung a short distance, for which latter purpose an old-fashioned catapult is quite adequate.

A bomb that can blow a hole in a rock face is bound to do a fair bit of damage at court or at a monopolists' ball. . . .

Whenever it proves impossible in the struggle against the private property monster and the government hyenas to pick off by means of explosives or fire bombs those whose elimination is of special importance for the social revolution, then, for good or ill, one or

John Most, *Revolutionäre Kriegswissenschaft* (New York, n.d.).

more revolutionaries will have to break their cover and put their lives at risk.

I am using the word "cover" here quite deliberately; the view some simpletons hold that the revolutionary's job is just to depart this life "courageously" when in fact his job is to make sure *others* depart this life, is absolute rubbish.

Any revolutionary who frivolously endangers his own life without making absolutely certain of the success of his undertaking is acting against the interests of the revolutionary cause.

Quite apart from the fact that the bullies of "law and order" are a hundred times more frightened if the man who commits the deed remains undiscovered than if he is caught or gets himself killed, it is one of the basic rules of military tactics that no group of men endangers itself during an operation more than is absolutely necessary. For this reason, two or three must never put themselves at risk when one is enough to carry out the revolutionary act.

If a revolutionary *must* undertake an action endangering his own life because there is no other way of eliminating the enemy in question, then he must make absolutely sure of the success of his mission. . . .

"The explosion was like a cannon firing. The stone slab disintegrated into about twenty pieces which were hurled at least ten to fifteen feet into the air. The bomb ripped a hole two feet in diameter and of similar depth in the ground. It took some time to find any remains of the bomb. Only after a considerable search were some jagged fragments the size of revolver bullets found about thirty to forty feet away."

Now, just imagine what a magnificent effect this bomb would have had if it had been placed under the table of some gluttons having a banquet or if it had been thrown through the window onto the table. . . .

It is no doubt unnecessary for me to say this, since only too many comrades have fallen into the hands of our opponents after unsuccessful missions and have perished. Knives have not been pushed in far enough and glancing shots have caused only slight wounds—not to mention shots and knives that have missed their mark entirely.

These failures have made people think of poisoning the weapons to be used in assassination attempts, but nothing has come of this idea as yet.

The reason for this is the difficulty in finding and getting hold of suitable poisons. Or to be more precise, it is revolutionaries' poverty that is to blame. . . .

Good revolvers, knives, poisons, and fuses are destined to play an important role at the moment of rebellion because it is impossible for the enemy to tell whether those carrying them are armed. He has no reason to avoid them and thus can be cornered and done away within his most private hideouts.

Above all, however, one must never forget modern explosives. To be sure of success, revolutionaries should always have on hand adequate quantities of nitroglycerin, dynamite, hand grenades, and blasting charges—all easily concealed under clothing.

These weapons, the proletariat's artillery, cause surprise, confusion, and panic among the ranks of the enemy. Efforts must therefore be made to ensure that there is a ready supply of these articles. . . .

A man or woman intending to carry out a revolutionary act should not discuss it with others; the deed should be kept to oneself until it is done. The only time this does not apply is when the success of the plan absolutely requires more than one person; then, he or she can select the necessary people. Naturally, to make a blunder here is simply to invite treachery!

Anyone planning an action must refrain from consorting in public with people already compromised as revolutionaries, since to do so would immediately attract the attention of spies and lead to police surveillance. From there it is only a short step to being neutralized.

If and when a revolutionary is about to be arrested, it is vital for him to remain calm and collected. Violent resistance or suicide are to be recommended only when there is a chance of destroying the aggressor or when it is already a matter of life and death. If, however, one is certain the arrest is being carried out only on the flimsiest grounds of suspicion, one should submit—with loud protestations—to the inevitable, for it will then be that much easier to save one's neck later.

A revolutionary should speak at a court hearing only if he is in a position (through an alibi, for example) to regain his freedom immediately. Otherwise he should refuse to make a statement of any kind. The lengthier the statements the law manages to wheedle out of a revolutionary, the greater the chances of his undoing.

If it actually comes to the pantomime of a court trial, then the revolutionary should only admit what has really been proven against him.

Finally, when all hope of rescue is gone, the revolutionary has a different duty, the noblest duty, to fulfil: he must defend his actions from the revolutionary-anarchist position and transform the witness stand into a tribune. In other words, one should protect one's person as long as possible so as to be available for further actions. But once it is clear that all is lost, one should use one's remaining time on earth to exploit the propaganda value of one's case as fully as possible. . . .

A tip. The "thorn-apple," which can frequently be seen on rubbish dumps, in ditches, or growing in gardens as a weed, is a vulgar breed of plant, but it has its uses. Its seeds can be used for truly humanitarian ends. Grind about twenty-five of its seeds (mature black ones, of course) into a flour, then bake them into a biscuit of some kind, like an almond biscuit, and offer them to a spy, denouncer, bailiff, or similar scum. The effects will be seen immediately. Within the next few days, the rat will go raving mad and snuff it. To be highly recommended . . .

To deliver letters of this kind, procure a tin box in the shape of a normal envelope, put into it a half-dozen or more letters (according to requirements), and place it—there is no danger—in your pocket. Go for a walk and empty the tin letter by letter into the letter boxes of various notorious houses. Success is ensured after a quarter of an hour.

Treated letters can be kept in a tightly closed tin for up to eight or ten hours without spontaneous combustion because no air reaches them.

For buildings such as churches and courts, you need a small wooden box that will fit easily into an overcoat pocket. Make a false bottom for it, fill the bottom part with pitch and the top with shavings soaked in phosphorus or similarly treated letters, and add potash to this. Carefully nail on the lid and then bore holes in it with a sharp, finely pointed instrument so as to allow a little air to enter. Place it in a suitable spot (on wood or upholstered seats). The desired effect will follow in three to four hours.

Phosphorus can also be used to trigger explosions. Attach to a container filled with dynamite a small box with a lid, from which the fuse runs to the container. Soak the fuse in phosphorus and close the lid. After placing the whole device in the desired spot, remove the lid so that the fuse is exposed to the air and then calmly walk away. By the time the explosion takes place—and it will—the person responsible is safe and sound. . . .

James Connolly

On Street Fighting

In the military sense of the term what after all is a *street?* A street is a defile in a city. A defile is a narrow pass through which troops can only move by narrowing their front, and therefore making themselves a good target for the enemy. A defile is also a difficult place for soldiers to maneuver in, especially if the flanks of the defile are held by the enemy.

A mountain pass is a defile the sides of which are constituted by the natural slopes of the mountainsides, as at the Scalp. A bridge over a river is a defile the sides of which are constituted by the river. A street is a defile the sides of which are constituted by the houses in the street.

To traverse a mountain pass with any degree of safety the sides of the mountain must be cleared by flanking parties ahead of the main body; to pass over a bridge the banks of the river on each side must be raked with gun or rifle fire whilst the bridge is being rushed; to take a street properly barricaded and held on both sides by forces in the houses, these houses must be broken into and taken by hand-to-hand fighting. A street barricade placed in position where artillery cannot operate from a distance is impregnable to frontal attack. To bring artillery within a couple of hundred yards—the length of the average street—would mean the loss of the artillery if confronted by even imperfectly drilled troops armed with rifles.

James Connolly in *Workers' Republic* (July 24, 1915) from *Revolutionary Warfare* (Dublin, 1968).

The Moscow revolution, where only eighty rifles were in the possession of the insurgents, would have ended in the annihilation of the artillery had the number of insurgent rifles been eight hundred.

The insurrection of Paris in June, 1848, reveals how districts of towns, or villages, should be held. The streets were barricaded at tactical points *not on the main streets* but commanding them. The houses were broken through so that passages were made inside the houses along the whole length of the streets. The party walls were loopholed, as were also the front walls, the windows were blocked by sandbags, boxes filled with stones and dirt, bricks, chests, and other pieces of furniture with all sorts of odds and ends piled up against them.

Behind such defenses the insurgents poured fire upon the troops through loopholes left for the purpose.

In the attack upon Paris by the allies fighting against Napoleon a village held in this manner repulsed several assaults of the Prussian allies of England. When these Prussians were relieved by the English these latter did not dare attempt a frontal attack but instead broke into an end house on one side of the village street and commenced to take the houses one by one. Thus all the fighting was inside the houses, and musket fire played but a small part. On one side of the street they captured all the houses, on the other they failed, and when a truce was declared the English were in possession of one side of the village, and their French enemies on the other.

The truce led to a peace. When peace was finally proclaimed, the two sides of the village street were still held by opposing forces.

The defense of a building in a city, town, or village is governed by the same rules. Such a building left unconquered is a serious danger even if its supports are all defeated. If it had been flanked by barricades, and these barricades were destroyed, no troops could afford to push on and leave the building in the hands of the enemy. If they did so, they would be running the danger of perhaps meeting a check farther on, which check would be disastrous if they had left a hostile building manned by an unconquered force in their rear. Therefore, the fortifying of a strong building, as a pivot upon which the defense of a town or village should hinge, forms a principal object of the preparations of any defending force, whether regular army or insurrectionary.

In the Franco–German War of 1870 the chateau, or castle, of

Geissberg formed such a position in the French lines on 4 August. The Germans drove in all the supports of the French party occupying this country house and stormed the outer courts, but were driven back by the fire from the windows and loopholed walls. Four batteries of artillery were brought up to within nine hundred yards of the house and battered away at its walls, and battalion after battalion was hurled against it. The advance of the whole German army was delayed until this one house was taken. To take it caused a loss of twenty-three officers and three hundred twenty-nine men, yet it had only a garrison of two hundred.

In the same campaign the village of Bazeilles offered a similar lesson in the tactical strength of a well-defended line of houses. The German army drove the French off the field and entered the village without a struggle. But it took a whole army corps seven hours to fight its way through to the other end of the village.

A mountainous country has always been held to be difficult for military operations owing to its passes or glens. A city is a huge mass of passes or glens formed by streets and lanes. Every difficulty that exists for the operation of regular troops in mountains is multiplied a hundredfold in a city. And the difficulty of the commissariat, which is likely to be insuperable to an irregular or popular force taking to the mountains, is solved for them by the sympathies of the populace when they take to the streets.

The general principle to be deducted from a study of the examples we have been dealing with, is that the defense is of almost overwhelming importance in such warfare as a popular force like the Citizen Army might be called upon to participate in. Not a mere passive defense of a position valueless in itself, but the active defense of a position whose location threatens the supremacy or existence of the enemy. The genius of the commander must find such a position, the skill of his subordinates must prepare and fortify it, the courage of all must defend it. Out of this combination of genius, skill, and courage alone can grow the flower of military success.

The Citizen Army and the Irish Volunteers are open for all those who wish to qualify for the exercise of these qualities.

V. I. Lenin

Guerrilla Warfare

. . . The phenomenon in which we are interested is the *armed* struggle. It is conducted by individuals and by small groups. Some belong to revolutionary organizations, while others (the *majority* in certain parts of Russia) do not belong to any revolutionary organization. Armed struggle pursues two *different* aims, which must be *strictly* distinguished: in the first place, this struggle aims at assassinating individuals, chiefs and subordinates in the army and police; in the second place, it aims at the confiscation of monetary funds both from the government and from private persons. The confiscated funds go partly into the treasury of the party, partly for the special purpose of arming and preparing for an uprising, and partly for the maintenance of persons engaged in the struggle we are describing. The big expropriations (such as the Caucasian, involving over 200,000 rubles, and the Moscow, involving 875,000 rubles) went in fact first and foremost to revolutionary parties—small expropriations go mostly, and sometimes entirely, to the maintenance of the "expropriators." This form of struggle undoubtedly became widely developed and extensive only in 1906, i.e., after the December uprising. The intensification of the political crisis to the point of an armed struggle and, in particular, the intensification of poverty, hunger, and unemployment in town and country, was one of the important causes of the struggle we are describing. This form of struggle was adopted as the preferable and even *exclusive* form of social struggle by the vagabond elements of the population, the lumpen proletariat and anarchist groups. Declaration of martial law, mobilization of fresh troops, Black Hundred pogroms (Sedlets), and military courts must be regarded as the "retaliatory" form of struggle adopted by the autocracy.

V. I. Lenin, "Guerrilla Warfare" in *Proletary*, No. 5, September 30, 1906.

The usual appraisal of the struggle we are describing is that it is anarchism, Blanquism, the old terrorism, the acts of individuals isolated from the masses, which demoralize the workers, repel wide strata of the population, disorganize the movement and injure the revolution. Examples in support of this appraisal can easily be found in the events reported every day in the newspapers.

But are such examples convincing? In order to test this, let us take a locality where the form of struggle we are examining is *most* developed—the Lettish Territory. This is the way *Novoye Vremya* (in its issues of September 9 and 12) complains of the activities of the Lettish Social Democrats. The Lettish Social Democratic Labor Party (a section of the Russian Social Democratic Labor Party) regularly issues its paper in 30,000 copies. The announcement columns publish lists of spies whom it is the duty of every decent person to exterminate. People who assist the police are proclaimed "enemies to the revolution," liable to execution and, moreover, to confiscation of property. The public is instructed to give money to the Social Democratic Party only against signed and stamped receipt. In the party's latest report, showing a total income of 48,000 rubles for the year, there figures a sum of 5,600 rubles contributed by the Libau branch for arms which was obtained by expropriation. Naturally, *Novoye Vremya* rages and fumes against this "revolutionary law," against this "terror government."

Nobody will be so bold as to call these activities of the Lettish Social Democrats anarchism, Blanquism, or terrorism. But why? Because here we have a *clear* connection between the new form of struggle and the uprising which broke out in December and which is again brewing. This connection is not so perceptible in the case of Russia as a whole, but it exists. The fact that "guerrilla" warfare became widespread precisely after December, and its connection with the accentuation not only of the economic crisis but also of the political crisis is beyond dispute. The old Russian terrorism was an affair of the intellectual conspirator; today as a general rule guerrilla warfare is waged by the worker combatant, or simply by the unemployed worker. Blanquism and anarchism easily occur to the minds of people who have a weakness for stereotype; but under the circumstances of an uprising, which are so apparent in the Lettish Territory, the inappropriateness of such trite labels is only too obvious.

The example of the Letts clearly demonstrates how incorrect, unscientific, and unhistorical is the practice so very common among us of analyzing guerrilla warfare without reference to the circumstances of an uprising. These circumstances must be borne in mind, we must reflect on the peculiar features of an intermediate period between big acts of insurrection, we must realize what forms of struggle inevitably arise under such circumstances, and not try to shirk the issue by a collection of words learned by rote, such as are used equally by the cadets and the *Novoye Vremya*-ites: anarchism, robbery, hooliganism!

It is said that guerrilla acts disorganize our work. Let us apply this argument to the situation that has existed since December, 1905, to the period of Black Hundred pogroms and martial law. What disorganizes the movement more in *such* a period: the absence of resistance or organized guerrilla warfare? Compare the center of Russia with her western borders, with Poland and the Lettish Territory. It is unquestionable that guerrilla warfare is far more widespread and far more developed in the western border regions. And it is equally unquestionable that the revolutionary movement in general, and the Social Democratic movement in particular, are *more disorganized* in central Russia than in the western border regions. Of course, it would not enter our heads to conclude from this that the Polish and Lettish Social Democratic movements are less disorganized *thanks* to guerrilla warfare. No. The only conclusion that can be drawn is that guerrilla warfare is not to blame for the state of disorganization of the Social Democratic working-class movement in Russia in 1906.

Allusion is often made in this respect to the peculiarities of national conditions. But this allusion very clearly betrays the weakness of the current argument. If it is a matter of national conditions then it is not a matter of anarchism, Blanquism, or terrorism—sins that are common to Russia as a whole and even to the Russians especially— but of something else. Analyze this something else *concretely,* gentlemen! You will then find that national oppression or antagonism explains nothing, because they have always existed in the western border regions, whereas guerrilla warfare has been engendered only by the present historical period. There are many places where there is national oppression and antagonism, but no guerrilla struggle, which sometimes develops where there is no national oppression whatever. A concrete analysis of the question will show that it is not a matter of national oppression, but of conditions of insurrection. Guerrilla warfare is an inevitable form of struggle at a time when the mass movement has actually reached the point of an uprising and when fairly large intervals occur between the "big engagements" in the civil war.

It is not guerrilla actions which disorganize the movement, but the weakness of a party which is incapable of taking such actions *under its control*. That is why the anathemas which we Russians usually hurl against guerrilla actions go hand in hand with secret, casual, unorganized guerrilla actions which really do disorganize the party. Being incapable of understanding what historical conditions give rise to this struggle, we are incapable of neutralizing its deleterious aspects. Yet the struggle is going on. It is engendered by powerful economic and political causes. It is not in our power to eliminate these causes or to eliminate this struggle. Our complaints against guerrilla warfare are complaints against our party weakness in the matter of an uprising.

What we have said about disorganization also applies to demoralization. It is not guerrilla warfare which demoralizes, but *unorganized, irregular, nonparty* guerrilla acts. We shall not rid ourselves one least bit of this *most unquestionable* demoralization by condemning and cursing guerrilla actions, for condemnation and curses are absolutely incapable of putting a stop to a phenomenon which has been engendered by profound economic and political causes. It may be objected that if we are incapable of putting a stop to an abnormal and demoralizing phenomenon, this is no reason why the *party* should adopt abnormal and demoralizing methods of struggle. But such an objection would be a purely bourgeois-liberal and not a Marxist objection, because a Marxist cannot regard civil war, or guerrilla warfare, which is one of its forms, as abnormal and demoralizing *in general*. A Marxist bases himself on the class struggle, and not social peace. In certain periods of acute economic and political crises the class struggle ripens into a direct civil war, i.e., into an armed struggle between two sections of the people. In such periods a Marxist is *obliged* to take the stand of civil war. Any moral condemnation of civil war would be absolutely impermissible from the standpoint of Marxism.

In a period of civil war the ideal party of the proletariat is a *fighting party*. This is absolutely incontrovertible. We are quite prepared to grant that it is possible to argue and prove the *inexpediency* from the standpoint of civil war of particular forms of civil war at any particular moment. We fully admit criticism of diverse forms of civil war from the standpoint of *military expediency* and absolutely agree that in *this* question it is the Social Democratic practical workers in each particular locality who must have the final say. But we absolutely demand in the name of the principles of Marxism that an analysis of the conditions of civil war should not be evaded by hackneyed and stereotyped talk about anarchism, Blanquism, and terrorism, and that senseless methods of guerrilla activity adopted by some organization or other of the Polish Socialist Party at some moment or other should not be used as a bogey when discussing the question of the participation of the Social Democratic Party as such in guerrilla warfare in general.

The argument that guerrilla warfare disorganizes the movement must be regarded critically. *Every* new form of struggle, accompanied as it is by new dangers and new sacrifices, inevitably "disorganizes" organizations which are unprepared for this new form of struggle. Our old propagandist circles were disorganized by recourse to methods of agitation. Our committees were subsequently disorganized by recourse to demonstrations. Every military action in any war to a certain extent disorganizes the ranks of the fighters. But this does not mean that one must not fight. It means that one must *learn* to fight. That is all.

When I see Social Democrats proudly and smugly declaring "we are not anarchists, thieves, robbers, we are superior to all this, we reject guerrilla warfare," I ask myself: Do these people realize what they are saying? Armed clashes and conflicts between the Black Hundred government and the population are taking place all over the country. This is an absolutely inevitable phenomenon at the present stage of development of the revolution. The population is spontaneously and in an unorganized way—and for that very reason often in unfortunate and *undesirable* forms—reacting to this phenomenon also by armed conflicts and attacks. I can understand us refraining from party leadership of *this* spontaneous struggle in a particular place or at a particular time because of the weakness and unpreparedness of our organization. I realize that this question must be settled by the local practical workers, and that the remolding of weak and unprepared organizations is no easy matter. But when I see a Social Democratic theoretician or publicist not displaying regret over this unpreparedness, but rather a proud smugness and a self-exalted tendency to repeat phrases learned by rote in early youth about anarchism, Blanquism, and terrorism, I am hurt by this degradation of the most revolutionary doctrine in the world.

It is said that guerrilla warfare brings the class-conscious proletarians into close association with degraded, drunken riffraff. That is true. But it only means that the party of the proletariat can never regard guerrilla warfare as the only, or even as the chief, method of struggle; it means that this method must be subordinated to other methods, that it must be commensurate with the chief methods of warfare, and must be ennobled by the enlightening and organizing influence of socialism. And without this *latter* condition, *all,* positively all, methods of struggle in bourgeois society bring the proletariat into close association with the various nonproletariat strata above and below it and, if left to the spontaneous course of events, become frayed, corrupted, and prostituted. Strikes, if left to the spontaneous course of events, become corrupted into "alliances"— agreements between the workers and the masters *against* the consumers. Parliament becomes corrupted into a brothel, where a gang of bourgeois politicians barter wholesale and retail "national freedom," "liberalism," "democracy," republicanism, anticlericalism, socialism and all other wares in demand. A newspaper becomes corrupted into a public pimp, into a means of corrupting the masses, of pandering to the low instincts of the mob, and so on and so forth. Social Democracy knows of no universal methods of struggle, such as would shut off the proletariat by a Chinese wall from the strata standing slightly above or slightly below it. At different periods Social Democracy applies different methods, *always* qualifying the choice of them by *strictly* defined ideological and organizational conditions.

The forms of struggle in the Russian revolution are distinguished by their colossal variety compared with the bourgeois revolutions in Europe. Kautsky partly foretold this in 1902 when he said that the future revolution (with the exception *perhaps* of Russia, he added) might be not so much a struggle of the people against the government as a struggle between two sections of the people. In Russia we undoubtedly see a wider development of this *latter* struggle than in the bourgeois revolutions in the West. The enemies of our revolution among the people are few in number, but as the struggle grows more acute they become more and more organized and receive the support of the reactionary strata of the bourgeoisie. It is therefore absolutely natural and inevitable that in *such* a period, a period of nationwide political strikes, an *uprising* cannot assume the old form of individual acts restricted to a very short time and to a very small area. It is absolutely natural and inevitable that the uprising should assume the higher and more complex form of a prolonged civil war embracing the whole country, i.e., an armed struggle between two sections of the people. Such a war cannot be conceived otherwise than as a series of a few big engagements at comparatively long intervals and a large number of small encounters during these intervals. That being so—and it is undoubtedly so—the Social Democrats must absolutely make it their duty to create organizations best adapted to lead the masses in these big engagements and, as far as possible, in these small encounters as well. In a period when the class struggle has become accentuated to the point of civil war, Social Democrats must make it their duty not only to participate but also to play the leading role in *this civil war*. The Social Democrats must train and prepare their organizations to be really able to act as a *belligerent side* which does not miss a single opportunity of inflicting damage on the enemy's forces.

This is a difficult task, there is no denying. It cannot be accomplished at once. Just as the whole people are being retrained and are learning to fight in the course of the civil war, so our organizations must be trained, must be reconstructed in conformity with the lessons of experience to be equal to this task.

We have not the slightest intentions of foisting on practical workers any artificial form of struggle, or even of deciding from our armchair what part any particular form of guerrilla warfare should play in the general course of the civil war in Russia. We are far from the thought of regarding a concrete assessment of particular guerrilla actions as indicative of a *trend* in Social Democracy. But we do regard it as our duty to help as far as possible to arrive at a correct *theoretical* assessment of the new forms of struggle engendered by practical life. We do regard it as our duty relentlessly to combat stereotypes and prejudices which hamper the class-conscious workers in correctly presenting a new and difficult problem and in correctly approaching its solution.

Mikhail Nikolayevich Tukhachevsky

The Struggle Against Banditry

On the basis of the foregoing I shall draw brief conclusions both about the character of banditry and the ways for its eradication.

Banditry, if we exclude from our considerations criminal brigandage, is a peasant uprising organized by the *kulaks*.[1] Depending on local conditions, it takes different forms.

In most cases it is a peasant uprising in affluent areas. This feature, however, is not always strictly characteristic of banditry. We know that the poor elements among the villagers are frequently drawn into banditry. One can expect the emergence of banditry especially in the border areas, even when poor elements predominate. This can be explained by the fact that the insurrection movement is being organized from abroad, from whence battle-trained manpower and arms are being sent. Finally, very frequently banditry takes on various national forms. In the Ukraine, for instance, banditry, which was essentially a pure class phenomenon, at times assumed national Ukrainian hues. In Turkestan, by contrast, banditry, or the Basmachi movement, assumed pronounced national features in addition to its class characteristics.

In all these cases banditry is the result of the breach of the union between workers and peasants, which is particularly complicated in conditions where culture is lacking. This breach results in the ousting of Soviet authorities from the villages and in their replacement by the local peasantry which is dominated almost always by White Guard elements.

The struggle against the peasant insurrection movement is made difficult in the extreme by the secret, permanent existence of this power combined with the secret existence of armed bandit forces. While an uprising in a city can easily be liquidated through a speedy

Mikhail Nikolayevich Tukhachevsky, from *Voina i Revolutsia*, No. 9, 1926.

[1] Rich peasants.

concentration of the necessary forces and means, and while all the
superiority of contemporary military technology can be put to use
there, in the village all this frequently proves to be of no avail. The
air force does not see a thing apart from peasants working in the
fields; the artillery has no target to fire at, etc. To liquidate a peasant
uprising, there is a need, besides military actions, for a broad political
campaign to explain the peasants' true interests.

Military actions should be closely combined with political and
economic measures and be accompanied by an explanation as to why
such measures are employed in the interests of unity between workers
and peasants.

The forms of peasant power are very diverse. They bear the character and title pertaining to those counterrevolutionary parties which
have seized and dominated the peasant uprising. This power penetrates to the lowest strata of village life. In a form secret to Soviet
power it pursues its activity by organizing resistance and anti-Soviet
education for the peasantry.

The armed forces of banditry do not everywhere have equal chances
to develop. Such chances depend directly on the quantity of arms
already possessed by the peasantry or which can be obtained from
outside. It happens at first that units of the Red army suffer setbacks
resulting in the increase of the arms reserves of the bandits. Moreover, the bandits obtain arms by seizing depots, planting agents in
artillery depots through whom they clandestinely procure arms, and
by making purchases in the cities. Last but not least, conditions in
the border areas enable them to receive arms from abroad.

The main strength of the banditry consists in its elusiveness which
is due to the militia-type territorially based organization of its military forces. Every village and rural district recruits such and such a
detachment which, when the time is opportune, seizes its territory.
Needless to say, this does not mean that the bandit detachments
always have to operate within their own district. Only in Fergana[2]
could we observe a considerable attachment by certain bandits to
their areas. This can be explained by the diversity of the national
and economic interests of the locality. But even there, under the
direction of the ringleaders of the Basmachi movement, the detachments could move freely. No attachment to the areas in which they

[2] A town and district in Turkestan.

were mobilized could be observed on the part of the Russian banditry. Quite the contrary, a characteristic feature of the bandits was the fact that they struck anywhere and, having dispersed, reassembled in their own bases.

The recruitment of the bandits was at first conducted on a voluntary basis. Gradually, however, as the influence of the bandits grew, we observed instances of recruitment by force. This was not done in organized ways but by means of direct threats. In both instances, recruitment was conducted on a territorial basis.

With regard to the replacement of horses, every bandit supplies a horse of his own. Furthermore, while operations continue, new mounts are furnished through the exchange of horses at the stations. The bandits select and constantly improve their stock of horses.

In the villages it is absolutely impossible to distinguish the bandits and their horses from peaceful peasants and theirs. Secrecy is ensured by mutual responsibility. Anyone breaking this secrecy is punished by death.

The bandits' arms are almost never of one type. Only in areas near the border can a tendency toward a more standardized type of arms be observed, attributable to their being sent from abroad. Very frequently the bandits shorten both the barrels of their rifles and their rifle stocks. Thus they acquire a sawn-off rifle which can be carried hidden under their clothes. Any artillery pieces or machine guns in the bandits' possession have been obtained by disarming units of the Red army.

Both communication and intelligence are employed by the bandits on a large scale, mainly through agents.

The strategic methods of the bandits' struggle sometimes assumes active forms that tend to spread the uprising into neighboring areas and into cities. This phenomenon, however, happens only rarely and haphazardly. Railway lines are usually not wrecked. The peasants are evidently intent on showing their practical instinct here. Isolated instances of wrecking have nevertheless occurred, and one has, therefore, to reinforce the railway guard detachments.

On the whole, the bandits strive to reduce the Red army forces to a state of strategic exhaustion. They force them to disperse their garrisons and detached units. They try to inflict upon them one loss after another by means of repeated surprise attacks, thereby demoralizing and undermining them. In this respect the bandits have an absolute advantage. While the troops intent on suppressing them are always visible and their disposition known, the location of the bandit gangs usually remains unknown. In order to inflict a serious defeat on garrisons and detached units, the bandits often organize themselves into sizable detachments and launch large-scale raids. These raids are carried out both in order to capture stocks of arms and to extend the bandits' power to neighboring areas.

The bandits also take action in order to achieve the political disruption of the Soviet forces. If the struggle against the insurrection is conducted ineptly and unsuccessfully, then their propagandistic activities can often be dangerous.

From the tactical point of view, the bandits' main trump card is surprise. The difficulty in locating the bandit gangs and in determining whether the bandits are inactive or prepared for war gives them an enormous advantage when they appear unexpectedly before the Red army detachments in terrain not suited for regular army units.

The bandits' reconnaissance is made easier by the support and organization of the local peasantry.

Ambushes, turning movements, and, in case of a setback, the dispersal of forces to their own territorial sectors are the bandits' favorite stratagems.

In a number of instances one can note large-scale activities in training and educating armed bandit forces.

The bandits deal savagely with captive prisoners.

These characteristics of banditry can take on other hues depending on the area and on the national and religious causes that engender its emergence. But on the whole, these activities are characteristic of banditry everywhere.

What are the general proposals for organizing the eradication of banditry? As was already noted, the basic question is the establishment of an indispensable political and economic union between the working class and the peasantry. From the national point of view, banditry, or the Basmachi movement, becomes even more complicated because of the necessity of outlining and putting into practice a correct national policy. Taking into account the cultural level of the native population, the Soviet power has to reckon not only with the national but also with the religious composition of the local population. When these questions, in addition to the formulation of a correct economic policy, are completely solved, then the ground will be cut from under the feet of the banditry and the Basmachi movement. Thus prerequisites are essential for the ultimate liquidation of banditry. Banditry cannot be radically overcome without action of a political, national, and economic kind. We can see examples in imperialist colonies where, despite the enormous expenditure on fighting the local population and the colossal military forces employed against it, constant riots and insurrections still take place, the capitalist governments being completely unable to cope with them.

From the organizational point of view it is necessary to have a representative of the state or the party on the territory affected by banditry. This representation should encompass the military, political, and economic officials of the particular territory. The military struggle should be adopted to local conditions; representative bodies uniting the military and civil power ought to be set up. Due to the nature of national banditry this work should be carried out strictly within the national framework of the Soviet administration. The militia also ought to be composed of members of the local nationality.

Armed forces act in two ways: first, by carrying out the tasks of an army of occupation stationed in garrisons in order to safeguard the corresponding administrative Soviet bodies and their work; secondly, as a raiding force against the active bands. Apart from the occupying military units, a reinforced Soviet militia is to be set up in the localities. It is advisable that this militia should not be composed of locally born people. Basing themselves on this military nucleus, the Soviet authorities will carry out a purge of the peasant population. This purge entails the elimination of the bandit elements. While doing so, it is necessary to draw to our side wide segments of the peasantry and to create in the villages resistance to the further encouragement and spread of banditry.

Depending upon the degree to which the area has been pacified and the extent to which pro-Soviet elements have installed themselves in the countryside, it might be useful to arm these elements against the bandits. Thus an implacable opposition to banditry would be created in the countryside. It is necessary to give these organizations the responsibility for intelligence and for warning about the activities of the bandit detachments.

At the same time, one should practice large-scale repression and employ incentives. The most effective methods of repression are the eviction of the families of bandits who hide relatives and the confiscation and subsequent distribution among pro-Soviet peasants of their property. In the event of difficulty in organizing immediate eviction, the establishment of large-scale concentration camps is necessary.

A system of collective responsibility should be introduced and applied about harboring bandits or not reporting their location and activities.

The program of introducing repression and incentives should be planned in accordance with the available resources and the general plan of action. Threats which are not implemented only undermine the authority of the administration and cause mistrust among the peasantry.

Before the start of the campaign of extirpation comes a preliminary period of organizational work to coordinate the measures of the Soviet administrative and military authorities. Only when everything is ready does it make sense to start decisive operations. Until this stage any action would only exhaust our troops.

The organs of the GPU and the intelligence detachments should establish the scope and composition of the bandit gangs, identify members of families involved in banditry, and ascertain the territorial origins of the bandit gangs. The origins of each gang must be established. Apart from this, one has to ascertain the composition of the personnel of the local bodies of the self-styled "peasant power." Once these conditions are met, the purge of the population will take place in complete congruence with the action of the Red army against these or other bandit gangs. The gangs either will be exterminated on the battlefield or will be detached from their territorial districts during the purge.

It is necessary to observe the promise of privileged treatment to those who surrender voluntarily with their arms. As the struggle against banditry succeeds, so will the number of those who surrender voluntarily increase. The general task of eradicating banditry will thereby be facilitated.

While occupying a territory, the garrisons should be of a numerical strength sufficient to enable them to beat off independently the attacks of bandit detachments. The raiding detachments should also be strong enough to enter independently into single combat with the bandits. There are particular advantages in the use of armored cars, which are the main scourge of the fast-moving bandits.

PART V

Guerrilla
Doctrine Today

Introductory Note

Recent writings on guerrilla warfare are much better known than earlier ones, but no collection of the classics of guerrilla doctrine would be complete without excerpts from Mao and some other contemporary authors. *On Protracted War* is the text of a series of lectures delivered by Mao at Yenan in May and June, 1938. Lin Piao (1907–1971) was at one time Mao's closest collaborator. One of the chief commanders in the war against Chiang and the Japanese, he was appointed Minister of Defense in 1959. *Long Live the Victory of People's War,* published in 1965, created a brief sensation by its emphasis on the encirclement of the "cities of the world" by the "rural areas of the world." Lin Piao died in a plane crash in September, 1971, apparently trying to escape to the Soviet Union.

Ernesto (Che) Guevara de la Serna (1928–1967) is the most important theoretician of the Cuban Revolution. The eldest son of an upper class Argentinian family, he studied medicine and joined the Castro brothers in their invasion of Cuba in November, 1956. "Guerrilla Warfare—A Method," Guevara's last theoretical essay, published in *Cuba Socialista III,* No. 25, deals with the prospects for revolution in other Latin American countries. Guevara's theoretical reflections about the lessons of the Cuban war are of great interest, but they do not pertain to what really happened during the war. Such discrepancies between guerrilla myth and reality can be found in most writings on the subject. In this case, however, the divergence is very pronounced indeed. Guevara, like Castro, was a firm believer in rural guerrilla warfare; the city, as he saw it, was the grave of the guerrilla. The same view was taken by Régis Debray (1941–), the chief interpreter of Castroism-Guevarism. A graduate of the Ecole Normale and a student of Althusser, he went to Cuba in 1961; he was arrested in Bolivia in 1967 and released in 1970. *Revolution in the Revolution* was published in 1967. According to Debray the guerrilla force is the Communist party in embryo (not vice versa); it should not be subordinated to the party. Insurrectional activity was the commandment of the hour, not political activity. In later years, having parted with his erstwhile comrades and returned to French politics, Debray admitted that his earlier views had been partly mistaken.

The shift from rural to urban guerrilla warfare is reflected in the writings of Abraham Guillen (1912?–) and, above all, Carlos Marighella (1911–1969). Guillen, Spanish by origin, emigrated to Latin America after the end of the Spanish Civil War and became one of the chief theoreticians of urban guerrillaism. For a time he had considerable influence upon the Tupamaros, but later on he disapproved of their policy. Marighella, a leading member of the Brazilian Communist party, broke with it in 1967 and set up a terrorist organization, the Action for National Liberation (ALN). While attributing equal importance to rural and urban guerrilla warfare in theory, he concentrated in practice entirely on urban terrorism. His *Minimanual,* published in June, 1969, became a guide for terrorists in many countries. Marighella and the other leaders of the ALN lost their lives in a shoot-out with the police.

Although the Vietnamese communists displayed courage, initiative, and great stamina in applying guerrilla warfare within their overall strategy, they were not innovative, and there is little in the theoretical writings of Vo Nguyen Giap and their other leaders that was not stated earlier by Mao and his comrades.

Of all the African guerrilla leaders, Amilcar Cabral (1926–1973) of Guiné-Bissau, a nonorthodox Marxist-Leninist, was the most successful, even though Portuguese Guiné was anything but ideal country from a guerrilla point of view.

Mao Tse-tung

The Three Stages
of the Protracted War

Since the Sino-Japanese War is a protracted one and final victory will belong to China, it can reasonably be assumed that this protracted war will pass through three stages. The first stage covers the period of the enemy's strategic offensive and our strategic defensive. The second stage will be the period of the enemy's strategic consolidation and our preparation of the counteroffensive. The third stage will be the period of our strategic counteroffensive and the enemy's strategic retreat. It is impossible to predict the concrete situation in the three stages, but certain main trends in the war may be pointed out in the light of present conditions. The course of objective events will be exceedingly rich and varied, with many twists and turns, and nobody can cast a "horoscope" for the Sino-Japanese War; nevertheless it is necessary for the strategic direction of the war to make an outline sketch of its trends. Although our sketch may not be in full accord with the subsequent facts and will be amended by them, it is still necessary to make such a sketch in order to give firm and purposeful strategic direction to the protracted war.

The first stage has not yet ended. The enemy's design is to occupy Canton, Wuhan, and Lanchow and link up these three points. To accomplish this aim the enemy will have to use at least fifty divisions, or about one and a half million men, spend from one and a half to two years, and expend more than ten thousand million yen. In penetrating so deeply, the enemy will encounter immense difficulties, with consequences disastrous beyond imagination. As for attempting to occupy the entire length of the Canton-Hankow Railway and the Sian-Lanchow Highway, he will have to fight perilous battles and, even so, may not fully accomplish his design. But in drawing up our

Mao Tse-tung: *On Protracted War* (1938).

operational plan we should base ourselves on the assumption that the enemy may occupy the three points and even certain additional areas, as well as link them up, and we should make dispositions for a protracted war, so that even if he does so, we shall be able to cope with him. In this stage the form of fighting we should adopt is primarily mobile warfare, to be supplemented by guerrilla and positional warfare. Through the subjective errors of the Kuomintang military authorities, positional warfare was assigned the primary role in the first phase of this stage, but, nevertheless, it is supplementary from the point of view of the stage as a whole. In this stage, China has already built up a broad united front and achieved unprecedented unity. Although the enemy has used and will continue to use base and shameless means to induce capitulation in the attempt to realize his plan for a quick decision and to conquer the whole of China without much effort, he has failed so far, nor is he likely to succeed in the future. In this stage, in spite of considerable losses, China has made considerable progress, which will become the main basis for her continued resistance in the second stage. In the present stage the Soviet Union has already given substantial aid to China. On the enemy side, there are already signs of flagging morale, and the momentum of attack of his army is less in the middle phase of this stage than in the initial phase and will diminish still further in the concluding phase. His finances and economy are beginning to show signs of exhaustion; war-weariness is beginning to set in among his people and troops; and within the clique that is running the war, "war frustrations" are beginning to manifest themselves and pessimism about the prospects of the war is growing.

The second stage may be termed one of strategic stalemate. At the tail end of the first stage, the enemy will be forced to fix certain terminal points to his strategic offensive owing to his shortage of troops and our firm resistance, and upon reaching them he will stop his strategic offensive and enter the stage of safeguarding his occupied areas. In the second stage, the enemy will attempt to safeguard the occupied areas and to make them his own by the fraudulent method of setting up puppet governments, while plundering the Chinese people to the limit; but again he will be confronted with stubborn guerrilla warfare. Taking advantage of the fact that the enemy's rear is unguarded, our guerrilla warfare will develop extensively in the first stage, and many base areas will be established, seriously threatening the enemy's consolidation of the occupied areas, and so in the second stage there will still be widespread fighting. In this stage, our form of fighting will be primarily guerrilla warfare, supplemented by mobile warfare. China will still retain a large regular army, but she will find it difficult to launch the strategic counteroffensive immediately because, on the one hand, the enemy will adopt a strategically defensive position in the big cities and along the main lines of communication under his occupation and, on the other hand, China will not yet be adequately equipped technically. Except for the troops engaged in frontal defense against the enemy, our forces will be switched in large numbers to the enemy's rear in comparatively dispersed dispositions, and, basing themselves on all the areas not actually occupied by the enemy and coordinating with the people's local armed forces, they will launch extensive, fierce guerrilla warfare against enemy-occupied places, keeping the enemy on the move as far as possible in order to destroy him in mobile warfare, as is now being done in Shansi Province. The fighting in the second stage will be ruthless, and the country will suffer serious devastation. But the guerrilla warfare will be successful, and if it is well conducted the enemy may be able to retain only about one third of his occupied territory, with the remaining two thirds back in our hands, which will constitute a great defeat for the enemy and a great victory for China. By then the enemy-occupied territory as a whole will fall into three categories: first, the enemy base areas; second, our base areas for guerrilla warfare; and, third, the guerrilla areas contested by both sides. The duration of this stage will depend on the degree of change in the balance of forces between us and the enemy and on the changes in the international situation; generally speaking, we should be prepared to see this stage last a comparatively long time and to weather its hardships. It will be a very painful period for China; the two big problems will be economic difficulties and the disruptive activities of the traitors. The enemy will go all out to wreck China's united front, and the traitor organizations in all the occupied areas will merge into a so-called unified government. Owing to the loss of big cities and the hardships of war, vacillating elements within our ranks will clamor for compromise, and pessimism will grow to a serious extent. Our tasks will then be to mobilize the whole people to unite as one man and carry on the war with unflinching perseverance, to broaden and consolidate the united front, sweep away all pessimism and ideas of compromise, promote the will to hard struggle and apply new wartime policies, and so to weather the hardships. In the second stage, we will have to call upon the whole country resolutely to maintain a united government, oppose splits, and systematically improve our fighting technique, reform the armed forces, mobilize the entire people, and prepare for the counteroffensive. The international situation will become still more unfavorable to Japan and the main international forces will incline toward giving more help to China, even though there may be talk of "realism" of the Chamberlain type which accommodates itself to *faits accomplis*. Japan's threat to Southeast Asia and Siberia will become greater, and there may even be another war. As regards Japan, scores of her divisions will be inextricably bogged down in China. Widespread guerrilla warfare and the people's anti-Japanese movement will wear down this big Japanese force, greatly reducing it and also disintegrating its morale by stimulating the growth of homesickness, war-weariness, and even anti-war sentiment. Though it would be wrong to say that Japan will achieve no results at all in her plunder of China, yet, being short of capital and harassed by guerrilla warfare, she cannot possibly achieve rapid or substantial results. This second stage will be the transitional stage of the entire war; it will be the most trying period but also the pivotal one. Whether China becomes an independent country or is reduced to a colony will be determined not by the retention or loss of the big cities in the first stage but by the extent to which the whole nation exerts itself in the second. If we can persevere in the War of Resistance, in the united front and in the protracted war, China will in that stage gain the power to change from weak to strong. It will be the second act in the three-act drama of China's War of Resistance. And through the efforts of the entire cast it will be possible to perform a most brilliant last act.

The third stage will be the stage of the counteroffensive to recover our lost territories. Their recovery will depend mainly upon the strength which China has built up in the preceding stage and which will continue to grow in the third stage. But China's strength alone will not be sufficient, and we shall also have to rely on the support of international forces and on the changes that will take place inside Japan, or otherwise we shall not be able to win; this adds to China's tasks in international propaganda and diplomacy. In the third stage, our war will no longer be one of strategic defensive, but will turn into a strategic counteroffensive manifesting itself in strategic offensives; and it will no longer be fought on strategically interior lines, but will shift gradually to strategically exterior lines. Not until we fight our way to the Yalu River can this war be considered over. The third stage will be the last in the protracted war, and when we talk of persevering in the war to the end, we mean going all the way through this stage. Our primary form of fighting will still be mobile warfare, but positional warfare will rise to importance. While positional defence cannot be regarded as important in the first stage because of the prevailing circumstances, positional attack will become quite important in the third stage because of the changed conditions and the requirements of the task. In the third stage guerrilla warfare will still provide strategic support by supplementing mobile and positional warfare, but it will not be the primary form as in the second stage.

It is thus obvious that the war is protracted and consequently ruthless in nature. The enemy will not be able to gobble up the whole of China but will be able to occupy many places for a considerable time. China will not be able to oust the Japanese quickly, but the greater part of her territory will remain in her hands. Ultimately the enemy will lose and we will win, but we shall have a hard stretch of road to travel.

The Chinese people will become tempered in the course of this long and ruthless war. The political parties taking part in the war will also be steeled and tested. The united front must be persevered in; only by persevering in the united front can we persevere in the war; and only by persevering in the united front and in the war can we win final victory. Only thus can all difficulties be overcome. After traveling the hard stretch of road we shall reach the highway to victory. This is the natural logic of the war.

In the three stages the changes in relative strength will proceed along the following lines. In the first stage, the enemy is superior and we are inferior in strength. With regard to our inferiority we must reckon on changes of two different kinds from the eve of the War of Resistance to the end of this stage. The first kind is a change for the worse. China's original inferiority will be aggravated by war losses, namely, decreases in territory, population, economic strength, military strength, and cultural institutions. Toward the end of the first stage, the decrease will probably be considerable, especially on the economic side. This point will be exploited by some people as a basis for their theories of national subjugation and of compromise. But the second kind of change, the change for the better, must also be noted. It includes the experience gained in the war, the progress made by the armed forces, the political progress, the mobilization of the people, the development of culture in a new direction, the emergence of guerrilla warfare, the increase in international support, etc. In the first stage, what is on the downgrade is the old quantity and the old quality, the manifestations being mainly quantitative. What is on the upgrade is the new quantity and the new quality, the manifestations being mainly qualitative. It is the second kind of change that provides a basis for our ability to fight a protracted war and win final victory.

In the first stage, changes of two kinds also occur on the enemy's side. The first kind is a change for the worse and manifests itself in hundreds of thousands of casualties, the drain on arms and ammunition, deterioration of troop morale, popular discontent at home, shrinkage of trade, the expenditure of over ten thousand million yen, condemnation by world opinion, etc. This trend also provides a basis for our ability to fight a protracted war and win final victory. But we must likewise reckon with the second kind of change on the enemy's side, a change for the better, that is, his expansion in territory, population, and resources. This too is a basis for the protracted nature of our War of Resistance and the impossibility of quick victory, but at the same time certain people will use it as a basis for their theories of national subjugation and of compromise. However, we must take into account the transitory and partial character of this change for the better on the enemy's side. Japan is an imperialist power heading for collapse, and her occupation of China's territory is temporary. The vigorous growth of guerrilla warfare in China will restrict her actual occupation to narrow zones. Moreover, her occupation of Chinese territory is creating and intensifying contradictions between Japan and other foreign countries. Besides, generally speaking, such occupation involves a considerable period in which Japan will make capital outlay without drawing any profits, as is shown by the experience in the three northeastern provinces. All of which again gives us a basis for demolishing the theories of national subjugation and of compromise and for establishing the theories of protracted war and of final victory.

In the second stage, the above changes on both sides will continue to develop. While the situation cannot be predicted in detail, on the whole Japan will continue on the downgrade and China on the upgrade. For example, Japan's military and financial resources will be seriously drained by China's guerrilla warfare, popular discontent will grow in Japan, the morale of her troops will deteriorate further, and she will become more isolated internationally. As for China, she will make further progress in the political, military, and cultural spheres and in the mobilization of the people; guerrilla warfare will develop further; there will be some new economic growth on the basis of the small industries and the widespread agriculture in the interior; international support will gradually increase; and the whole picture will be quite different from what it is now. This second stage may last quite a long time, during which there will be a great reversal in the balance of forces, with China gradually rising and Japan gradually declining. China will emerge from her inferior position, and Japan will lose her superior position; first the two countries will become evenly matched, and then their relative positions will be reversed. Thereupon, China will in general have completed her preparations for the strategic counteroffensive and will enter the stage of the counteroffensive and the expulsion of the enemy. It should be reiterated that the change from inferiority to superiority and the completion of preparations for the counteroffensive will involve three things, namely, an increase in China's own strength, an increase in Japan's difficulties, and an increase in international support; it is the combination of all these forces that will bring about China's superiority and the completion of her preparations for the counteroffensive.

Because of the unevenness in China's political and economic development, the strategic counteroffensive of the third stage will not present a uniform and even picture throughout the country in its initial phase but will be regional in character, rising here and subsiding there. During this stage, the enemy will not relax his divisive tricks to break China's united front, hence the task of maintaining internal unity in China will become all the more important, and we shall have to ensure that the strategic counteroffensive does not collapse halfway through internal dissension. In this period the international situation will become very favorable to China. China's task will be to take advantage of it in order to attain complete liberation and establish an independent democratic state, which at the same time will mean helping the world anti-Fascist movement.

China moving from inferiority to parity and then to superiority, Japan moving from superiority to parity and then to inferiority; China moving from the defensive to stalemate and then to the counteroffensive, Japan moving from the offensive to the safeguarding of her gains and then to retreat—such will be the course of the Sino-Japanese War and its inevitable trend.

Hence the questions and the conclusions are as follows: Will China be subjugated? The answer is, No, she will not be subjugated, but will win final victory. Can China win quickly? The answer is, No, she cannot win quickly, and the war must be a protracted one. Are these conclusions correct? I think they are.

At this point, the exponents of national subjugation and of compromise will again rush in and say, "To move from inferiority to parity China needs a military and economic power equal to Japan's, and to move from parity to superiority she will need a military and economic power greater than Japan's. But this is impossible, hence the above conclusions are not correct."

This is the so-called theory that "weapons decide everything," which constitutes a mechanical approach to the question of war and a subjective and one-sided view. Our view is opposed to this; we see not only weapons but also people. Weapons are an important factor in war, but not the decisive factor; it is people, not things, that are decisive. The contest of strength is not only a contest of military and economic power, but also a contest of human power and morale. Military and economic power is necessarily wielded by people. If the great majority of the Chinese, of the Japanese, and of the people of other countries are on the side of our War of Resistance Against Japan, how can Japan's military and economic power, wielded as it is by a small minority through coercion, count as superiority? And if not, then does not China, though wielding relatively inferior military and economic power, become the superior? There is no doubt that China will gradually grow in military and economic power, provided she perseveres in the War of Resistance and in the united front. As for our enemy, weakened as he will be by the long war and by internal and external contradictions, his military and economic power is bound to change in the reverse direction. In these circumstances, is there any reason why China cannot become the superior? Nor is that all. Although we cannot as yet count the military and economic power of other countries as being openly and to any great extent on our side, is there any reason why we will not be able to do so in the future? If Japan's enemy is not just China, if in future one or more other countries make open use of their considerable military and economic power defensively or offensively against Japan and openly help us, then will not our superiority be still greater? Japan is a small country, her war is reactionary and barbarous, and she will become more and more isolated internationally; China is a big country, her war is progressive and just, and she will enjoy more and more support internationally. Is there any reason why the long-period development of these factors should not definitely change the relative position between the enemy and ourselves?

Lin Piao

Encircling the Cities of the World

. . . What should the oppressed nations and the oppressed people do in the face of wars of aggression and armed suppression by the imperialists and their lackeys? Should they submit and remain slaves in perpetuity? Or should they rise in resistance and fight for their liberation?

Comrade Mao Tse-tung answered this question in vivid terms. He said that after long investigation and study the Chinese people discovered that all the imperialists and their lackeys "have swords in their hands and are out to kill. The people have come to understand this and so act after the same fashion." This is called doing unto them what they do unto us.

In the last analysis, whether one dares to wage a tit-for-tat struggle against armed aggression and suppression by the imperialists and their lackeys, whether one dares to fight a people's war against them, means whether one dares to embark on revolution. This is the most

Lin Piao, *Long Live the Victory of People's War* (Peking, 1965).

effective touchstone for distinguishing genuine from fake revolutionaries and Marxist-Leninists.

In view of the fact that some people were afflicted with the fear of the imperialists and reactionaries, Comrade Mao Tse-tung put forward his famous thesis that "the imperialists and all reactionaries are paper tigers." He said,

> All reactionaries are paper tigers. In appearance, the reactionaries are terrifying, but in reality they are not so powerful. From a long-term point of view, it is not the reactionaries but the people who are really powerful.

The history of people's war in China and other countries provides conclusive evidence that the growth of the people's revolutionary forces from weak and small beginnings into strong and large forces is a universal law of development of class struggle, a universal law of development of people's war. A people's war inevitably meets with many difficulties, with ups and downs and setbacks in the course of its development, but no force can alter its general trend toward inevitable triumph.

Comrade Mao Tse-tung points out that we must despise the enemy strategically and take full account of him tactically.

To despise the enemy strategically is an elementary requirement for a revolutionary. Without the courage to despise the enemy and without daring to win, it will be simply impossible to make revolution and wage a people's war, let alone to achieve victory.

It is also very important for revolutionaries to take full account of the enemy tactically. It is likewise impossible to win victory in a people's war without taking full account of the enemy tactically and without examining the concrete conditions, without being prudent and giving great attention to the study of the art of struggle and without adopting appropriate forms of struggle in the concrete practice of the revolution in each country and with regard to each concrete problem of struggle.

Dialectical and historical materialism teaches us that what is important primarily is not that which at the given moment seems to be durable and yet is already beginning to die away, but that which is arising and developing, even though at the given moment it may not appear to be durable, for only that which is arising and developing is invincible.

Why can the apparently weak newborn forces always triumph over the decadent forces which appear so powerful? The reason is that truth is on their side and that the masses are on their side, while the reactionary classes are always divorced from the masses and set themselves against the masses.

This has been borne out by the victory of the Chinese revolution, by the history of all revolutions, the whole history of class struggle and the entire history of mankind.

The imperialists are extremely afraid of Comrade Mao Tse-tung's thesis that "imperialism and all reactionaries are paper tigers," and the revisionists are extremely hostile to it. They all oppose and attack this thesis and the philistines follow suit by ridiculing it. But all this cannot in the least diminish its importance. The light of truth cannot be dimmed by anybody.

Comrade Mao Tse-tung's theory of people's war solves not only the problem of daring to fight a people's war, but also that of how to wage it.

Comrade Mao Tse-tung is a great statesman and military scientist, proficient at directing war in accordance with its laws. By the line and policies, the strategy and tactics he formulated for the people's war, he led the Chinese people in steering the ship of the people's war past all hidden reefs to the shores of victory in most complicated and difficult conditions.

It must be emphasized that Comrade Mao Tse-tung's theory of the establishment of rural revolutionary base areas and the encirclement of the cities from the countryside is of outstanding and universal practical importance for the present revolutionary struggles of all the oppressed nations and peoples, and particularly for the revolutionary struggles of the oppressed nations and peoples in Asia, Africa, and Latin America against imperialism and its lackeys.

Many countries and peoples in Asia, Africa, and Latin America are now being subjected to aggression and enslavement on a serious scale by the imperialists headed by the United States and their lackeys. The basic political and economic conditions in many of these countries have many similarities to those that prevailed in old China. As in China, the peasant question is extremely important in these regions. The peasants constitute the main force of the national-democratic revolution against the imperialists and their lackeys. In committing aggression against these countries, the imperialists usually begin by seizing the big cities and the main lines of communication, but they are unable to bring the vast countryside completely under their control. The countryside, and the countryside alone, can provide the broad areas in which the revolutionaries can maneuver freely. The countryside, and the countryside alone, can provide the revolutionary bases from which the revolutionaries can go forward to final victory. Precisely for this reason, Comrade Mao Tse-tung's theory of establishing revolutionary base areas in the rural districts and encircling the cities from the countryside is attracting more and more attention among the people in these regions.

Taking the entire globe, if North America and western Europe can be called "the cities of the world," then Asia, Africa, and Latin America constitute "the rural areas of the world." Since World War II, the proletarian revolutionary movement has for various reasons been temporarily held back in the North American and western European capitalist countries, while the people's revolutionary movement in Asia, Africa, and Latin America has been growing vigorously. In a sense, the contemporary world revolution also presents a picture of the encirclement of cities by the rural areas. In the final analysis, the whole cause of world revolution hinges on the revolutionary struggles of the Asian, African, and Latin American peoples who make up the overwhelming majority of the world's population. The socialist countries should regard it as their internationalist duty to support the people's revolutionary struggles in Asia, Africa, and Latin America.

The October Revolution opened up a new era in the revolution of the oppressed nations. The victory of the October Revolution built a bridge between the socialist revolution of the proletariat of the West and the national-democratic revolution of the colonial and semi-colonial countries of the East. The Chinese revolution has successfully solved the problem of how to link up the national-democratic with the socialist revolution in the colonial and semicolonial countries.

Comrade Mao Tse-tung has pointed out that, in the epoch since the October Revolution, anti-imperialist revolution in any colonial or semicolonial country is no longer part of the old bourgeois, or capitalist world revolution, but is part of the new world revolution, the proletarian-socialist world revolution.

Comrade Mao Tse-tung has formulated a complete theory of the new democratic revolution. He indicated that this revolution, which is different from all others, can only be, nay, must be, a revolution against imperialism, feudalism, and bureaucrat capitalism waged by the broad masses of the people under the leadership of the proletariat.

This means that the revolution can only be, nay, must be, led by the proletariat and the genuinely revolutionary party armed with Marxism-Leninism, and by no other class or party.

This means that the revolution embraces in its ranks not only the workers, peasants, and the urban petty bourgeoisie, but also the national bourgeoisie and other patriotic and anti-imperialist democrats.

This means, finally, that the revolution is directed against imperialism, feudalism, and bureaucrat capitalism.

The new-democratic revolution leads to socialism, and not to capitalism.

Comrade Mao Tse-tung's theory of the new-democratic revolution is the Marxist-Leninist theory of revolution by stages as well as the Marxist-Leninist theory of uninterrupted revolution.

Comrade Mao Tse-tung made a correct distinction between the two revolutionary stages, i.e., the national-democratic and the socialist revolutions; at the same time he correctly and closely linked the two. The national-democratic revolution is the necessary preparation for the socialist revolution, and the socialist revolution is the inevitable sequel to the national-democratic revolution. There is no Great Wall between the two revolutionary stages. But the socialist revolution is only possible after the completion of the national-democratic revolution. The more thorough the national-democratic revolution, the better the conditions for the socialist revolution.

The experience of the Chinese revolution shows that the tasks of the national-democratic revolution can be fulfilled only through long and tortuous struggles. In this stage of revolution, imperialism and its lackeys are the principal enemy. In the struggle against imperialism and its lackeys, it is necessary to rally all anti-imperialist patriotic forces, including the national bourgeoisie and all patriotic personages. All those patriotic personages from among the bourgeoisie and other exploiting classes who join the anti-imperialist struggle play a progressive historical role; they are not tolerated by imperialism but welcomed by the proletariat.

It is very harmful to confuse the two stages, that is, the national-democratic and the socialist revolutions. Comrade Mao Tse-tung criticized the wrong idea of "accomplishing both at one stroke," and pointed out that this utopian idea could only weaken the struggle against imperialism and its lackeys, the most urgent task at that time. The Kuomintang reactionaries and the Trotskyites they hired during the War of Resistance deliberately confused these two stages of the Chinese revolution, proclaiming the "theory of a single revolution" and preaching so-called socialism without any Communist party. With this preposterous theory they attempted to swallow up the Communist party, wipe out any revolution, and prevent the advance of the national-democratic revolution, and they used it as a pretext for their nonresistance and capitulation to imperialism. This reactionary theory was buried long ago by the history of the Chinese revolution.

The Khrushchev revisionists are now actively preaching that socialism can be built without the proletariat and without a genuinely revolutionary party armed with the advanced proletarian ideology, and they have cast the fundamental tenets of Marxism-Leninism to the four winds. The revisionists' purpose is solely to divert the oppressed nations from their struggle against imperialism and sabotage their national-democratic revolution, all in the service of imperialism.

The Chinese revolution provides a successful lesson for making a thoroughgoing national-democratic revolution under the leadership of the proletariat; it likewise provides a successful lesson for the timely transition from the national-democratic revolution to the socialist revolution under the leadership of the proletariat.

Mao Tse-tung's thought has been the guide to the victory of the Chinese revolution. It has integrated the universal truth of Marxism-Leninism with the concrete practice of the Chinese revolution and creatively developed Marxism-Leninism, thus adding new weapons to the arsenal of Marxism-Leninism.

Ours is the epoch in which world capitalism and imperialism are heading for their doom and socialism and communism are marching to victory. Comrade Mao Tse-tung's theory of people's war is not only a product of the Chinese revolution, but has also the characteristics of our epoch. The new experience gained in the people's revolutionary struggles in various countries since World War II has provided continuous evidence that Mao Tse-tung's thought is a common asset of the revolutionary people of the whole world. This is the great international significance of the thought of Mao Tse-tung.

Che Guevara

Guerrilla Warfare—A Method

During the waging of the armed struggle two moments of extreme danger for the future of the revolution appear. The first arises during the preparatory stage, and the manner in which it is resolved determines the decision to struggle and the clear understanding that the popular forces have of the ends. When the bourgeois state advances against the positions of the people, obviously a defensive process against the enemy must be created which, once it achieves superiority, attacks. If minimum objective and subjective conditions have already developed, the defense should be armed, but in such a way that the popular forces are not converted into mere recipients of the blows of enemies; nor should the stage for armed defense simply be a last refuge for the persecuted. The guerrilla, the people's defensive movement at a given moment, has in itself, and constantly should develop, its ability to attack the enemy. In time, this ability is what will determine its nature as a catalyst of the popular forces. It merits being said that guerrilla activity is not passive self-defense; it is defense with attack, and from the moment it establishes itself as such, its final goal is the conquest of political power.

This moment is important. In the social processes, the difference between violence and nonviolence cannot be measured by the number of shots that are exchanged; it yields to concrete and fluctuating situations. And it is necessary to be able to see the instant in which the popular forces, aware of their relative weakness, but, at the same time, of their strategic strength, must force the enemy to take the necessary steps so that the situation does not retrocede. The balance between the oligarchic dictatorship and popular pressure must be upset. The dictatorship constantly tries to operate without the showy use of force. Forcing the dictatorship to appear undisguised—that is, in its true aspect of violent dictatorship of the reactionary classes—will contribute to its unmasking, which will intensify the struggle to such extremes that then there is no turning back. The manner in which the people's forces, dedicated to the task of making the dictatorship define itself—holding back or unleashing the battle—carry out their function depends on the firm beginning of a long-range armed action.

Escape from the other dangerous moment depends on the power of growing development which the popular forces possess. Marx always maintained that once the revolutionary process had begun, the proletariat had to strike and strike unceasingly. Revolution that does not constantly become more profound is a regressive revolution. Tired soldiers begin to lose faith and then some of the maneuvers to which the bourgeoisie has so accustomed us may appear. These can be elections with the transfer of power to another gentleman with a more mellifluous voice and a more angelic countenance than the current dictator, or a coup by reactionaries generally led by the army and directly or indirectly supported by progressive forces. There are others, but we do not intend to analyze tactical stratagems.

Principally, we are calling attention to the maneuvers of the military coup that was previously mentioned. What can the military give to the true democracy? What loyalty can one ask of them if they are mere tools of the domination of the reactionary classes and of the imperialist monopolies, and, as a caste, whose value depends upon the weapons it possesses, aspire merely to maintain their privileges?

In situations difficult for oppressors, when the military plot and oust a dictator who de facto has already been beaten, it must be supposed that they do it because the dictator is not capable of preserving their class privileges without extreme violence, which, in general, now does not suit the interest of oligarchies.

This in no way means rejecting the use of the military as individual fighters, separated from the social milieu in which they have operated and, in fact, rebelled against. But this use must be made in the framework of the revolutionary course to which they will belong as fighters and not as representatives of a caste.

In times past, in the preface to the third edition of *The Civil War in France,* Engels said, "After each revolution, the workers were armed; for that reason, the disarmament of the workers was the first order of the bourgeoisie who headed the State. Hence, after each revolution won by the workers, a new struggle developed that culminated with their overthrow . . ." (Quoted from Lenin, *The State and the Revolution*).

This game of continual struggles, in which formal changes of any type are attained only to strategically regress, has been repeated for decades in the capitalist world. But still, permanent deception of the proletariat in this aspect has been going on periodically for more than a century.

It is also dangerous that, moved by the desire to maintain for some time the conditions most favorable for revolutionary action by means of the use of certain aspects of bourgeois legality, the leaders of the progressive party confuse the terms—which is very common during the course of the action—and forget the final strategic objective: seizure of power.

These two difficult moments of the revolution, which we have briefly analyzed, are obviated when the leading Marxist-Leninist parties are able to see clearly the implications of the moment and to mobilize the masses, to the greatest extent, by correctly leading them to resolve fundamental contradictions.

In discussing the subject, we have assumed that, eventually, the idea of armed struggle and also the formula of guerrilla warfare as a method of combat will be accepted. Why do we estimate that guerrilla warfare is the correct method under the present conditions in America? There are basic arguments which, to our mind, determine the necessity of guerrilla action in America as the central axis of the struggle.

First: Accepting as a truth the fact that the enemy will struggle to keep himself in power, it is necessary to consider the destruction of the oppressing army; but to destroy it, it is necessary to oppose it with a popular army. This army is not created spontaneously but must arm itself from its enemy's arsenal, and this causes a hard and very long struggle in which the popular forces and their leaders would be continually exposed to attack from superior forces without suitable conditions for defense and maneuverability.

On the other hand, the guerrilla nucleus, settled in terrain favorable to the struggle, guarantees the security and permanence of the revolutionary command. The urban forces, directed from the general staff of the army of the people, can carry out actions of incalculable importance. The possible destruction of these groups would not kill the soul of the revolution; its leadership, from its rural fortress, would continue to catalyze the revolutionary spirit of the masses and organize new forces for other battles.

Furthermore, the organization of the future state apparatus begins in this zone. It is in charge of efficiently guiding the class dictatorship during the entire transition period. The longer the battle, the greater and more complex will be the administrative problems, and in solving them, cadres will be trained for the difficult task of consolidating power and economic development in a future stage.

Second: We have to look at the general situation of the Latin American peasants and the progressively more explosive nature of their struggle against feudal structures in the framework of a social situation of alliance between local and foreign exploiters.

Returning to the Second Declaration of Havana: "The peoples of America freed themselves from Spanish colonialism at the beginning of the last century, but they did not free themselves from exploitation. The feudal landlords took over the authority of the Spanish governors, the Indians continued in grinding slavery, the Latin American man in one form or another followed in the steps of the slave, and the slightest hopes of the people crumbled under the power of oligarchies and the yoke of foreign capital. This has been the situation in [Latin] America, in one form or another. Today Latin America is under an even more ferocious imperialism, far more powerful and ruthless than Spanish colonial imperialism.

"And faced with the objective and historically inexorable reality of the Latin American revolution, what is the attitude of Yankee imperialism? To prepare to begin a colonial war with the peoples of Latin America; to create an apparatus of force, political pretexts, and pseudo-legal instruments signed with the representatives of reactionary oligarchies to repress by blood and fire the struggle of the Latin American peoples."

This objective situation demonstrates the force that slumbers, unproductive, in our peasants and the need for using it for the liberation of America.

Third: The continental character of the struggle.

Could this new stage of the emancipation of America be conceived as the meeting of two local forces struggling for power in a given territory? Only with difficulty. The struggle will be to the death between all the popular forces and all the forces of repression. The paragraphs quoted above also predict it.

The Yankees will intervene out of solidarity of interests and because the struggle in America is a decisive one. In fact, they are already intervening in the preparation of repressive forces and in the organization of a continental fighting apparatus. But, from now on, they will do it with all their energies; they will punish the popular forces with all the destructive weapons at their disposal; they will not permit the revolutionary power to consolidate, and if anyone should do so, they will again attack, they will not recognize it, they will try to divide the revolutionary forces, they will introduce saboteurs of every kind, they will create border problems, they will turn other reactionary states against them, they will try to smother the economy of the new state, in one word, to annihilate it.

With this American panorama, it is difficult to achieve and consolidate victory in an isolated country. The unity of repressive forces must be answered with the unity of popular forces. In all countries where oppression reaches unbearable levels, the banner of rebellion must be raised, and this banner will have, because of historical need, continental features. The Andes Cordillera is called on to be the Sierra Maestra of America, as Fidel has said, and all the vast territories of the continent are called to be the scene of the struggle to the death against the imperialist power.

We cannot say when it will achieve these continental features, nor how long the struggle will last; but we can predict its coming and its success, because it is the result of inevitable historical, economic, and political circumstances, and the course cannot be turned aside. To begin it when conditions are propitious, regardless of the situation in other countries, is the task set for the revolutionary force in each country. The waging of the struggle will continue the general strategy. The prediction on the continental character is the fruit of the analysis of the forces of each contender, but this does not exclude, not by a long shot, an independent outburst. Just as the beginning of the struggle at a point in a country is intended to carry it throughout the country, the beginning of the revolutionary war contributes to the development of new conditions in neighboring countries.

The development of revolutions has come about normally by inversely proportional ebbs and flows. The revolutionary flow corresponds to the counterrevolutionary ebb, and vice versa, at the mo-

ment of the revolutionary decline, there is a counterrevolutionary
rise. At times like this, the situation of the popular forces becomes
difficult and they must resort to the best means of defense to suffer
the least damage. The enemy is extremely strong, continentally. For
this reason, the relative weaknesses of the local bourgeoisie cannot be
analyzed for purposes of making decisions of a limited scope. Even
more remote is the possible alliance of these oligarchies with the people under arms. The Cuban Revolution has sounded the alarm. The
polarization of forces will be total: exploiters from one side and the
exploited from another; the masses of the petty bourgeoisie will lean
toward one or the other, depending on their interests and the political
skill with which they are handled. Neutrality will be an exception.
This is what the revolutionary war will be like.

Let us think about how a guerrilla focus could begin.

Relatively small nuclei of people choose favorable places for guerrilla warfare, either to begin a counterattack, or to weather the storm,
and thus they begin to act. The following must be clearly established:
at first, the relative weakness of the guerrilla movement is such that
it must work only to settle in the terrain, establishing connections
with the populace and reinforcing the places that will possibly become
its base of support.

There are three conditions for the survival of a guerrilla movement
that begins its development under the situation just described: constant mobility, constant vigilance, constant distrust. Without the adequate use of these three elements of military tactics, the guerrilla will
survive only with difficulty. It must be remembered that the heroism
of the guerrilla warrior at this moment consists in the extent of his
established ends and the enormous sacrifices he must make to achieve
them.

These sacrifices will not be the daily combat, or face-to-face fighting with the enemy. They will take forms that are more subtle and
more difficult to resist for the body and mind of the individual who
is in the guerrilla movement.

These guerrillas will perhaps be severely punished by the enemy
armies. Sometimes they will be divided into groups; those who have
been made prisoners, martyrized; persecuted like hunted animals in
those areas where they have chosen to operate, with the constant
worry of having the enemy one step behind; with the constant distrust
of everyone since the frightened peasants will hand them over, in

some cases, to be rid of the repressive troops; with no other alternative but death or victory, at times when death is an ever present thought, and victory is the myth about which only a revolutionary can dream.

That is the heroism of the guerrilla. That is why it is said that walking is a form of fighting, that retreat from combat at a given moment is but another form of combat. Faced with the general superiority of the enemy, the plan is to find the tactical form of achieving a relative superiority at a selected point, whether it be to concentrate more effectives than the enemy, or to assure an advantage in making use of the terrain, thus upsetting the balance of forces. Under these conditions a tactical victory is assured. If the relative superiority is not clear, it is preferable not to act. Combat that will not lead to victory should not be carried out, as long as the "how" and the "when" can be chosen.

In the framework of the large political and military action of which it is a part, the guerrilla movement will grow and consolidate. Bases of support, a basic element for the prosperity of the guerrilla army, will then appear. These bases of support are points which the enemy's army can penetrate only with great losses. They are bastions of the revolution, the refuge and springboard of the guerrilla for excursions which are farther away and more daring.

This moment arrives if the tactical and political difficulties have been simultaneously overcome. The guerrillas can never forget their function as the vanguard of the people, a mandate which they personify, and consequently, they must create the necessary political conditions for the establishment of a revolutionary power based on the total support of the masses. The great claims of the peasants must be satisfied to the extent and in the way circumstances warrant, making the population a compact and decided unit.

If the military situation will be difficult at first, the political will be no less ticklish. And if one single military error can liquidate the guerrilla movement, a political error can stop its development for long periods.

The struggle is political and military. That is the way it must be waged and, consequently, understood.

The guerrilla movement, in its growth period, reaches a point where its capacity for action covers a specific region for which there is a surplus of men and an overconcentration in the zone. The bee swarming begins when one of the leaders, an outstanding guerrilla, moves to another region and repeats the chain of developments of guerrilla warfare, subject, of course, to a central command.

Now, it is necessary to point out that it is not possible to aspire to victory without the formation of a popular army. The guerrilla forces can expand only to a certain size; the popular forces in the cities and other penetrable zones of the enemy can inflict damages on him but the military potential of the reaction could still remain intact. It must always be remembered that the final result must be the annihilation of the enemy. Therefore, every new zone which is created, plus the zones of penetration of the enemy behind his lines, plus the forces that operate in the principal cities, must be subordinate to the [central] command. It cannot be claimed that the tight chain of command that characterizes an army exists, but certainly there must be a strategic chain of command. Within determined conditions of freedom of action, guerrilla units must obey all strategic orders from the central command, set up in one of the most secure and strongest posts, preparing the conditions for the union of the forces at a given moment.

Guerrilla warfare or war of liberation will, in general, have three stages: the first, a strategic defense, in which a small hunted force bites the enemy; it is not protected for a passive defense in a small circle, but its defense consists in limited attacks which it can carry out. After this, a state of equilibrium is reached in which the possibilities of action of the enemy and the guerrilla unit are stabilized; and later the final moment of overrunning the repressive army that will lead to the taking of the great cities, to the great decisive encounters, to the total annihilation of the enemy.

After the point of equilibrium is reached, when both forces respect one another, guerrilla warfare acquires new characteristics along the way of its development. The concept of the maneuver begins to appear. Large columns attack strong points. It is a war of movement with a transfer of forces and means of attack of relative strength. But, due to the capacity for resistance and counterattack that the enemy still has, this war of maneuvers does not definitely replace the guerrilla units. It is merely another way they act. It is a greater magnitude of the guerrilla forces until finally a popular army crystallizes into army corps. Even at this moment, marching at the head of the action of the main forces, the guerrilla units will go in their state of "purity," destroying communications, sabotaging the enemy's entire defensive apparatus.

We had predicted that the war would be continental. This means also that it will be prolonged; there will be many fronts, it will cost much blood, innumerable lives for a long time. But, even more, the phenomena of polarization of forces that are occurring in America, the clear division between exploiters and exploited that will exist in future revolutionary wars, means that when power is taken over by the armed vanguard of the people, the country, or countries, that obtain it will have liquidated simultaneously, in the oppressor, the imperialist, and the national exploiters. The first stage of socialist revolution will have crystallized; the peoples will be ready to stanch their wounds and begin the construction of socialism. . . .

Régis Debray

The Guerrilla as the Political Vanguard

In Cuba, military (operational) and political leadership have been combined in one man: Fidel Castro. Is this the result of mere chance, without significance, or is it an indication of a historically different situation? Is it an exception or does it foreshadow something fundamental? What light does it throw on the current Latin American experience? We must decipher this experience in time, and we must not rush to condemn history in the making because it does not conform to received principles. Fidel Castro said recently:

> I am accused of heresy. It is said that I am a heretic within the camp of Marxism-Leninism. Hmm! It is amusing that so-called Marxist organizations, which fight like cats and dogs in their dispute over possession of revolutionary truth, accuse us of wanting to apply the Cuban formula mechanically. They reproach us with a lack of understanding of the party's role; they reproach us as heretics within the camp of Marxism-Leninism.

Régis Debray, *Revolution in the Revolution* (New York, 1967).

The fact is that those who want mechanically to apply formulas to the Latin American reality are precisely these same "Marxists," since it is always in the interest of the man who commits a robbery to be the first to cry thief. But what does Fidel Castro say that causes him to be characterized as "a heretic," "subjective," and "petty bourgeois"? What explosive message of his causes people in the capitals of America and of the socialist countries of Europe and Asia, all those who "want to wage revolutionary war by telepathy," "the un-principled ones," to join in the chorus against the Cuban Revolution?

"Who will make the revolution in Latin America? Who? The people, the revolutionaries, with or without a party." (Fidel.)

Fidel Castro says simply that there is no revolution without a vanguard; that this vanguard is not necessarily the Marxist-Leninist party; and that those who want to make the revolution have the right and the duty to constitute themselves a vanguard, independently of these parties.

It takes courage to state the facts out loud when these facts contradict a tradition. There is, then, no metaphysical equation in which vanguard = Marxist-Leninist party; there are merely dialectical conjunctions between a given function—that of the vanguard in history—and a given form of organization—that of the Marxist-Leninist party. These conjunctions arise out of prior history and depend on it. Parties exist here on earth and are subject to the rigors of terrestrial dialectics. If they have been born, they can die and be reborn in other forms. How does this rebirth come about? Under what form can the historic vanguard reappear?

Let us proceed systematically.

First question: How can we think or state that under the present circumstances there can be a revolution "with or without a party"? This question must be asked, not in order to revive useless and sterile animosities (of which the chief beneficiary is the counterrevolution everywhere), but because the answer to the second question is contingent on it.

Second question: In what form can the historic vanguard appear?

What is depends on what was, what will be on what is. The question of parties, as they are today, is a question of history. To answer it we must look to the past.

A party is marked by its conditions of birth, its development, the class or alliance of classes that it represents, and the social milieu in which it has developed. Let us take the same counter-examples in order to discover what historic conditions permit the application of the traditional formula for party and guerrilla relationships: China and Vietnam.

The Chinese and Vietnamese parties were involved from the beginning with the problem of establishing revolutionary power. This link was not theoretical but *practical* and manifested itself very early, in the form of a grievous experience. The Chinese party was born in 1921, when Sun Yat-sen's bourgeois revolution—in which it participated by reason of its affiliation with the Kuomintang—was in the ascendancy. From its inception it received direct aid from the Soviet mission, including military advisers led by Joffe and later by Borodin. The latter, on his arrival, organized the training of Chinese Communist officers at the Whampoa Military Academy, which soon permitted the Chinese party, as Mao said in 1938, "to recognize the importance of military matters." Three years after it was organized it underwent the disastrous experience of the first revolutionary civil war (1924–7), the urban insurrection, and the Canton strike in which it took a leading role. It assimilated this experience and, under the aegis of Mao Tse-tung, transmuted it into self-critical understanding, which led to the adoption of an antithetical line, contrary even to the advice of the Third International, i.e., the withdrawal to the countryside and the rupture with the Kuomintang.

The Vietnamese party came into being in 1930, immediately organized peasant insurrections in the hinterland which were quickly repressed, and two years later defined its line, under the aegis of Ho Chi Minh, in its first program of action: "The only path to liberation is that of armed mass struggle." "Our party," wrote Giap, "came into being when the Vietnamese revolutionary movement was at its peak. From the beginning it led the peasants, encouraged them to rise up and establish Soviet power. Thus, at an early stage, it became aware of the problems of revolutionary power and of armed struggle." In brief, these parties transformed themselves, within a few years of their founding, into vanguard parties, each one with its own political line, elaborated independently of international social forces, and each profoundly linked to its people.

In the course of their subsequent development, international contradictions were to place these parties—like the Bolshevik party some years earlier—at the head of popular resistance to foreign imperialism: in China, against the Japanese invasion in 1937; in Vietnam also, against the Japanese in 1939, and against the French colonialists in 1945. The antifeudal revolt was thus transformed into an anti-imperialist revolt, the latter giving impetus to the former. The class struggle took the form of a patriotic war, and the establishment of socialism corresponded to the restoration of national independence: the two are linked. These parties, spearheading the war of the people against the foreigners, consolidated themselves as the standard-bearers of the fatherland. They became an integral part of it.

The circumstances of this same war of liberation led certain parties originally composed of students and of the best of the workers' elite to withdraw to the countryside to carry on a guerrilla war against the occupying forces. They then merged with the agricultural workers and small farmers; the Red army and the Liberation Forces (Vietminh) were transformed into peasant armies under the leadership of the party of the working class. They achieved *in practice* the alliance of the majority class and the vanguard class: the worker–peasant alliance. The Communist party, in this case, was the result and the generative force of this alliance. So were its leaders, not artificially appointed by a congress or coopted in traditional fashion, but tested, molded, and tempered by this terrible struggle which they led to victory. Function makes the functionary, but paradoxically only historic individuals "make history."

Without going into detail, historic circumstances have not permitted Latin American Communist parties, for the most part, to take root or develop in the same way. The conditions of their founding, their growth, their link with the exploited classes are obviously different. Each one may have its own history but they are alike in that they have not, since their founding, lived through the experience of winning power in the way the Chinese and Vietnamese parties have; they have not had the opportunity, existing as they do in countries possessing formal political independence, of leading a war of national liberation; and they have therefore not been able to achieve the worker–peasant alliance—an interrelated aggregation of limitations arising from shared historical conditions.

The natural result of this history is a certain structure of directive bodies and of the parties themselves, adopted to the circumstances in which they were born and grew. But, by definition, historic situa-

tions are not immutable. The Cuban Revolution and the processes it
has set in motion throughout Latin America have upset the old per-
spectives. A revolutionary armed struggle, wherever it exists or is in
preparation, requires a thoroughgoing transformation of peacetime
practices. War, as we know, is an extension of politics, but with
specific procedures and methods. The effective leadership of an
armed revolutionary struggle requires a new style of leadership, a
new method of organization, and new physical and ideological responses on the part of leaders and militants.

A new style of leadership: It has been widely demonstrated that
guerrilla warfare is directed not from outside but from within, with
the leadership accepting its full share of the risks involved. In a
country where such a war is developing, most of the organization's
leaders must leave the cities and join the guerrilla army. This is, first
of all, a security measure, assuring the survival of the political leaders.
One Latin American party has already taken this decision. This same
party has likewise transformed its central committee, replacing most
of the old leaders with young men directly involved in the war or in
the underground struggle in the cities. The reconstitution of the party
thus goes hand in hand with its rejuvenation.

In Latin America, wherever armed struggle is the order of the day,
there is a close tie between biology and ideology. However absurd
or shocking this relationship may seem, it is nonetheless a decisive
one. An elderly man, accustomed to city living, molded by other
circumstances and goals, will not easily adjust himself to the mountain nor—though this is less so—to underground activity in the cities.
In addition to the moral factor—conviction—physical fitness is the
most basic of all skills needed for waging guerrilla war; the two
factors go hand in hand. A perfect Marxist education is not, at the
outset, an imperative condition. That an elderly man should be proven
militant—and possess a revolutionary training—is not, alas, sufficient
for coping with guerrilla existence, especially in the early stages.
Physical aptitude is the prerequisite for all other aptitudes; a minor
point of limited theoretical appeal, but the armed struggle appears
to have a rationale of which theory knows nothing.

A new organization: The reconstitution of the party into an effective directive organism, equal to the historic task, requires that an
end be put to the plethora of commissions, secretariats, congresses,
conferences, plenary sessions, meetings, and assemblies at all levels—

national, provincial, regional, and local. Faced with a state of emergency and a militarily organized enemy such a mechanism is paralyzing at best, catastrophic at worst. It is the cause of the vice of excessive deliberation which Fidel has spoken of and which hampers executive, centralized, and vertical methods, combined with the large measure of tactical independence of subordinate groups which is demanded in the conduct of military operations . . .

New ideological reflexes: Certain behavior patterns become inappropriate under conditions of an objective state of war: the basing of an entire political line on existing contradictions between enemy classes or between groups with differing interests within the same bourgeois social class; the consequent obsessive pursuit of alliances with one or another fraction of the bourgeoisie, of political bargaining, and of electoral maneuvers, from which the ruling classes have so far reaped all the benefits; the safeguarding of unity at any price, regardless of revolutionary principles and interests, which has gradually turned the party and its survival in a given form into an end in itself, more sacred even than the revolution; the siege fever, heritage of the past, and its accompanying mistrust, arrogance, rigidity, and fitfulness.

Addressing himself fraternally to party comrades during the struggle against Batista, Che Guevara made the following mordant comment: "You are capable of creating cadres who can endure torture and imprisonment in silence but not of training cadres who can capture a machine-gun nest." This remark in no way constitutes an appraisal of courage; it is a political evaluation. It is not a matter of replacing cowardice with courage, still less one ideology with another, but of one form of courage with another, one pattern of action (and of psychic identification) with another; that is to say, of accepting the ultimate consequences of one's principles, right up to the point where they demand of the militant other forms of action and other responses from his nervous system.

We can now pose the second question.

How to overcome these deficiencies? Under what conditions can these parties resume their vanguard function, including guerrilla warfare? Is it by their own political work on themselves, or is some other form of education historically necessary? If we are to answer these questions regarding the future, we must look not at the past but at the present. Briefly, the question might be posed as follows:

How is a vanguard party formed? Can the party, under existing Latin American conditions, create the popular army, or is it up to the popular army to create the vanguard? Which is the nucleus of which?

For reasons beyond their control, many Latin American Communist parties made a false start, thirty or forty years ago, thus creating a complicated situation. But parties are never anything but instruments of class struggle. Where the instrument no longer serves its purpose, should the class struggle come to a halt or should new instruments be forged? A childish question: no one can make such a decision. The class struggle, especially in Latin America today, can be curbed, eroded, deflected, but it cannot be stopped. The people devise their own vanguards, making do with what is available, and the duty of revolutionaries is to hasten this development. But the development of what, precisely?

We are witnessing today, here and there, strange reversals. Che Guevara wrote that the guerrilla movement is not an end in itself, nor is it a glorious adventure; it is merely a means to an end: the conquest of political power. But, lo and behold, guerrilla forces were serving many other purposes: a form of pressure on bourgeois governments; a factor in political horse-trading; a trump card to be played in case of need—such were the objectives with which certain leaderships were attempting to saddle their military instrumentalities. The revolutionary method was being utilized for reformist ends. Then, after a period of marking time, the guerrillas turned away from and rejected these goals imposed from outside and assumed their own political leadership. To become reconciled with itself the guerrilla force set itself up as a political leadership, which was the only way to resolve the contradictions and to develop militarily. Let it be noted that no part of the guerrilla movement has attempted to organize a new party; it seeks rather to wipe out doctrinal or party divisions among its own combatants. The unifying factors are the war and its immediate political objectives. The guerrilla movement begins by creating unity within itself around the most urgent military tasks, which have already become political tasks, a unity of nonparty elements and of all the parties represented among the *guerrilleros*. The most decisive political choice is membership in the guerrilla forces, in the Armed Forces of Liberation. Thus gradually this small army creates rank-and-file unity among all parties, as it grows and wins its first victories. Eventually the future people's army will beget the party of which it is to be, theoretically, the instrument: essentially the party is the army.

Did not the Cuban Revolution experience this same paradox? It has been said with dismay that the party, the usual instrument for the seizure of power, was developed *after* the conquest of power. But no, it already existed in embryo—in the form of the rebel army. Fidel, its commander-in-chief, was already an unofficial party leader by early 1959. A foreign journalist in Cuba was astonished one day to see many communist leaders in battle-dress; he had thought that battle-dress and pistols belonged to the folklore of the Revolution, that they were really a kind of martial affectation. Poor man! It was not an affectation, it was the history of the Revolution itself appearing before his eyes, and most certainly the future history of America. Just as the name of socialism was formally applied to the Revolution after a year of socialist practice, the name of the party came into use three years after the proletarian party had begun to exist in uniform. In Cuba it was not the party that was the directive nucleus of the popular army, as it had been in Vietnam according to Giap; the rebel army was the leading nucleus of the party, the nucleus that created it. The first party leaders were created on 26 July 1953 at Moncada. The party is the same age as the revolution; it will be fourteen on 26 July 1967. Moncada was the nucleus of the rebel army, which was in turn the nucleus of the party. Around this nucleus, and only because it already had its own political-military leadership, other political forces have been able to assemble and unite, forming what is today the Communist party of Cuba, of which both the base and the head continue to be made up of comrades from the guerrilla army.

The Latin American revolution and its vanguard, the Cuban revolution, have thus made a decisive contribution to international revolutionary experience and to Marxism-Leninism.

Under certain conditions, the political and the military are not separate, but form one organic whole, consisting of the people's army, whose nucleus is the guerrilla army. The vanguard party can exist in the form of the guerrilla foco *itself. The guerrilla force is the party in embryo.*

This is the staggering novelty introduced by the Cuban Revolution.

Carlos Marighella

From the "Minimanual"

A Definition of the Urban Guerrilla

The chronic structural crisis characteristic of Brazil today, and its resultant political instability, are what have brought about the upsurge of revolutionary war in the country. The revolutionary war manifests itself in the form of urban guerrilla warfare, psychological warfare, or rural guerrilla warfare. Urban guerrilla warfare or psychological warfare in the city depends on the urban guerrilla.

The urban guerrilla is a man who fights the military dictatorship with arms, using unconventional methods. A political revolutionary and an ardent patriot, he is a fighter for his country's liberation, a friend of the people and of freedom. The area in which the urban guerrilla acts is in the large Brazilian cities. There are also bandits, commonly known as outlaws, who work in the big cities. Many times assaults by outlaws are taken as actions by urban guerrillas.

The urban guerrilla, however, differs radically from the outlaw. The outlaw benefits personally from the action, and attacks indiscriminately without distinguishing between the exploited and the exploiters, which is why there are so many ordinary men and women among his victims. The urban guerrilla follows a political goal and only attacks the government, the big capitalists, and the foreign imperialists, particularly North Americans.

Another element just as prejudicial as the outlaw and also operating in the urban area is the right-wing counterrevolutionary who creates confusion, assaults banks, hurls bombs, kidnaps, assassinates, and commits the worst imaginable crimes against urban guerrillas,

Carlos Marighella, *Minimanual of the Urban Guerrilla* (London, n.d.).

revolutionary priests, students, and citizens who oppose fascism and seek liberty.

The urban guerrilla is an implacable enemy of the government and systematically inflicts damage on the authorities and on the men who dominate the country and exercise power. The principal task of the urban guerrilla is to distract, to wear out, to demoralize the militarists, the military dictatorship and its repressive forces, and also to attack and destroy the wealth and property of the North Americans, the foreign managers, and the Brazilian upper class.

The urban guerrilla is not afraid of dismantling and destroying the present Brazilian economic, political, and social system, for his aim is to help the rural guerrilla and to collaborate in the creation of a totally new and revolutionary social and political structure, with the armed people in power . . .

Personal Qualities of the Urban Guerrilla and How He Subsists

The urban guerrilla is characterized by his bravery and decisive nature. He must be a good tactician and a good shot. The urban guerrilla must be a person of great astuteness to compensate for the fact that he is not sufficiently strong in arms, ammunition, and equipment.

The career militarists or the government police have modern arms and transport, and can go about anywhere freely, using the force of their power. The urban guerrilla does not have such resources at his disposal and leads a clandestine existence. Sometimes he is a convicted person or is out on parole, and is obliged to use false documents.

Nevertheless, the urban guerrilla has a certain advantage over the conventional military or the police. It is that, while the military and the police act on behalf of the enemy, whom the people hate, the urban guerrilla defends a just cause, which is the people's cause.

The urban guerrilla's arms are inferior to the enemy's, but from a moral point of view, the urban guerrilla has an undeniable superiority.

This moral superiority is what sustains the urban guerrilla. Thanks to it, the urban guerrilla can accomplish his principal duty, which is to attack and to survive.

The urban guerrilla has to capture or divert arms from the enemy to be able to fight. Because his arms are not uniform, since what he has are expropriated or have fallen into his hands in different ways, the urban guerrilla faces the problem of a variety of arms and a shortage of ammunition. Moreover, he has no place to practice shooting and marksmanship.

These difficulties have to be surmounted, forcing the urban guerrilla to be imaginative and creative, qualities without which it would be impossible for him to carry out his role as a revolutionary.

The urban guerrilla must possess initiative, mobility, and flexibility, as well as versatility and a command of any situation. Initiative especially is an indispensable quality. It is not always possible to foresee everything, and the urban guerrilla cannot let himself become confused, or wait for orders. His duty is to act, to find adequate solutions for each problem he faces, and not to retreat. It is better to err acting than to do nothing for fear of erring. Without initiative there is no urban guerrilla warfare.

Other important qualities in the urban guerrilla are the following: to be a good walker, to be able to stand up against fatigue, hunger, rain, heat. To know how to hide and to be vigilant. To conquer the art of dissembling. Never to fear danger. To behave the same by day as by night. Not to act impetuously. To have unlimited patience. To remain calm and cool in the worst conditions and situations. Never to leave a track or trail. Not to get discouraged.

In the face of the almost insurmountable difficulties of urban warfare, sometimes comrades weaken, leave, give up the work.

The urban guerrilla is not a businessman in a commercial firm nor is he a character in a play. Urban guerrilla warfare, like rural guerrilla warfare, is a pledge the guerrilla makes to himself. When he cannot face the difficulties, or knows that he lacks the patience to wait, then it is better to relinquish his role before he betrays his pledge, for he clearly lacks the basic qualities necessary to be a guerrilla.

The urban guerrilla must know how to live among the people and must be careful not to appear strange and separated from ordinary city life.

He should not wear clothes that are different from those that other people wear. Elaborate and high fashion clothing for men or women may often be a handicap if the urban guerrilla's mission takes him into working-class neighborhoods or sections where such dress is uncommon. The same care has to be taken if the urban guerrilla moves from the south to the north or vice versa.

The urban guerrilla must live by his work or professional activity. If he is known and sought by the police, if he is convicted or is on parole, he must go underground and sometimes must live hidden. Under such circumstances, the urban guerrilla cannot reveal his activity to anyone, since that is always and only the responsibility of the revolutionary organization in which he is participating.

The urban guerrilla must have a great capacity for observation, must be well informed about everything, principally about the enemy's movements, and must be very searching and knowledgeable about the area in which he lives, operates, or through which he moves.

But the fundamental and decisive characteristic of the urban guerrilla is that he is a man who fights with arms; given this condition, there is very little likelihood that he will be able to follow his normal profession for long without being identified. The role of expropriation thus looms as clear as high noon. It is impossible for the urban guerrilla to exist and survive without fighting to expropriate.

Thus, within the framework of the class struggle, as it inevitably and necessarily sharpens, the armed struggle of the urban guerrilla points toward two essential objectives:

(a) the physical liquidation of the chiefs and assistants of the armed forces and of the police;

(b) the expropriation of government resources and those belonging to the big capitalists, latifundists, and imperialists, with small expropriations used for the maintenance of individual urban guerrillas and large ones for the sustenance of the revolution itself.

It is clear that the armed struggle of the urban guerrilla also has other objectives. But here we are referring to the two basic objectives, above all expropriation. It is necessary for every urban guerrilla to keep in mind always that he can only maintain his existence if he is disposed to kill the police and those dedicated to repression, and if he is determined—truly determined—to expropriate the wealth of the big capitalists, the latifundists, and the imperialists.

One of the fundamental characteristics of the Brazilian revolution is that from the beginning it developed around the expropriation of the wealth of the major bourgeois, imperialist, and latifundist interests, without excluding the richest and most powerful commercial elements engaged in the import–export business.

And by expropriating the wealth of the principal enemies of the people, the Brazilian revolution was able to hit them at their vital center, with preferential and systematic attacks on the banking network—that is to say, the most telling blows were leveled against capitalism's nerve system.

The bank robberies carried out by the Brazilian urban guerrillas hurt such big capitalists as Moreira Salles and others, the foreign firms which insure and reinsure the banking capital, the imperialist companies, the federal and state governments—all of them systematically expropriated as of now.

The fruit of these expropriations has been devoted to the work of learning and perfecting urban guerrilla techniques, the purchase, the production, and the transportation of arms and ammunition for the rural areas, the security apparatus of the revolutionaries, the daily maintenance of the fighters, of those who have been liberated from prison by armed force and those who are wounded or persecuted by the police, or to any kind of problem concerning comrades liberated from jail, or assassinated by the police and the military dictatorship.

The tremendous costs of the revolutionary war must fall on the big capitalists, on imperialism, and the latifundists and on the government too, both federal and state, since they are all exploiters and oppressors of the people.

Men of the government, agents of the dictatorship and of North American imperialism principally, must pay with their lives for the crimes committed against the Brazilian people.

In Brazil, the number of violent actions carried out by urban guerrillas, including deaths, explosions, seizures of arms, ammunition, and explosives, assaults on banks and prisons, etc., is significant enough to leave no room for doubt as to the actual aims of the revolutionaries. The execution of the CIA spys Charles Chandler, a member of the US Army who came from the war in Vietnam to infiltrate the Brazilian student movement, the military henchmen killed in bloody encounters with urban guerrillas, all are witness to the fact that we are in full revolutionary war and that the war can be waged only by violent means.

This is the reason why the urban guerrilla uses armed struggle and why he continues to concentrate his activity on the physical extermination of the agents of repression, and to dedicate twenty-four hours a day to expropriation from the people's exploiters.

Technical Preparation of the Urban Guerrilla

No one can become an urban guerrilla without paying special attention to technical preparation.

The technical preparation of the urban guerrilla runs from the concern for his physical preparedness, to knowledge of and apprenticeship in professions and skills of all kinds, particularly manual skills.

The urban guerrilla can have strong physical resistance only if he trains systematically. He cannot be a good fighter if he has not learned the art of fighting. For that reason the urban guerrilla must learn and practice various kinds of fighting, of attack, and personal defense.

Other useful forms of physical preparation are hiking, camping, and practice in survival in the woods, mountain climbing, rowing, swimming, skin diving, training as a frogman, fishing, harpooning, and the hunting of birds, small and big game.

It is very important to learn how to drive, pilot a plane, handle a motorboat and a sailboat, understand mechanics, radio, telephone, electricity, and have some knowledge of electronic techniques.

It is also important to have a knowledge of topographical information, to be able to locate one's position by instruments or other available resources, to calculate distances, make maps and plans, draw to scale, make timings, work with an angle protractor, a compass, etc.

A knowledge of chemistry and of color combination, of stamp-making, the domination of the technique of calligraphy and the copying of letters and other skills are part of the technical preparation of the urban guerrilla, who is obliged to falsify documents in order to live within a society that he seeks to destroy.

In the area of auxiliary medicine he has the special role of being a doctor or understanding medicine, nursing, pharmacology, drugs, elementary surgery, and emergency first aid.

The basic question in the technical preparation of the urban guerrilla is nevertheless to know how to handle arms such as the machine gun, revolver, automatic, various types of shotguns, carbines, mortars, bazookas, etc.

A knowledge of various types of ammunition and explosives is another aspect to consider. Among the explosives, dynamite must be well understood. The use of incendiary bombs, of smoke bombs, and other types is indispensable prior knowledge.

To know how to make and repair arms, prepare Molotov cocktails, grenades, mines, home-made destructive devices, how to blow up bridges, tear up and put out of service rails and sleepers, these are requisites in the technical preparation of the urban guerrilla that can never be considered unimportant.

The highest level of preparation or the urban guerrilla is the center for technical training. But only the guerrilla who has already passed the preliminary examination can go on to this school—that is to say, one who has passed the proof of fire in revolutionary action, in actual combat against the enemy. . . .

The Seven Sins of the Urban Guerrilla

Even when the urban guerrilla applies his revolutionary technique with precision and rigorously abides by security rules, he can still be vulnerable to errors. There is no perfect urban guerrilla. The most he can do is to make every effort to diminish the margin of error since he cannot be perfect.

One of the methods we should use to diminish the margin of error is to know thoroughly the seven sins of the urban guerrilla and try to fight them.

The first sin of the urban guerrilla is inexperience. The urban guerrilla, blinded by this sin, thinks the enemy is stupid, underestimates his intelligence, believes everything is easy and, as a result, leaves clues that can lead to his disaster.

Because of his inexperience, the urban guerrilla can also overestimate the forces of the enemy, believing them to be stronger than they really are. Allowing himself to be fooled by this presumption, the urban guerrilla becomes intimidated, and remains insecure and indecisive, paralyzed and lacking in audacity.

The second sin of the urban guerrilla is to boast about the actions he has completed and broadcast them to the four winds.

The third sin of the urban guerrilla is vanity. The urban guerrilla who suffers from this sin tries to solve the problems of the revolution by actions erupting in the city, but without bothering about the beginnings and the survival of the guerrilla in rural areas. Blinded by success, he winds up organizing an action that he considers decisive and that puts into play all the forces and resources of the organization. Since the city is the area of the strategic circle which we cannot avoid or break while rural guerrilla warfare has not yet erupted and is not at the point of triumph, we always run the fatal error of permitting the enemy to attack us with decisive blows.

The fourth sin of the urban guerrilla is to exaggerate his strength and to undertake projects for which he lacks forces and, as yet, does not have the required infrastructure.

The fifth sin of the urban guerrilla is precipitous action. The urban guerrilla who commits this sin loses patience, suffers an attack of nerves, does not wait for anything, and impetuously throws himself into action, suffering untold reverses.

The sixth sin of the urban guerrilla is to attack the enemy when he is most angry.

The seventh sin of the urban guerrilla is to fail to plan things, and to act out of improvisation.

Popular Support

One of the permanent concerns of the urban guerrilla is his identification with popular causes to win public support.

Where government actions become inept and corrupt, the urban guerrilla should not hesitate to step in to show that he opposes the government and to gain mass sympathy. The present government, for example, imposes heavy financial burdens and excessively high taxes on the people. It is up to the urban guerrilla to attack the dictatorship's tax collection system and to obstruct its financial activity, throwing all the weight of violent revolutionary action against it.

The urban guerrilla fights not only to upset the tax and collection system; the arm of revolutionary violence must also be directed against those government organs that raise prices and those who direct them, as well as against the wealthiest of the national and foreign profiteers and the important property owners; in short, against all those who accumulate huge fortunes out of the high cost of living, the wages of hunger, excessive prices and rents.

Foreign trusts, such as refrigeration and other North American plants that monopolize the market and the manufacture of general food supplies, must be sytematically attacked by the urban guerrilla.

The rebellion of the urban guerrilla and his persistence in intervening in public questions is the best way of insuring public support of the cause we defend. We repeat and insist on repeating: *it is the best way of insuring public support.* As soon as a reasonable section of the population begins to take seriously the action of the urban guerrilla, his success is guaranteed.

The government has no alternative except to intensify repression. The police networks, house searches, arrests of innocent people and of suspects, closing off streets, make life in the city unbearable. The military dictatorship embarks on massive political persecution. Political assassinations and police terror become routine.

In spite of all this, the police systematically fail. The armed forces, the navy, and the air force are mobilized and undertake routine police functions. Even so they find no way to halt guerrilla operations, nor to wipe out the revolutionary organization with its fragmented groups that move around and operate throughout the national territory persistently and contagiously.

The people refuse to collaborate with the authorities, and the general sentiment is that the government is unjust, incapable of solving problems, and resorts purely and simply to the physical liquidation of its opponents.

The political situation in the country is transformed into a military situation in which the "gorillas" appear more and more to be the ones responsible for errors and violence, while the problems in the lives of the people become truly catastrophic.

When they see the militarists and the dictatorship on the brink of the abyss, and fearing the consequences of a revolutionary war which is already at a fairly advanced and irreversible level, the pacifiers, always to be found within the ruling classes, and the right-wing opportunists, partisans of nonviolent struggle, join hands and circulate rumors behind the scenes, begging the hangmen for elections, "redemocratization," constitutional reforms, and other tripe designed to fool the masses and make them stop the revolutionary rebellion in the cities and the rural areas of the country.

But, watching the revolutionaries, the people now understand that it is a farce to vote in elections which have as their sole objective guaranteeing the continuation of the military dictatorship and covering up its crimes.

Attacking wholeheartedly this election farce and the so-called political solution so appealing to the opportunists, the urban guerrilla must become more aggressive and violent, resorting without let-up to sabotage, terrorism, expropriations, assaults, kidnappings, executions, etc.

This answers any attempt to fool the masses with the opening of Congress and the reorganization of political parties—parties of the government and of the opposition it allows—when all the time the parliament and the so-called parties function thanks to the license of the military dictatorship in a true spectacle of marionettes and dogs on a leash.

The role of the urban guerrilla, in order to win the support of the people, is to continue fighting, keeping in mind the interests of the masses and heightening the disastrous situation in which the government must act. These are the circumstances, disastrous for the dictatorship, which permit the revolutionaries to open rural guerrilla warfare in the midst of the uncontrollable expansion of urban rebellion.

The urban guerrilla is engaged in revolutionary action in favor of the people and with it seeks the participation of the masses in the struggle against the military dictatorship and for the liberation of the country from the yoke of the United States. Beginning with the city and with the support of the people, the rural guerrilla war develops rapidly, establishing its infrastructure carefully while the urban area continues the rebellion.

Abraham Guillen

Urban Guerrilla Strategy

If 70 percent of a country's population is urban, the demography and the economy must dictate the specific rules of the strategy of revolutionary combat. The center of operations should never be in the mountains or in the villages, but in the largest cities where the population suffices to form the army of the revolution. In such cases, the countryside must support the actions of urban guerrillas through its clandestine local militias (groups of self-defense), who work during the day and fight at night, encouraged by a program of agrarian reform that gives the land to those who cultivate it.

Some of the urban centers in underdeveloped countries such as Buenos Aires and Montevideo have respectively more than 30 percent and 50 percent of the total population of the country. The capitals of these countries including their suburban zones constitute a sea of houses which extends for miles. But in the interior of the country the population of the ranches consists more of animals than men. There are fewer inhabitants per square mile than there were in the Middle Ages in Europe. The great cattle ranges have contributed to transferring population from the countryside to the slums of the city. At the same time, capitalist monopoly concentrates the workers in the cities, extracting them from the marginal population of the countryside. Strategically, in the case of a popular revolution in a country in which the highest percentage of the population is urban, the center of operations of the revolutionary war should be in the city. Operations should consist of scattered surprise attacks by quick and mobile units superior in arms and numbers at designated points,

Abraham Guillen, *Estrategia de la guerrilla urbana* (c. 1971), translated in Donald C. Hodges (ed.), *Philosophy of the Urban Guerrilla* (New York, 1973).

but avoiding barricades in order not to attract the enemy's attention at one place. The units will then attack with the greatest part of their strength the enemy's least fortified or weakest links in the city.

In those countries with more than 50 percent urban population (72 percent in Argentina and 84 percent in Uruguay), the revolutionary battle should preferably be not in the mountains and countrysides but in the urban areas. For the revolution's potential is where the population is. In the provinces without a dense population there are possibilities of creating hundreds of incidents in order to attract a part of the enemy troops (the more the better) through hundreds of separate guerrilla actions. Thus when the enemy is dispersed throughout the country, it is conquered by the concentration of the revolutionary army upon the cities, the rear guard of the revolution. To achieve victory over a powerful army that is hated by the population, it is necessary to scatter it, attracting it here and there, defeating it in small battles in a suitable field for the urban guerrillas, until the population turns against it and more and more people join the army of liberation, regional echelons, and groups of self-defense (local guerrillas).

Each system of production contains its law of the social division of labor, which allocates in time and space the means of production and the population. The city regularly produces machinery and other goods for the countryside, receiving food and raw materials in return. If the rural guerrillas interrupt the communication between city and countryside by means of nocturnal sabotage, food and raw materials will not flow normally into the city. It is the purpose of this strategy to shatter the functioning of the law of the division of labor, the exchange between countryside and city. The city without food is a disintegrating world. The countryside, however, can subsist for a longer period of time without manufactured goods from the cities. Consequently, not even in those countries with a high percentage of urban population is an effective strategy possible without including the countryside. Cooperation between the laborer and the peasant is essential to the revolution.

In those countries with a high percentage of urban population in which the economic system is concentrated upon one, two, or three cities, revolutionary warfare must preferably be urban, without excluding the cooperation of the rural militias, whose job is to attract part of the urban military forces in order to preserve the initiative of the army of liberation. . . . Buenos Aires represents approximately 70 percent of the wealth, the consumption of energy, the transportation, the industry, the commerce, and in general the greater part of the Argentine economy. Santiago de Chile, Lima, Rio de Janeiro, Mexico City, Bogotá, and other Latin American capitals do not have the concentrated economic power of Buenos Aires and Montevideo. . . . Revolutionary warfare is preferably rural in Brazil, although it has its center of operations in the cities of the River Plate. Brazil is a country in which the war must be conducted against an enormous mass of counterrevolutionary troops, while Uruguay and Argentina must undertake prolonged urban warfare based on many small military victories which together will render the final victory.

* * *

Assessment of the Uruguayan Tupamaros

To the credit of the Uruguayan guerrillas, they were the first to operate in the cement jungles of a capitalist metropolis, to endure during the first phase of a revolutionary war thanks to an efficient organization and tactics, and to confound the police and armed forces for a considerable period. . . . With its failures as well as successes, the Movement of National Liberation (Tupamaros) has contributed a model of urban guerrilla warfare that has already made a mark on contemporary history—the scene of a struggle between capitalism and socialism with its epicenter in the great cities. The lessons that can be learned from the Tupamaros can be summarized in the following ten points.

1. *Fixed or Mobile Front?* When urban guerrillas lack widespread support because of revolutionary impatience or because their actions do not directly represent popular demands, they have to provide their own clandestine infrastructure by renting houses and apartments. By tying themselves to a fixed terrain in this way, the Tupamaros have lost both mobility and security: two prerequisites of guerrilla strategy. In order to avoid encirclement and annihilation through house-to-house searches, the guerrillas can best survive not by establishing fixed urban bases, but by living apart and fighting together.

2. *Mobility and Security.* If urban guerrillas rent houses for their

commandos, they are in danger of leaving a trail that may be followed by the police who review monthly all registered rentals. Should most of their houses be loaned instead of leased, then the guerrillas should refrain as a general rule from building underground vaults or hideouts which would increase their dependence on the terrain. To retain their mobility and a high margin of security they must spread out among a favorable population. Guerrillas who fight together and then disperse throughout a great city are not easily detected by the police. When dragnets are applied to one neighborhood or zone, guerrillas without a fixed base can shift to another neighborhood. Such mobility is precluded by a reliance on rented houses or hideouts in the homes of sympathizers, heretofore a major strategical error of the Tupamaros.

3. *Heavy or Light Rear Guard?* Urban guerrillas who develop a heavy infrastructure in many rented houses commit not only a military error, but also an economic and logistical one. For a heavy rear guard requires a comparatively large monthly budget in which economic and financial motives tend to overshadow political considerations. Lacking enough houses, the guerrillas tend to upgrade to positions of command those willing to lend their own. Among the Tupamaros detained in 1972 was the owner of the hacienda "Spartacus," which housed an armory in an underground vault. At about the same time the president of the frigorific plant of Cerro Largo was detained and sentenced for aiding the Tupamaros. He may well have embraced the cause of the Tupamaros with loyalty and sincerity; but as a businessman he responded as any other bourgeois would to his workers' demands for higher wages. Thus when promotion through the ranks is facilitated by owning a big house, a large farm or enterprise, the guerrillas become open to bourgeois tendencies. When guerrillas rely for cover not on a people in arms but on people of property, then urban guerrilla warfare becomes the business of an armed minority, which will never succeed in mobilizing in this manner the majority of the population.

4. *Logistical Infrastructure.* Although a mobile front is preferable to a fixed one, there are circumstances in which a fixed front is unavoidable, e.g., in the assembly, adjustment, and adaptation of arms. These fixed fronts, few and far between, must be concealed from the guerrillas themselves; they should be known only to the few who work there, preferably one person in each, in order to avoid discovery

by the repressive forces. In the interest of security it is advisable not to manufacture arms, but to have the parts made separately by various legal establishments, after which they can be assembled in the secret workshops of the guerrillas.

It is dangerous to rely on a fixed front for housing, food, medical supplies, and armaments. If the guerrillas are regularly employed, they should live as everybody else does; they should come together only at designated times and places. Houses that serve as barracks or hideouts tend to immobilize the guerrillas and to expose them to the possibility of encirclement and annihilation. Because the Tupamaros immobilized many of their commandos in fixed quarters, they were exposed in 1972 to mass detentions; they lost a large part of their armaments and related equipment and were compelled to transfer military supplies to the countryside for hiding.

In abusing control over their sympathizers and keeping them under strict military discipline, the Tupamaros had to house them together. But they were seldom used in military operations at a single place or in several simultaneously, indicating the absence of strategical preparation. If urban guerrillas cannot continually disappear and reappear among the population of a great city, then they lack the political prerequisites for making a revolution, for creating the conditions of a social crisis through the breakdown of "law and order." Despite their proficiency during the first hit-and-run phase of a revolutionary war, the Tupamaros have failed to escalate their operations by using larger units at more frequent intervals for the purpose of paralyzing the existing regime.

5. *Heroes, Martyrs, and Avengers.* In revolutionary war any guerrilla action that needs explaining to the people is politically useless: it should be meaningful and convincing by itself. To kill an ordinary soldier in reprisal for the assassination of a guerrilla is to descend to the same political level as a reactionary army. Far better to create a martyr and thereby attract mass sympathy than to lose or neutralize popular support by senseless killings without an evident political goal. To be victorious in a people's war one has to act in conformity with the interests, sentiments, and will of the people. A military victory is worthless if it fails to be politically convincing.

In a country where the bourgeoisie has abolished the death penalty, it is self-defeating to condemn to death even the most hated enemies of the people. Oppressors, traitors, and informers have condemned themselves before the guerrillas; it is impolitic to make a public show of their crimes for the purpose of creating a climate of terror, insecurity, and disregard for basic human rights. A popular army that resorts to unnecessary violence, that is not a symbol of justice, equity, liberty, and security, cannot win popular support in the struggle against a dehumanized tyranny.

The Tupamaros' "prisons of the people" do more harm than benefit to the cause of national liberation. Taking hostages for the purpose of exchanging them for political prisoners has an immediate popular appeal; but informing the world of the existence of "people's prisons" is to focus unnecessarily on a parallel system of repression. No useful purpose can be served by such politically alienating language. Moreover, it is intolerable to keep anyone hostage for a long time. To achieve a political or propaganda victory through this kind of tactic, the ransom terms must be moderate and capable of being met; in no event should the guerrillas be pressed into executing a prisoner because their demands are excessive and accordingly rejected. A hostage may be usefully executed only when a government refuses to negotiate on any terms after popular pressure has been applied; for then it is evident to everyone that the government is ultimately responsible for the outcome.

So-called people's prisons are harmful for other reasons: they require several men to stand guard and care for the prisoners; they distract guerrillas from carrying out alternative actions more directly useful to the population; and they presuppose a fixed front and corresponding loss of mobility. At most it is convenient to have a secure place to detain for short periods a single hostage.

To establish people's prisons, to condemn to death various enemies of the people, to house the guerrillas in secret barracks or underground hideouts is to create an infrastructure supporting a miniature state rather than a revolutionary army. To win the support of the population, arms must be used directly on its behalf. Whoever uses violence against subordinates in the course of building a miniature counterstate should be removed from his command. Surely, there is little point in defeating one despotism only to erect another in its place!

6. *Delegated Commands.* In a professional army the leadership is recruited from the military academies within a hierarchical order of command. In a guerrilla organization the leaders emerge in actual

revolutionary struggles, elected because of their capacity, responsibility, combativity, initiative, political understanding and deeds rather than words. However, at pain of forfeiting the democratic character of a revolutionary army and the function of authority as a delegated power, not even the best guerrilla commander can be allowed to remain long at the helm. A rotating leadership is necessary to avoid the "cult of personality"; power should be alternately exercised by those commanders with the most victories, by those most popular with their soldiers and most respected by the people. Inasmuch as guerrilla warfare takes the form of self-defense, its success depends on the exercise of direct democracy, on guerrilla self-management and self-discipline—a far cry from the barracks discipline typical of a bureaucratic or professional army. . . .

The people have more need of many revolutionary heroes than of a single outstanding leader like Julius Caesar or Napoleon Bonaparte. Epaminondas, the Theban general who defeated the Spartans, held a command that lasted only two years. Although the greatest strategist of his time, he became an ordinary soldier when his command expired. Only because of his extraordinary skill was he made a military adviser to the new commander-in-chief. Guerrillas can benefit by his example.

A delegated command is unlimited except for the time determining its delegation. The responsibility of subordinates is to discuss in advance each operation, to make recommendations, etc. But the discussion ends when the supreme command assumes responsibility for the outcome of a particular battle or engagement. If the commander is mistaken in his judgment, if the result is defeat rather than victory, his duty is to resign. Should he succeed in a vote of confidence he may retain his command; but two successive defeats should make his resignation irrevocable.

One of the most common errors of Latin American guerrillas is to make legends of their leaders as they did of Fidel Castro and Che Guevara. The resulting messianism conceals the incapacity of many guerrilla commanders who take their troops into the countryside— like the Tupamaros in 1972—without revising mistaken strategies. Perhaps the leaders of the Uruguayan guerrillas have come to believe in their providential powers, thereby reducing the ordinary guerrilla to a political and military zero, to the status of a soldier in a conventional army . . .

In their endeavor to create a state within the state through highly disciplined guerrilla columns, secret barracks, "prisons of the people," underground arsenals, and a heavy logistical infrastructure, the Tupamaros have become overly professionalized, militarized, and isolated from the urban masses. Their organization is closer to resembling a parallel power contesting the legally established one, a microstate, rather than a movement of the masses.

7. *Strategy, Tactics, and Politics.* If the tactics adopted are successful but the corresponding strategy and politics mistaken, the guerrillas cannot win. Should a succession of tactical victories encourage a strategical objective that is impossible to attain, then a great tactical victory can culminate in an even greater strategical defeat.

The kidnappings of the Brazilian consul Días Gomide and the CIA agent Dan Mitrione are instances of tactical successes by the Tupamaros. But in demanding in exchange a hundred detained guerrillas, the Tupamaros found the Uruguayan government obstinate, in order not to lose face altogether. Here a successful tactic contributed to an impossible strategical objective. In having to execute Mitrione because the government failed to comply to their demands, the Tupamaros not only failed to accomplish a political objective, but also suffered a political reversal in their newly acquired role of assassins—the image they acquired through hostile mass media.

The Tupamaros would have done better by taping Mitrione's declarations and giving the story to the press. The population would have followed the incidents of his confession with more interest than the interminable serials. Mitrione's confessed links with the CIA should have been fully documented and sent to Washington in care of Senator Fulbright. With this incident brought to the attention of Congress, the operation against the CIA would have won world support for the Tupamaros. Once the Uruguayan government had lost prestige through this publicity, the Uruguayan press might be asked to publish a manifesto of the Tupamaros explaining their objectives in the Mitrione case. Afterward his death sentence should have been commuted out of respect for his eight sons, but on condition that he leave the country. Such a solution to the government's refusal to negotiate with the guerrillas would have captured the sympathies of many in favor of the Tupamaros. Even more than conventional war, revolutionary war is a form of politics carried out by violent means.

With respect to Días Gomide the Tupamaros lost an opportunity to embarrass politically the Brazilian government. They should never have allowed matters to reach the point at which his wife could appear as an international heroine of love and marital fidelity by collecting sums for his release. Every cruzeiro she collected was a vote against the Tupamaros and indirectly against the Brazilian guerrillas. In exchange for Días Gomide, a man of considerable importance to the military regime, the Tupamaros should have demanded the publication of a manifesto in the Brazilian press. Its contents might have covered the following items: a denunciation of the "death squad" as an informal instrument of the Brazilian dictatorship; a demand for free, secret, and direct elections; the legalization of all political parties dissolved by the military regime; the restitution of political rights to Brazil's former leaders and exiles including Quadros, Kubitschek, Brizola, Goulart, and even reactionaries like Lacerda; the denunciation of government censorship of the press; and a demand that popular priests be set free. With such a political response the revolutionary war might have been exported to Brazil. Guerrilla actions should not be narrowly circumscribed when they can have regional and international repercussions. . . .

The Tupamaros are perilously close to resembling a political Mafia. In demanding large sums of money in ransom for political hostages they have sometimes appeared to be self-serving. It matters little to the average citizen whether bank deposits pass into the hands of "expropriators" who do little directly to lighten the public burden— not because they do not want to but because they cannot do so in isolation from the people and without popular support. There is an historical irony about these would-be liberators who indirectly live off the surplus of the people they liberate. . . .

Amilcar Cabral

Revolutionary War in Africa

We have already made a critical review of our armed forces, just as we had previously praised them. In Africa, our armed forces were among the best, and today we can say that in our country we have one of the foremost armed forces of Africa. We have really known how to fight. We have fought with the utmost courage, and with extreme courage we have achieved wonderful things; in a country as small as Guinea, we have managed to withstand an enemy strength of over forty thousand men possessing tanks, aircraft, ships, and bombs of the most fearful kind. We have laid ambushes and so destroyed hundreds of enemy vehicles; we have sunk ships. We managed to begin a new phase: we attacked enemy barracks—and we shall do it again. Our armed forces and our country's valiant fighters deserve all praise. Our responsible agents, too, especially those who have carried out our party leadership's commands concerning the armed forces, deserve all our respect and esteem.

We must not forget that there have been mistakes, lapses, and delays such as, for example, ill-conceived ambushes, a tendency to arrive late at rendezvous, a lack of watchfulness, notably on rivers (although we are well equipped to fire on ships), and a want of courage in shooting at aircraft (although we know that the more we fire on them, the more fear is felt by the airmen). Although it was known that at Quitapine and in other regions such as Boe our comrades fought with extraordinary courage against Portuguese aircraft, many did not follow their example. In many districts, we delayed our attacks and immobilized our infantry for a long time. "Patchanga"*

Amilcar Cabral, *Unité et lutte, Vol. II: La pratique révolutionnaire* (Paris, 1973).

* The PPSM, a Soviet-made automatic weapon.

loaders were often damaged by loading without being emptied in firing. We failed to make the necessary reconnaissance before attacking. As a result, we frequently discovered mines in our path as we attacked. We could not lay down the plans needed for an attack; a general plan of action might be directed from above, but when the men were actually on the field at the point of attack, some commanders discovered they were unable to make specific plans. We therefore could not achieve the maximum advantage from these attacks. For instance, we must admit that to this day Portuguese prisoners have been taken in only two attacks: at Cantacunda and Bissassema—little enough considering all the assaults we have made on barracks. At a time when the Portuguese are fleeing from over twenty barracks, we can assess all the chances we have missed of killing or taking prisoner great numbers of the enemy. Unfortunately, a lack of watchfulness, constancy, and tenacity is the most typical fault in our armed forces.

The prerequisite for improving our armed forces is for our commanders to improve their work. We must have no more commanders who command nothing but simply make a profit out of their commands; no more coordinators who coordinate nothing but their private lives; and no men in charge of the armed conflict who, because they are near the border, spend most of their time away from their posts. We must finish with them, for they deceive themselves and us. Therefore, it is the men in charge who must be improved. In fact, everyone of you here today knows that the value of a fighting man depends largely on his leader. If he is good, so will the fighters be. If he is in an attacking frame of mind, there will be an attack every day. If the leader advances, if he is brave, the fighters will attack. It may not be absolutely necessary for the commanders to attack barracks, but it is fundamental that they carry their men with them in attacking. You may well say, "Cabral, it is not always so easy; there are men who drop down squirming in agony as soon as fighting is mentioned." Yes, it is true; I know, and I know too that in every country in the world and in all wars there are men who are afraid at the moment of truth.

If, when we order a man to attack, he runs away and so unsettles his group, we have the right to kill him. That is so in any army in the world, whether it is an invading army or—and then with even more cause—an army defending its own country. Generally speaking, good commanders have good troops. Our own case shows it. Within one month, Baro Seidi twice entered Pitche with his men, showing that when the commander is good, so are the men, for the same men were at Gabu for three months without ever firing a shot . . .

However, most of the plans we had worked out were only half-executed, or not at all. Not one corps of our armed forces can say that it halted for lack of knowing what to do. What is to be done is clearly laid down; I have never had a meeting with anyone directing or responsible for armed conflict without giving him clear-cut orders in writing so that he should know what he had to do and do it. They dare not tell me to my face that they could do nothing for want of instructions. We must keep on exerting ourselves more and more to carry out the demands placed upon us, but we must also show initiative as far as our opportunities and sphere of action allow. We must follow the party line as laid down by the leadership and at the same time give proof of initiative, since no leader or leadership engaged in an armed struggle can spell out every detail of the task. Close liaison with our people must show them that our *Forces Armées Révolutionnaires du Peuple* is the FARP of our people. It is not just a name—the People's Revolutionary Armed Forces—it is our people's children who fight for the people. We must go on recruiting more men without ever deceiving our people for that purpose. We have the right to recruit our country's children. The Portuguese recruit them by force—so why should we not recruit them? We should tell them that we wish to recruit them: we should convince them by persuasion and reason, and not until we have exhausted all means of persuasion should we take the necessary measures so as not to be defeated in our struggle.

But let us avoid recruiting men we should not recruit. Among the recruits are to be seen men older than my own father; others are frail, ill, or crippled. This only compounds our difficulties, for they are often forcibly impressed and bear a grudge against us ever after. Some youngsters, too, are soon seen to be worth little and to lack courage. We should likewise fight shy of recruiting them. As a further example, we should avoid recruiting for our people's militia without knowing just who ought to be recruited. The mistakes already made in this respect might have spoiled all our work for the militia regardless of what was required by the men in charge. Remember that the militia is an armed force too. As you know, our FARP today com-

prises the people's army, the people's militia, and the people itself
in arms.

Within our armed forces we should pay paramount respect to the
principle of discipline. This is not our invention. In any army or
armed band, there must be a leader and the leader should be obeyed.
A leader is no man's master; he is leader in order to set an example
and give commands, but no man is his slave. Discipline and respect
work both ways, from lower to higher and from higher to lower. In
our armed forces we must be fully aware that an armed force is more
efficient the more mobile, trained, and active it is. Our armed forces
must recognize the principles of economy, economy of human life
and of supplies and weapons. We live off the land and our numbers
are few; thus the principles of unceasing initiative, boldness, courage,
heroism, and the principles of mobility, speed, and swiftness are essential to armed forces struggling for their country's liberation. We
should therefore arrange for our forces to be here, there, and everywhere. If we make up a group which can make repeated attacks on
the enemy and which constantly changes its position, he will think
we are many in number and our threat will frighten him. We members
of the armed forces should respect all the principles that our party
has always clearly set before our leaders and men in charge . . .

At a time when we have so many liberated zones under our command and so many men under our orders it is ridiculous that Spinola,
the governor of Bissau, should display himself with his monocle and
gloves in the towns of our country and no one even gives him a scare.
Some days ago, three schools were opened in Bissora. Spinola was
there with his gloves and his monocle. He walked through the streets
in the midst of our people . . . No one can convince me that it is
impossible to mingle disguised among the people and throw a grenade.
We might be indebted for this to members of our security forces or
our armed forces supervised by political commissars and commanders
and helped by the latter's diligent work. A grenade would kill Spinola
or would stop him from calmly walking about in urban centers . . .

A Selective Bibliography

K. Adaridi, *Freischaren und Freikorps. Auf Grund von Kriegserfahrungen*, Berlin, 1925.

F. R. Allemann, *Macht und Ohnmacht der Guerrilla*, Munich, 1974.

T. Argiolas, *La guerriglia. Storia e dottrina*, Florence, 1967.

J. A. Armstrong, K. de Witt (eds.), *Soviet Partisans in World War II*, Madison, Wisconsin, 1964.

V. Bambirra (ed.), *Diez Años de Insurrección*, 2 vols., Santiago, 1971.

A. Bayo, *150 Questions to a Guerrila*, Boulder, Colorado, 1963.

H. Bejar, *Peru 1965, Notes on a Guerrilla Experience*, New York, 1970.

J. Bowyer Bell: *Myth of the Guerrilla*, New York, 1971.

Carlo Bianco di St. Jorioz, *Della guerra nazionale d'insurrezione per bande applicata all'Italia*, Italia, 1830.

H. Blanco, *El camino de nuestra revolución*, Lima, 1964.

A. von Boguslawski, *Der kleine Krieg und seine Bedeutung für die Gegenwart*, Berlin, 1881.

G. Bonnet, *Les guerres insurrectionelles et révolutionaires de l'antiquité à nos jours*, Paris, 1958.

A. F. de Brack, *Advanced Posts of Light Cavalry*, London, 1850.

H. von Brandt, *Der kleine Krieg in seinen verschiedenen Beziehungen*, Berlin, 1850.

G. Budini, *Alcune idee sull'Italia*, London, 1843.

D. von Bülow, *Militärische und vermischte Schriften*, Leipzig, 1853.

A. Cabral, *Revolution in Guinea*, London, 1969.

A. Cabral, *Unité et lutte*, 2 vols., Paris, 1973.

C. E. Callwell, *Small Wars: Their Principles and Practice*, London, 1899.

G. Cardinal von Widdern, *Der kleine Krieg und der Etappendienst. Aus dem deutsch-französischen Krieg 1870–71*, Leipzig, 1892–97.

F. Castro, *Selected Works: Vol. I, Revolutionary Struggle*, Cambridge, Massachusetts, 1971.

L. M. Chassin, *La conquête de la Chine par Mao Tse-tung (1945–1949)*, Paris, 1952.

Chizzolini, *Della guerra nazionale*, Milan, 1863.

W. Chrzanowski, *O wojnie partyzanckiej*, Paris, 1835.

C. von Clausewitz, *Schriften-Aufsätze-Studien-Briefe*, ed. W. Hahlweg, Vol. I, Göttingen, 1966.

J. Connolly, *Revolutionary Warfare*, Dublin, 1968.

De la Croix, *Traité de la petite guerre*, Paris, 1752.

H. von Dach, *Der totale Widerstand*, Bern, 1966.

D. Davydov, *Voennie Zapiski*, Moscow, 1940.

R. Debray, *Revolution in the Revolution*, New York, 1967.

R. Debray, *Strategy for Revolution*, London, 1973.

R. Debray, *La critique des armes*, 2 vols., Paris, 1974.

C. von Decker, *Der Kleine Krieg im Geiste der neueren Kriegsführung*, Berlin, 1822.

G. Desroziers, *Combats et partisans*, Paris, 1883.

H. Eckstein (ed.), *Internal War*, New York, 1964.

A. Ehrhardt, *Kleinkrieg*, Potsdam, 1935.

J. Ellis, *A Short History of Guerrilla Warfare*, London, 1975.

A. Emmerich, *The Partisan in War*, London, 1789.

A. Emmerich, *Der Parteigänger im Kriege oder der Nutzen eines Corps leichter Truppen für eine Armes*, Dresden, 1791.

F. Engels, *Ausgewählte militärische Schriften*, 2 vols., Berlin, 1958, 1964.

J. von Ewald, *Abhandlungen über den kleinen Krieg*, Kassel, 1785.

G. Fairbarn, *Revolutionary Guerrilla Warfare*, London, 1974.

F. Fanon, *The Wretched of the Earth*, New York, 1963.

D. Galula, *Counterinsurgency Warfare, Theory, and Practice*, London, 1964.

E. Gentilini, *Guerra degli stracorridori*, Capolago, 1848.

F. Gershelman, *Partisanskaia Voina*, St. Petersburg, 1885.

Vo Nguyen Giap, *People's War, People's Army*, Hanoi, 1962.

Vo Nguyen Giap, *The Military Art of People's War*, New York, 1970.

A. Gingins-La Sarra, *Les partisans et la défense de la Suisse*, Lausanne, 1861.

B. Goldenberg, *Kommunismus in Latein Amerika*, Stuttgart, 1970.

R. Gott, *Guerrilla Movements in Latin America*, London, 1970.

De Grandmaison, *De la petite guerre ou traité du service des troupes légères en campagne*, Paris, 1756.

T. N. Greene (ed.), *The Guerrilla and How to Fight Him*, Marine Corps Gazette, 1962.

G. Grivas, *General Grivas on Guerrilla Warfare*, New York, 1965.

C. Grosse, *Kurzgefasste Geschichte der Parteigängerkriege in Spanien 1833–1836*, Leipzig, 1837.

E. (Che) Guevara, *Guerrilla Warfare*, London, 1969.

W. Hahlweg, *Krieg ohne Fronten*, Stuttgart, 1968.

B. Liddell-Hart, *T. E. Lawrence in Arabia and After*, London, 1934.

C. Helmuth, *Der kleine Krieg*, Magdeburg, 1855.

Ho Chi-Minh, *Selected Works: Vol. I and II*, Hanoi, 1961.

D. C. Hodges (ed.), *Philosophy of the Urban Guerrilla*, New York, 1973.

K. Hron, *Der Parteigänger-Krieg*, Vienna, 1885.

M. Jähns, *Geschichte der Kriegswissenschaften*, Munich, 1891.

A. Jelowicki, *O powstaniu i wojnie partyzanckiej*, Paris, 1835.

W. de Jeney, *Le partisan, ou l'art de faire la petite guerre avec succès, selon le génie de nos jours*, La Haye, 1759.

R. F. Johnson, *Night Attacks*, London, 1886.

A. H. de Jomini, *Précis de l'art de la guerre*, Paris, 1838.

H. M. Kamienski, *Wojna Ludowa*, Paris, 1866.

R. E. Kiessler, *Guerrilla und Revolution*, Bonn, 1975.

V. N. Klembovski, *Partisanskie Deistviia*, St. Petersburg, 1894.

P. Klent, *Partizanska Taktika*, Belgrade, 1965.

J. Kohl, J. Litt, *Urban Guerrilla Warfare in Latin America*, Cambridge, Massachusetts, 1974.

Kollektiv RAF, *Über den bewaffneten Kampf in Westeuropa*, Berlin, 1971.

H. Kühnrich, *Der Partisanenkrieg in Europa 1939–1945*, Berlin, 1965.

T. E. Lawrence, *Revolt in the Desert*, London, 1927.

T. E. Lawrence, *The Seven Pillars of Wisdom*, London, 1935.

J. F. A. Lemière de Corvey, *Des partisans et des corps irréguliers*, Paris, 1823.

E. Liberti (ed.), *Techniche della guerra partigiana nel Risorgimento*, Florence, 1972.

Lin Piao, *Long Live the Victory of People's War*, Peking, 1965.

E. Lussu, *Teoria dell' insurrezione*, Milan, 1969.

G. B. Malleson, *Ambushes and Surprises*, London, 1885.

T. Miller Maguire, *Guerrilla or Partisan Warfare*, London, 1904.

Mao Tse-tung, *On Guerrilla Warfare*, London, 1961.

Mao Tse-tung, *Selected Works: Vol. I*, Peking, 1965.

Mao Tse-tung, *Basic Tactics*, London, 1967.

C. Marighella, *For the Liberation of Brazil*, London, 1971.

A. R. Martin, *Mountain and Savage Warfare*, Allahabad, 1898.

Marx-Engels Werke, Berlin [East], 1960.

G. la Masa, *Della guerra insurrezionale in Italia*, Turin, 1856.

G. Maschke, *Kritik des Guerilleros*, Frankfurt, 1973.

E. Mayans (ed.), *Tupamaros: antologia documental*, Cuernavaca, 1971.

J. J. McCuen, *The Art of Counter-Revolutionary War*, London, 1966.

A. Mercader, J. de Vega, *Tupamaros: estrategia y acción*, Montevideo, 1969.

L. V. Mieroslawski, *Kritische Darstellungen des Feldzuges vom Jahre 1831 und hieraus abgeleitete Regeln für Nationalkriege*, 2 vols., Berlin, 1847.

F. O. Miksche, *Secret Forces: The Technique of Underground Movements*, London, n.d.

R. Moss, *Urban Guerrillas*, London, 1972.

J. Most, *Revolutionäre Kriegswissenschaft*, New York, 1884.

H. J. Müller Borchert, *Guerrilla im Industriestaat*, Hamburg, 1973.

A. H. Nasution, *Fundamentals of Guerrilla Warfare*, London, 1963.

A. Neuberg, *Armed Insurrection*, London, 1970.

W. Nieszokoc, *O Systemie wojny partyzanskiej wzniesionym wsrod emigracji*, Paris, 1835.

A. Orlov, *Handbook of Intelligence and Guerrilla Warfare*, Ann Arbor, Michigan, 1963.

F. M. Osanka (ed.), *Modern Guerrilla Warfare*, Glencoe, Illinois, 1962.

J. Paget, *Counter-Insurgency Campaigning*, London, 1967.

P. Paret, "French Revolutionary Warfare from Indochina to Algeria" in *Princeton Studies in World Politics*, No. 6, 1964.

P. Paret, J. W. Shy, "Guerrillas in the 1960s" in *Princeton Studies in World Politics*, No. 1, 1962.

G. Pepe, *Memoria su i mezzi che menano all Italiana indipendenza*, Paris, 1833.

G. Pisacane, *Saggi storici-politici-militari sull' Italia*, new ed., Milan, 1957.

W. J. Pomeroy (ed.), *Guerrilla Warfare and Marxism*, New York, 1968.

Ray de Saint Genies, *L'officier partisan*, 6 vols., Paris, 1769.

De la Roche-Aymon, *Essai sur la petite guerre*, Paris, 1770.

F. W. Rüstow, *Die Lehre vom kleinen Krieg*, Zurich, 1864.

Felipe de San Juan, *Instrucción de Guerrilla*, Santiago, 1823.

J. B. Schels, *Der Kleine Krieg*, Vienna, 1848.

J. B. Schels, *Leichte Truppen, kleiner Krieg*, 2 vols., Vienna, 1813–14.

C. Schmitt, *Theorie des Partisanen*, Berlin, 1963.

K. B. Stolzman, *Partyzanka czyli wojna dla ludow powstajacych najwlasciwza*, Paris, 1844.

R. Taber, *The War of the Flea*, New York, 1965.

M. Talas, *Harb al isabat*, Damascus, 1966.

E. V. Tarle (ed.), *Partisanskaia Voina*, Moscow, 1943.

L. Taruc, *Born of the People*, New York, 1953.

M. Tevis, *La petite guerre*, Paris, 1855.

Ch. W. Thayer, *Guerrillas*, London, 1964.

R. Thompson, *Defeating Communist Insurgency*, London, 1966.

J. Broz Tito, *Selected Military Works*, Belgrade, 1966.

R. Trinquier, *La guerre moderne*, Paris, 1961.

F. Tudman, *Rat Protiv Rat*, Zagreb, 1957.

T. Mitev Urkovachev, *Partisanskata Voina*, Sofia, 1966.

G. W. von Valentini, *Abhandlung über den kleinen Krieg*, Berlin, 1799.

Ritter de Ville, *Von Parteyen*, Breslau, 1755.

Vuich, *Malaia Voina*, St. Petersburg, 1850.

W. St. Ritter von Wilczynski, *Theorie des grossen Krieges mit Hilfe des kleinen oder Partisanen-Krieges bei theilweiser Verwendung der Landwehr*, Vienna, 1869.

De Wüst, *L'art militaire du partisan*, La Haye, 1768.

G. S. Zafferoni, *L'insurrezione armata*, Milan, 1868.

WALTER LAQUEUR is Chairman of the International Research Council of the Center for Strategic and International Studies, and Director of the Institute of Contemporary History and Wiener Library, London. He is also editor of *The Washington Papers* and co-editor of the *Journal of Contemporary History*. He is at present Visiting Professor of History at Harvard. An eminent scholar and commentator on international politics, Mr. Laqueur is author of a number of highly acclaimed and widely translated books on recent European and Middle Eastern history.